Death, Heaven
and the Victorians

Death, Heaven and the Victorians

John Morley

University of Pittsburgh Press

'Mr Mould and his men had not exaggerated the grandeur of the arrangements. They were splendid. The four hearse-horses especially, reared and pranced, and showed their highest action, as if they knew a man was dead, and triumphed in it. "They break us, drive us, ride us, ill-treat, abuse, and maim us for their pleasure—But they die: Hurrah, they die!" '

From *Martin Chuzzlewit* (1843–4) by Charles Dickens

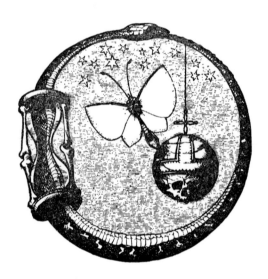

© John Morley 1971
Designed by Gillian Greenwood
First published in Great Britain 1971
by Studio Vista, Blue Star House, Highgate Hill, London N19
Printed and bound in Great Britain by R. J. Acford Ltd., Chichester, Sussex

Library of Congress Catalogue Card Number 78-173852
ISBN 0-8229-1103-5

Contents

'This book is not the hasty effusion of morbid sentiment.' I hope not. It is an attempt to place in context some of the more astonishing objects that have survived from the Victorian age. I am aware that the picture is not complete; moreover, I have tried to avoid subjects that are already adequately covered, and have not approached architecture, a subject in itself. I have tried, where possible, to leave contemporary comments in contemporary language, which has nuances lost in modern paraphrase.

I have to thank Mrs Barbara Morris, who urged me to write this book, and Mr Martin Battersby, who did not rest until I had committed myself to doing so. Dr E. J. Dingwall kindly read the chapter on Spiritualism; Miss Anne Buck and Mrs Elizabeth Taylor gave much help on costume. Dr Geoffrey Rowell put me on the track of essential ecclesiastical material. I have also to thank for their help and advice Mr Harold Berkley, Mrs Shirley Bury, Lady Chapman, Dr Phillis Cunnington, Mr Denis Geroult (BBC), Miss Zillah Halls, Mr Ronald Horton, Miss Barbara Jones, Mr Tom Last, Mrs Doris Langley Moore, Mrs Betty O'Looney, Mr Richard Ormond, Miss Patricia Ranger, Mrs Kildale Robinson, Mr Edward Sibbick and Dr Phoebe Stanton. The staff of Brighton Reference Library gave invaluable help.

Her Majesty the Queen graciously gave permission to reproduce objects and photographs from the Royal Collection. I am also very grateful to all those others who gave permission to reproduce objects in their possession, and to Mr David Rumsey who took all but a handful of the photographs. Miss Diana Holman Hunt kindly gave permission to quote telegrams sent to Lady Lytton after Queen Victoria's death, Evans Bros to quote from *My Memories of Six Reigns* by HRH Princess Marie Louise, Miss Nancy Mitford to quote from her *Ladies of Alderley* and Dr Windle to quote from the diary of William Windle, in his possession.

I am greatly indebted to my wife for her encouragement, for her help with the text, and for her removal of obscurities and solecisms.

1 Introduction

> ' "It is good when it happens", say the children
> "That we die before our time." '[1]

Wickedness has never been the monopoly of any one period, but few periods appear, in some ways, more singularly wicked than the first half of the English nineteenth century. The gap between pretension and performance was great; hypocrisy is a vice without glamour; misery, where it existed, was intense and intensely concentrated. Men found themselves chastised by scorpions that they themselves had created. The age that saw the fictitious birth of Frankenstein's monster saw the shaping of a real force, invented and developed by men, which had acquired an impetus that placed it quite beyond their techniques of control. The unchecked inventiveness, industry and ambition of their contemporaries condemned many ordinary men and women to an existence that was a living death—if by chance they escaped death itself. Industrialization was eventually to bring certain benefits; with its beginnings it brought terrible evils. The search for a cure for the degradations allowed by *laissez-faire* eventually destroyed *laissez-faire* itself, but meanwhile squalor, urban filth and disease affected more people than ever before.

In 1790 twice as many labourers worked on the land as in the towns; by 1840 the situation had been reversed. Between 1801 and 1831 the population increased generally by sixteen per cent every ten years, making a total increase of forty-seven per cent; during that thirty years the populations of Liverpool, Glasgow and Manchester had increased by 100 per cent, 108 per cent and 109 per cent. The result was hideous. In Liverpool, by 1840, 30,000 people, one fifth of the working class, lived in 7800 'inhabited cellars'.[2] In London, in Marylebone, 382 families each lived in one room, sixty-one families lived in two rooms, five families lived in three rooms. Only one family lived in four rooms, but 159 families each lived in *part* of a room. Not more than one family in a hundred had a third room. In the parish of St Martin-in-the-Fields some houses contained from forty-five to sixty persons.[3]

The consequences were predictable. By the third decade of the century *The Lancet* could cite the fact that mortality in city dwellers was forty per cent higher than amongst the rest of the population; in London, in 1830, the average age at death was estimated at forty-four years for gentry, professional persons, and their families; at twenty-five years for tradesmen, clerks, and their families; and at twenty-two for labourers and their families.[4] These figures are qualified in the text, but they are accurate enough as an indication. They were not stable. In Glasgow, for instance, the rate of mortality in 1821 was 1 in 31; in 1831, 1 in 30; in 1835, 1 in 29; in 1838, 1 in 26. For children under ten years of age, the rate rose from 1 in 75 in 1821 to 1 in 48 in 1839.[5] (In Manchester, in 1840, more than fifty-seven out of every hundred working-class children died before reaching the age of five.) The empty cradle (plate 1) was a reality in many homes (plates 3, 4,

FIG I

'Who'll carry him to the grave?
I, said the Kite,
If it's not in the night . . .'

From *Popular Nursery Tales and Rhymes* with 170 illustrations by John Absolon, H. K. Brown, E. H. Courbould, Harrison Weir, J. Wolf and others. Engraved by the Brothers Dalziel. George Routledge and Sons.   Collection Ronald Horton.

54): sentimentality must have given a valuable defence against hard fact (plate 2), although children were early taught in a hard school (fig 1, plates 5, 6, 20, 100). Dr Cowan of Glasgow, who provided the statistics quoted above, commented: 'The mortality bill of 1837 exhibits a rate of mortality inferring an intensity of misery and suffering unequalled in Britain, and not surpassed in any towns we are acquainted with on the Continent of Europe.' Such was the state of the largest town in Scotland in the year of the new Queen's accession.

A description of Leeds in 1845 gives a physical impression of a typical industrial town; it is by no means an extreme example, and more highly coloured descriptions could easily be found:

'. . . there are many cheerful, open streets where the better classes reside. The lower classes here, as elsewhere, inhabit the less comfortable and less healthy localities . . . A number of dwellings which, from the damp and the pestilent effluvia arising from the decaying matter in the bottom of the Beck, combined with the smoke and fumes arising from the various works, are most unhealthy.

But by far the most unhealthy localities of Leeds are close squares of houses, or yards, as they are called, which have been erected for the accommodation of working people. Some of these, though situated in comparatively high ground, are airless from the enclosed structure, and *being wholly unprovided with any form of under-drainage* [my italics], or convenience, or arrangements for cleansing, are one mass of damp and filth . . . . The ashes, garbage, and filth of all kinds are

8

thrown from the doors and windows of the houses upon the surface of the streets and courts . . . . The privies are few in proportion to the number of inhabitants. They are open to view both in front and rear, are invariably in a filthy condition, and often remain without the removal of any portion of the filth for six months. The feelings of the people are blunted to all seeming decency, and from the constantly contaminated state of the atmosphere, a vast amount of ill-health prevails, leading to listlessness, and inducing a desire for spirits and opiates; the combined influence of the whole condition causing much loss of time, increasing poverty, and terminating the existence of many in premature death.'[6]

The 'cheerful, open streets' lived in by 'the better classes' had a sanitary as well as a social meaning; this is emphasized by another observation, referring in this instance to Bath. 'An epidemic smallpox raged at the end of the year 1837, and carried off upwards of 300 persons; yet of all that number I do not think there was a single gentleman, and not above two or three tradesmen. The residences of the labouring classes were pretty regularly visited . . . .' The writer continues, 'we find health rising in proportion to the improvements in residences; we find morality, in at least a great measure, following the same law'.[7] It is interesting to hear a clergyman make this last admission, in an age that believed,

> The rich man in his castle
> The poor man at his gate
> God made them, high or lowly
> And ordered their estate.[8]

Edwin Chadwick did not carry his conclusions so far, but he did assert in 1842:

'That the annual loss of life from filth and bad ventilation are greater than the loss from death or wounds in any wars [fig 2] in which the country has been engaged in

FIG 2 'The Angel of Death', an illustration to the poem 'The Volunteer' by Thomas Hood, from *Whims and Oddities in Prose and Verse* 1836. *Collection Ronald Horton*

9

modern times. That of the 43,000 cases of widowhood, and 112,000 cases of destitute orphanage relieved from the poor's rate in England and Wales alone, it appears that the greatest proportion of the deaths of the heads of families occurred from the above specified and removable causes: that their ages were under forty-five years . . . .'

By implementing his suggested sanitary reforms 'it is probable that the full *ensurable* period of life indicated by the Swedish tables; that is, an increase of thirteen years at least, may be extended to the whole of the labouring classes . . . .'[9]

His similar conclusion in 1843 has a note of wry humour—it was that sanitary measures that decreased deaths and increased the duration of life would be the most effective means to abate the evils of interment![10] By 1849, when cholera killed 16,000 people in London (in some cases three corpses lay in the one room that was a family's entire living space) the need for those sanitary measures had been recognized by the legislators.

The Industrial Revolution brought wealth and death; impartiality in their distribution was not observed. The connexion between death and poverty was close. A story told in 1868 by a clergyman illustrates how close it was, and shows also how poverty made it necessary to portray death as the only way to taste even the basic necessities of life. This appears to us paradoxical, but the technique helped to satisfy several needs. The story is called, 'Willie's Tomorrow'.

'It was in a very miserably poor room, and it was night. In the grate there was a poor little fire . . . —almost going out; and one poor rush-light candle upon the table. In this wretched room—far on in the night, a mother was at her hard work—to be ready to take home the next morning, to get some money to buy bread: and near this wretched fire was a poor little boy—"Willie"—on his dying bed.

This poor boy lifted up his little pale face, looking so old, though he was young (poverty made him so) and said, "I am very hungry, mother!" His mother said to him—"To-morrow, dear Willie, we'll have some bread." Little Willie said, "To-morrow! To-morrow! Didn't I pray to God this morning, 'Give me *this day*, my daily bread?' Has God forgotten me? Why to-morrow? Didn't He say THIS DAY, and I said, 'Give me *this day* my daily bread!' "

Then little Willie laid very still a little while—eleven o'clock was striking, and little Willie looked up and said, "Is it to-morrow?" His mother could not speak, but took little Willie in her arms to soothe him. She had no bread to give. Little Willie soon became very much worse; and his thoughts wandered; he thought of all kinds of strange things—but every now and then he said, "To-morrow! to-morrow!"

Presently he was silent; and his mother saw a smile on his lips . . . . She knew that he was dying. He just said to her, "To-morrow, to-morrow, mother," and he died.

Just then the cathedral clock struck twelve—the mother counted it. God *had* given him *that* day his "daily bread". O what bread! What a feast! He was gone *before* tomorrow—where "they hunger no more, neither thirst any more". He had found his "place of refuge".

"The eternal God is thy refuge, and underneath are the everlasting arms."

Look! "the eternal God is thy refuge"—and underneath are the wings to bear thee over every trouble here, so waft thee, like little Willie, into the bliss of heaven. "The eternal God is thy refuge; and underneath are the everlasting arms." '[11]

GENTILITY

'It is within the last half century that prodigious funerals, awful hearses drawn by preternatural quadrupeds, clouds of black plumes, solid and magnificent oak coffins instead of the sepulchral elm, coffin within coffin, lead, brick graves, and capacious catacombs have spread downwards far beyond the select circle once privileged to illustrate the vanity of human greatness.' (*The Times*, 2 February 1875)

Industry created wealth, and the Napoleonic wars that provided favourable conditions for the growth of industry also eased into the world a new affluent class of farmers and landlords. A new rural and urban middle class arose, accompanied by a new class of rural and urban poor.

This huge new middle class began to ape the gentry; it did so at a time when the impedimenta of 'gracious living' were becoming rapidly more numerous and diversified. An intense social competition was generated; despite the ridicule of satirists such as Cruikshank, Cobbett and Dickens, the urge towards visible display found ever more opulent expression; the Veneerings and Mrs Merdle's bosom are fictitious representations of a type common in real life. Display did not stop short at life; death also had its consumer goods, and Mrs Merdle's husband would have incurred as proportionately lavish an expenditure on her funeral as on the ornaments displayed on her bosom, and with a like social purpose. 'Oh! do not let us say that gold is dross, when it can buy such things as these . . .' cried Mr Mould the undertaker, in an ecstasy, after detailing his fantastic stock[12]—a stock that would, in the new urban context, find its maximum audience. The middle class did not adopt aristocratic values unchanged; it gave them a definite middle-class tinge, and to secure the double crown of respectability in life, and salvation after it, became the aim of the typical Victorian. Wealth was intimately linked with respectability and salvation; a phrase—one of many—of 1842 makes it quite clear that respectability and riches were practically synonymous: 'In the case of funerals of persons of moderate respectability costing say, about £60 . . . . '[13]

Over and over again one meets evidence that it was thought as necessary to maintain the standards of one's class in death as in life, and, if possible, even to use death as a means of further social advancement. This feeling was present with the lowest classes. In 1843 it was reported that paupers sometimes abandoned their children's bodies in the street rather than subject them to the shame of a parish funeral;[14] many a workhouse inmate, like old Sally in *Oliver Twist*, was secretly saving money in order to avoid that disgrace.

It was declared that the desire for a good funeral was the strongest feeling amongst the working classes. Subscriptions towards funeral expenses could be easily obtained, at the cost of insurances against illness, the education of children, etc. A letter of 1848 illustrates the second point:

'One woman who was keeping a "chance child" from charity, a fine boy of 9, said she would like to send him [to school] but could not afford 2d a week as she paid id for a burial club for him, poor fellow he was so desolate like in the world and it was comfortable to be sure to be well buried.'[15]

From a total of £24 million deposited with savings banks, £6 to £8 million was saved in order to meet funeral expenses.[16] The Committee of 1843 spoke with regret of 'persons in inferior conditions and of limited means, who are governed by the examples of those above them, and who are put to ruinous expense' but itself suggested that people should be buried by occupations, and that with such groups should be buried famous people of the same calling; it remarked that 'the humblest class of artisans would find consolation and honour in interment in the same cemetery with Brindley, with Crompton, or with Murdoch . . .'; it did not notice that if it perpetuated class distinctions in death, it could not prevent the same lobbying for position that occurred in life. Great indignation was shown when distinctions were ignored: in 1857 the London Necropolis and National Mauso-leum Company protested to the Home Secretary that it faced unfair competition from cemeteries that, in defiance of the regulations, were practising 'pit burial' for paupers; one of its complaints was that at Victoria Park 'all funerals seemed to be conducted alike, and the coffins placed in the graves irrespective of class; some that came in a two horse-hearse were put into the same grave as those that were brought in cabs.'[17]

Dickens, whose works are a major source for almost all aspects of his period, and especially for the manners and aspirations of the lower middle class, had no doubts in allocating blame for this funereal competition. His 'Black Jobmaster', surveying one of his own funerals, comments, 'That was the sort of turn-out to do a gen-teel party credit'. The narrator then asks:

'Shall I tell you what I know? . . . The Black Jobmaster is right. The root of all this, is the gen-teel party.

You don't mean to deny it, I hope? You don't mean to tell me that this non-sensical mockery isn't owing to your gentility . . . . Don't I know that you always begin [the Burial Service] with the words, "We brought nothing into this world, and it is certain that we can carry nothing out"? Don't I know that in a monstrous satire on those words, you carry your hired velvets, and feathers [plate 7], and scarves, and all the rest of it, to the edge of the grave, and get plundered (and serve you right!) in every article, because you WILL be gen-teel parties to the last?'[18]

Dickens' example of the undertaker's technique shows this competitive gentility:

' "Hearse and four, Sir?" says he. "No, a pair will be sufficient." "I beg your pardon, Sir, but when we buried Mr Grundy at number twenty, there were four on 'em, Sir; I think it right to mention it." "Well, perhaps there had better be four." "Thank you, Sir. Two coaches and four, Sir, shall we say?" "No, coaches and pair." "You'll excuse my mentioning it, Sir, but pairs to the coaches and four to the hearse would have a singular appearance to the neighbours . . . ." "Well, say four!" "Thank you, Sir. Feathers of course?" "No. No feathers. They're absurd." "Very good, Sir, *No* feathers?" "No." "*Very* good Sir. We *can* do four without feathers, Sir, but it's what we never do. When we buried Mr Grundy, there was feathers, and—I only throw it out, Sir—Mrs Grundy might think it strange." "Very well! Feathers!" "Thank you, Sir,"—and so on.

Is it and so on, or not, through the whole black job of jobs, because of Mrs Grundy and the gen-teel party?'[19]

He attempted, like many others, to appeal to the sense of social responsibility, an appeal that succeeded only when fashion lent powerful aid: 'You perfectly understand—you who are not the poor, and ought to set 'em an example—that besides making the whole thing costly, you've confused their minds about this burying, and have taught 'em to confound expense and show, with respect and affection. You know all you've got to answer for, you gen-teel parties?'[20]

The reformers, at least in the early days, were equally bound by convention. Mrs Stone, writing in 1858, condemned excessive expenditure on both mourning and burial. 'Mourning in our country is regulated now by a power hardly less stringent than those laws by which the royalty and *noblesse* of France used to be governed. This power is Custom or Fashion . . . .' To her, the power of custom and fashion was harsh and unhealthy: 'The wholesome and heart-softening tears of a survivor are checked in their source, by terror of the inevitable expense of that which custom prescribes as "a decent funeral".' In a lofty strain, Mrs Stone, following earlier writers on the subject, quoted St Basil: 'For what need have you of a sumptuous monument or a costly entombing? What advantage is there in a fruitless expense? Prepare your own funeral while you live. Works of charity and mercy are the funeral obsequies you can bestow upon yourself.' Charity and mercy, however, seem to have been powerless against the respectability of wealth; Mrs Stone herself reneged by adding, with a conviction given by general assent: 'There can be no impropriety, so that it be done with good taste and modesty, in maintaining that distinction of style and expenditure to the grave which it has pleased Providence to appoint in life.'[21] Those high-sounding Victorian passwords —'propriety', 'modesty', 'distinction', 'style', 'providence'—chime like bells, combining to form an irreproachable sentiment. The flaw was that the only persons who could judge the status afforded in life to the deceased were the surviving relatives, and they were not disinterested.

ROMANTICISM

> Young soul put off your flesh and come
> With me into the quiet tomb,
>   Our bed is lovely, dark, and sweet
> The earth will swing us, as she goes,
> Beneath our coverlids of snows,
>   And the warm leaden sheet.
> Dear and dear is their poisoned note,
> The little snakes' of silver throat,
> In mossy skulls that nest and lie,
> Ever singing, 'Die, oh! die!'[22]

The aspirations of the lovers in *The Magic Flute*, one of the most noble exemplars of late-eighteenth-century sensibility, were directed towards the Temple of

Reason and Virtue, an already old-fashioned construction. Had such an opera been attempted in 1840, what part would Reason and Virtue have played in its theme? It is likely that Love and Death would have occupied their place; the violent passions, violent actions, and violent deaths of Werther and Hamlet dominated the new aesthetic.

The early deaths of so many Romantic heroes, in fact as in fiction, strengthened the Romantic obsession with youth and death (plate 23); this quickly decayed, especially in connexion with youthful deaths, into sentimentality (plates 4, 22, 24). The reweaving of the spells of the Middle Ages brought back a dark gothic element (together with lighter manifestations (plate 45)). Chateaubriand, in a Gothic cathedral, was transported into remote ages, and 'the more remote were these times the more they inspired ideas that end always with a reflexion upon the nothingness of man and the speed of life': he found death 'so poetic because it bordered upon things immortal, so mysterious because of its silence . . . .'[23] De Musset lamented that Byron and Goethe, 'two poets, whose genius was second only to that of Napoleon, consecrated their lives to the work of collecting all the elements of anguish and of grief scattered over the universe'; he apostrophied them—'death was in your eyes, and you were the very Colossi of grief'.[24] This element, added to the Romantic cult of the heart, to Coleridge's pregnant definition of the role of 'Imagination', and to the revival of the supernatural and of the irrational, made a potent mixture.

This was the background of early Victorian sensibility; other influences made their impression, but it was Romanticism that largely determined the nature and form of early Victorian emotion. And death calls for emotion in the most stoic society—save where the stoicism stems from atheism. The sources of the Romantic attitude were primarily literary; an increasing literacy made them the more available. In England, Martin and Pugin helped to give Romanticism its visual clothing, its gothicism and melodrama; indeed, if one wished to look at the world through early Victorian spectacles, one might do worse than to use Martin as one lens and Pugin as the other.

The congealed romanticism that encapsuled Victorian family life, that produced the keepsake and sentimental ballad, and that effloresced in the Valentine, found its reverse expression in objects, poems, ceremonies, and clothes in remembrance of the defunct. Such objects as memorial cards (plates 7, 9, 66), samplers stitched intricately by children with epitaphs for parents and grandparents (plate 8), ceramic memorials of disasters at sea and on land (plates 10, 13); a marble cross set in mauve velvet and carved by 'her mother's hand' (plate 11), a black wedding dress worn in memory of a father (plate 102), photographs set in jet (plate 93), a beloved's hair formed into a ring, a bracelet, a necklace (plate 91) or a watch chain, the family dogs, immortalized by the taxidermist or the bronze founder . . . make an endless list. Queen Victoria, in her grand grief for the Prince Consort (plate 32), assembled an array of mourning objects almost Egyptian in their comprehensiveness, ranging from the handkerchief embroidered with tears (plate 33), the firescreen painted with a family mausoleum (plate 27), through bric-à-brac to architecture and to an ostensible christening present that resolved itself into yet another memorial (plates 34, 35, 36, 37). Her subjects were scarcely less enthusiastic

14

(plates 25, 30, 34, 38). Crime itself had its horrid romanticism (plates 15, 16, 18), which was shared by the criminals themselves (plate 17).

The artist who, perhaps, most convincingly reflects the morbid romanticism of the period is Hans Andersen, admired to idolatry by Dickens and the mass of the mid-Victorian reading public. Touched by his genius, morbidity gains a poetic intensity; it is, nevertheless, akin to that of many inferior productions. In his stories death is a constant theme, treated usually in the lilies-and-maidens style, the style of the languishing epitaphs and flowered memorial cards that were to come later in the century. The tale of 'The Hyacinths', for example, contains

'three fair sisters—transparent and delicate they were . . . . Hand in hand they danced in the moonlight, beside the quiet lake; they were not fairies, but daughters of men. Sweet was the fragrance when the maidens vanished into the wood; the fragrance grew stronger: three biers, whereon lay the fair sisters, glided out from the depths of the wood and floated upon the lake, the glow-worms flew shining around like little hovering lamps. Sleep the dancing maidens, or are they dead? The odour from the flowers tells us they are corpses. The evening bells peal out their dirge.'

In 'Story of a Mother' the child, despite a long and painful search by the mother, is not redeemed from Death's conservatory, since God's will is paramount. This theme, in various guises, recurs constantly in Victorian fiction; the language, as in the extract below (from *Why Weepest Thou? A Book for Mourners*) is the language of Romanticism. The anguished resignation of grief comes through the now (1888) hackneyed tags and images of the poem:

The lambs safely folded

I loved them so,
That when the elder Shepherd of the fold
Came, covered with the storm and pale and cold,
And begged of one of my sweet lambs to hold,
    I bade him go . . . .

I laid him down,
In those white shrouded arms, with bitter tears;
For some voice told me that, in after years,
He should know naught of passion, grief, or fears,
    As I had known.

And yet again
That elder Shepherd came: my heart grew faint—
He claimed another lamb; with sadder plaint,
Another!—she who, gentle as a saint,
    Ne'er gave me pain . . . .

15

> Oh, how I wept,
> And clasped her to my bosom, with a wild
> And yearning love—my lamb! my pleasant child!
> Her, too, I gave: the little angel smiled,
>   And slept!
>
> 'Go! go!' I cried;
> For once again that Shepherd laid his hand
> Upon the noblest of our household band:
> Like a pale spectre, there he took his stand,
>   Close to his side . . . .
>
> He will not take
> Another lamb, I thought; for only one
> Of the dear fold is spared to be my sun,
> My guide, my mourner, when this life is done—
>   My heart would break . . . .

Death does, of course, take all, and the mother is resigned.

There is another, and very different, aspect of Romanticism—an aspect which carries a strong whiff of the theatre; this can be seen in the personalization of Death, and in the Victorian funeral. Andersen himself could pull out the full funeral stops:

'The poor Emperor could hardly breathe; it appeared to him as though something were sitting on his chest; he opened his eyes, and saw that it was Death, who had put on the Emperor's crown, and held with one hand the golden scimitar, with the other the splendid imperial banner; whilst, from under the folds of the thick velvet hangings, the strangest looking heads were seen peering forth . . . the good and bad deeds of the Emperor, which were now all fixing their eyes upon him, whilst Death sat upon his heart.'[25]

The baroque drama of this passage has affinities with the black pageant of the early-nineteenth-century funeral:

'Suddenly a huge black object was dimly discernible entering the avenue and dragging its ponderous length towards the castle . . . the snow ceased, the clouds rolled away, and the red brassy glare of the setting sun fell abruptly on the moving phenomenon, and disclosed to view a stately full-plumed hearse. There was something so terrific, yet so picturesque, in its appearance, as it ploughed its way through waves of snow—its sable plumes and gilded skulls nodding and grinning in the now lurid glimmering of the fast-sinking sun—that all stood transfixed with alarm and amazement.'[26]

A letter in *Country Life* on Victorian funerals brings out the same theatrical menace: 'I well remember one dreary, foggy morning, on my way to school, seeing two jet black horses, complete with plumes and drivers' hats enwreathed with crape, suddenly loom out of the mist, making my blood run cold.'

The Victorians did, perhaps, calculate their effects. We know, for instance, that the Select Committee of 1856 on capital punishment paid careful attention to the arrangements proposed to replace public executions and the 'riot of drunkenness and debauchery' that accompanied them. It decided that 'the imagination of an evil-doer would draw a far more impressive picture of an execution taking place within the gaol, out of his sight, than would be actually presented to his eyes in public' (plate 15) and that '. . . the tolling of a bell, or . . . raising a black flag . . . would be attended with a better and more awful effect'. Eventually, the power of an exact temporal symbolism was evoked; it was resolved that the exact time of the execution should be marked by the 'tolling of a bell, which shall cease at the moment of execution, and the hoisting at the same time of a black flag'. One person asked whether '. . . a procession . . . or any graver solemnities than those which now attend an execution, would have a good effect upon the multitude?' The suggestion was made that, to supplement the bell and the flag, the churches might be opened and a service given, a prayer said, a sermon delivered.

This concern for a telling and dramatic, not to say theatrical, effect, appeared also in ideas aired in 1843 concerning cemetery burial. The Rev. H. Milman asked 'whether the very numbers of funerals, which must take place for a large town, with the extent of the burial places, may not be made a source for solemnity and impressiveness' in the new cemeteries? He mentioned that the cemetery bells should be deep in tone, not a 'quick shrill gingle'. The Vicar of Spitalfields had a similar idea concerning the dramatic possibilities of a large concourse of people—he thought that a combined burial service, with flocks of mourners from several different parties, would be most impressive: indeed, 'this aggregation of burials need only be limited by the effective power of the human voice . . . These salutary effects would be heightened to a thrilling degree by music . . . . I presume that the introduction of music . . . is not inconsistent with the rubric.'[27] Obviously this was a daring suggestion.

James Mill, the disciple of Bentham, 'regarded as an aberration of the moral standards of modern times . . . the great stress laid upon feeling. Feelings, as such, he considered to be no proper subjects of praise or blame. Right or wrong, good and bad, he regarded as qualities solely of conduct . . . .'[28] This strict rationalism was not in harmony with the predilections of Romanticism; the display of feeling soon became a necessary part of the social equipment of every polite person and, as such, it percolated to the lower classes. Grief was a pre-eminent feeling; even where there was a cause for grief, it seems that it often became necessary to force it, and it is quite clear that a show of exaggerated grief became a mark of would-be gentility. Dickens thus described the stance of Sally Flanders, a character based on his former nurse, when he visited her after her husband's death:

'Sally was an excellent creature . . . but the moment I saw her I knew she was not in her own real natural state. She formed a sort of Coat of Arms grouped with a smelling bottle, a handkerchief, an orange, a bottle of vinegar, Flander's sister, her own sister, Flander's brother's wife, and two neighbouring gossips—all in mourning, and all ready to hold her whenever she fainted. At sight of poor little me she became much agitated . . . became hysterical, and swooned . . . . An affecting scene followed . . . . Reviving a little, she embraced me, said, "You knew him well . . ." and fainted again, which, as the rest of the Coat of Arms soothingly said, "done her credit". Now, I know that she needn't have fainted unless she liked, and that she wouldn't have fainted unless it had been expected of her . . . . I was not sure but that it might be manners in *me* to faint next . . . .'[29]

It may seem difficult to reconcile Dickens's unease over Sally Flanders' histrionics with the behaviour of himself and his friends over the fictional death of Little Nell; in fact, the combination of hard-headedness and sentiment is often encountered in Victorian England. For Little Nell, even the satiric Tom Hood and the neo-classical Walter Savage Landor wept; Macready begged Dickens to save her life, and the fatal scene 'gave a dead chill' to his blood. Daniel O'Connell burst into tears, said 'He should not have killed her', and threw the book out of the window. Mrs Henry Siddons found Francis Jeffrey with his head on the table, his eyes suffused with tears. 'You'll be sorry to hear', he told her, 'that Little Nelly, Boz's Little Nelly, is dead.' Carlyle was greatly affected. Dickens was moved to forget his grammar: 'Nobody shall miss her like I shall. It is such a very painful thing to me, that I really cannot express my sorrow.'

The death of Paul Dombey, another child, produced similar scenes. Jeffrey wrote to Dickens: 'I have sobbed and cried over it last night and again this morning.' Macready, seeing Dickens for the first time after Paul's death, could not speak for sobs. And Dickens was susceptible to the pathos of other authors: 'I cried most bitterly,' he wrote to Thackeray, 'over your affecting picture of that cock-boat manned by babies and shall never forget it.'[30]

In the funeral itself, feeling found formal expression. Mr Mould asked the question: 'Why do people spend more money . . . upon a death, Mrs Gamp, than upon a birth?' and himself answered, 'It's because the laying out of money with a well-conducted establishment, where the thing is performed upon the very best scale, binds the broken heart, and sheds balm upon the wounded spirit. Hearts want binding, and spirits want balming when people die; not when people are born.'[31] Here, sentiment and gentility join together to assist in producing that quintessence of sentiment and gentility, the Victorian funeral.

2 The Victorian Funeral

'. . . the fat atmosphere of funerals . . .'[1]

A passage from the *Supplementary Report . . . into the Practice of Interment in Towns* (1843) gives a fair idea of the standard panoply of a funeral:

'Are you aware that the array of funerals, commonly made by undertakers, is strictly the heraldic array of a baronial funeral, the two men who stand at the doors being supposed to be the two porters of the castle, with their staves, in black; the man who heads the procession, wearing a scarf, being a representative of a herald-at-arms; the man who carries a plume of feathers on his head being an esquire, who bears the shield and casque, with its plume of feathers; the pall-bearers, with batons, being representatives of knights-companions-at-arms; the men walking with wands being supposed to represent gentlemen-ushers with their wands:—are you aware that this is said to be the origin and type of the common array usually provided by those who undertake to perform funerals?'

The undertaker to whom this question was put replied in the negative; Loudon, writing in 1843, could still assert that these facts were not generally known. This ignorance of the symbolic meanings of the items of funeral pomp is curious so long after Sir Walter Scott and in an age that delighted in symbolic allusiveness, in the corporealization of an idea; whether aware of it or not, such an array would have appealed to the generation that had organized the Eglinton Tournament and, earlier, the Coronation of King George IV.

A list of the various 'classes of funerals', given in *Cassell's Household Guide* in about 1870, details the combinations possible; they are graded by cost. Eight are described, costing from £3 5s to £53; hearses (plates 52, 53), velvets (plate 49), pairs of horses, mutes (plate 19), silk velvets, feathers (plate 49), and lead coffins are gradually brought in, until the full middle-class complement is achieved:

'Hearse and four horses, two mourning coaches with fours, twenty-three plumes of rich ostrich-feathers, complete velvet covering for carriages and horses, and an esquire's plume of best feathers; strong elm shell, with tufted mattress, lined and ruffled with superfine cambric, and pillow; full worked glazed cambric winding-sheet, stout outside lead coffin, with inscription plate [plate 46] and solder complete; one-and-a-half-inch oak case, covered with black or crimson velvet, set with three rows round, and lid panelled with best brass nails; stout brass plate of inscription, richly engraved; four pairs of best brass handles and grips, lid ornaments to correspond; use of silk velvet pall; two mutes with gowns, silk hat-bands and gloves; fourteen men as pages, feathermen, and coachmen, with truncheons and wands, silk hat-bands [plate 44], etc.; use of mourners' fittings; and attendant with silk hat-band etc. (Appendix A).

It is indispensable, in this context, once again to quote Dickens; the master-journalist's picture of his world, incomparably vivid, seems unobscured by the veil time normally casts between us and the past. Hostility or scorn concentrated his gifts—he was recognized as a pioneer of funeral reform—and his descriptions of the early Victorian funeral present an even clearer picture than do contemporary prints, which lack his physical immediacy. One constant factor is a kind of horrid exultation shared by Dickens and his undertakers; it is obvious that the whole business repelled and fascinated him, as death did Queen Victoria: 'I have orders, Sir, to put on my whole establishment of mutes; and mutes come very dear, Mr Pecksniff; not to mention their drink. To provide silver-plate handles of the very best description, ornamented with angels' heads from the most expensive dies. To be perfectly profuse in feathers. In short, Sir, to turn out something absolutely gorgeous.'[2] The concept of expense and the sanction of money are intimately associated with funeral paraphernalia. 'My four long-tailed prancers, never harnessed under ten pund ten' (plate 40).[3] Gold, says the undertaker, can give the mourner 'four horses to each vehicle; it can give him velvet trappings; it can give him drivers in cloth cloaks and top-boots; it can give him the plumage of the ostrich, dyed black; it can give him any number of walking attendants, dressed in the first style of funeral fashion, and carrying batons tipped with brass [plate 49]; it can give him a handsome tomb; it can give him a place in Westminster Abbey itself, if he choose to invest it in such a purchase.'[4]

This particular funeral was to be a grand spectacle; more often, Dickens emphasized the sordid and the ludicrous. The baroque was not in his style, and one would not recognize, from his accounts, how impressive a Victorian funeral could be, nor that, as Washington Irving said, 'Few pageants can be more stately and frigid than an English funeral in town' (plates 46, 47).[5] The funeral of Pip's sister in *Great Expectations* (1861), a decidedly lower-middle-class affair, is a typical Dickens affair; it would have been managed by a small town undertakers (plate 43), the pretensions of which might have been advertised by a hatchment-like sign (plate 42), imitating the aristocratic signal of death (plate 41). The squalor of it all seems largely due to the fact that its imitations of gentility were compromised by poverty.

Pip approached the house and saw that

'Trabb and Co. had put in a funeral execution and taken possession. Two dismally absurd persons, each ostentatiously exhibiting a crutch done up in a black bandage . . . were posted at the front door . . . in one of them I recognized a postboy discharged from the Boar . . . as I came up, [he] knocked at the door—implying that I was far too much exhausted by grief, to have strength remaining to knock for myself.

Another sable warder [a carpenter . . .] opened the door, and showed me into the best parlour. Here, Mr Trabb . . . was holding a kind of black Bazaar, with the aid of a quantity of black pins . . . he had just finished putting somebody's hat into black long clothes, like an African baby . . . .'

Joe was 'entangled in a little black cloak tied in a large bow under his chin . . . as chief mourner'; the other mourners 'were all going to follow and were all in course of being tied up separately into ridiculous bundles . . .' with 'Pumblechook in a black cloak and several yards of hatband'. The cortège being ready to start, the statutory grief had to be displayed: ' "Pocket-handkerchiefs out, all!" cried

Mr Trabb at this point, in a depressed business-like voice—"Pocket-handkerchiefs out! We are ready!" ... So, we all put our pocket-handkerchiefs to our faces, as if our noses were bleeding', and left the parlour, the air of which was 'faint with the smell of sweet cake ... cut up plum cake, cut up oranges, and sandwiches and biscuits, and two decanters ... port and sherry.' The coffin was followed; it was a 'point of Undertaking ceremony that the six bearers must be stifled and blinded under a horrible black velvet housing with a white border, the whole looked like a blind monster with twelve human legs [plate 46]'. It was all very much appreciated: 'the neighbourhood, however, highly approved ... we were all but cheered ....'

Funeral hospitality was all important, especially in the north where, in certain areas, the town criers invited all to the funeral feast. Mrs Gaskell mentions with horror the disorderly 'arvills' or funeral celebrations at Haworth, which often ended in riot and bloodshed; one member from every family in the village—a large village—was invited to Charlotte Brontë's funeral. If tea were served, a funeral teapot (plate 14) and tea service might have been used.

The item that was almost synonymous with funerals was the ostrich feather, real or imitation; 'Funeral and Featherman' often appears on undertakers' trade-cards (plate 50). It is probable that the general use of feathers entered England as a French fashion after the Restoration; the growing magnificence of funerals was noted by Wren and others. One of the most extraordinary nineteenth-century exaggerations was the 'feather-tray' (plate 39); unfortunately, it seems unlikely that any example of this piece of arch-equipment has survived. Dickens, of course, was hostile: 'because there were not feathers enough yet, there was a fellow in the procession carrying a board of 'em on his head, like Italian images'. He was accompanied by the mutes—'about five-and-twenty or thirty other fellows (all hot and red in the face with eating and drinking) dressed up in scarves and hat-bands, and carrying—shut-up fishing rods, I believe.'[6]

There was, however, romance in funerary customs; images of a different order are conjured up by a 'most delicate and beautiful rite' observed in some of the more remote southern villages at the funeral of a young virgin: 'A chaplet of flowers is borne before the corpse by a young girl ... and is afterwards hung up in the church over the accustomed seat of the deceased. These chaplets are sometimes made of white paper, in imitation of flowers, and inside of them is generally a pair of white gloves.'[7] This custom has been witnessed in Sussex within living memory. The symbolism of white and black gloves in English funerals is curious and ubiquitous. At a large funeral crape scarves and hat-bands were given to relatives, silk scarves and hat-bands to friends and the clergymen, and black kid gloves to all; if economy had to be observed, the gloves only were given. The memorial cards that were sent to distant friends originally accompanied a pair of gloves; later, the importance of the gloves was usurped by the cards (plates 7, 9).

It can be imagined with what jealous eyes the neighbours, in this class-conscious society, would have watched the arrangements, and how keenly they would have weighed whether or not the precept of the 'judicious Hooker' (often quoted by the Victorians in this context, together with Jeremy Taylor) had been fulfilled in respect of the corpse. To Hooker, the purpose of funeral duties was to 'show that love

21

towards the party deceased which Nature requireth; then to do him that honour which is fit both generally for men, and particularly for the honour of his person; last of all, to testify the care which the Church hath to comfort the living, and the hope which we all have concerning the resurrection of the dead.'[8] The love and honour, at least, cost money.

The 1843 Committee gave a broad breakdown of the average expenses of funerals in a table (repeated below);[9] the comment was appended that, although an approximation, the total was far more likely to be an underestimate than otherwise. This total figure, in its context, is staggering.

Average and aggregate expenses of funerals

Class	Total Number of Funerals of each Class that have taken place in the Metropolis in the Year 1839	Number of Children under 10 Years of Age	Present Average Expenses of each Funeral of each Class, inclusive of burial dues		Total Expenses of the Funerals of all the Persons of each Class, inclusive of Children	Annual Expense of Funerals in England and Wales: estimating the proportions of Deaths of each Class to be the same as in the Metropolis, and the Average Expenses of each Class to be the same
			Adults	Children		
			£ s	£ s	£	£
Gentry, &c. . .	2,253	529	100 0	30 0	188,270	1,735,040
Tradesmen, 1st clss.	5,757	2,761	50 0	14 0	250,792	2,370,379
Tradesmen, 2nd clss. and undescribed .	7,682	3,703	27 10	7 15	103,728	..
Artisans, &c. . .	25,930	13,885	5 0	1 10	81,053	766,074
Paupers . .	3,655	593	13s		2,761	..
Total Expense for the Metropolis					626,604	
Proximate Estimate of the Expense for the Total Number of Funerals in one Year, England and Wales						4,871,493

The commentary enlarges on the information supplied in the table: the average expenses of persons of rank and title varied from £1500 to £800, according to whether the funeral took place in country or town, the former being the more expensive: the expenses of the upper gentry varied from £400 to £200, seldom being as low as £150. The average expense of all in London above the status of paupers was calculated at £14 19s 9d per head; an undertaker stated that £5 was the lowest average expense of a poor man's burial. In Scotland the expenses of the decent burial of a labouring man were not less than £5, exclusive of mourning costs. The *Quarterly Review* gives figures slightly different in detail: £60 to £100 for an upper tradesman, £250 for a gentleman, £500 to £1500 for a nobleman, all in the metropolis.[10] The heroine of *Jane Eyre* (1848) received £30 a year as a governess, a sum meant to reflect the generosity of Mr Rochester.

The insistence on 'respectability' was ruthless; this can be seen in an interesting analysis of the costs of various items of funeral equipment (Appendix B). Again, class and station was everything: what was respectable for one class ceased to be so when adopted by another (Appendix D).

The Report's main conclusion, that £4 to £5 million was 'annually thrown into the grave, at the expense of the living', was not contested; it was repeated with eager indignation by the Press. The Committee did not restrain itself in judging the evil effects of this expenditure, although it must have been still very generally socially accepted. This acceptance was sanctioned by law; it was the practice of the offices of Masters in Chancery, where executors' accounts were examined, to allow undertakers' bills of from £60 to £70 (exclusive of burial dues) as a matter of course, *even where the estate was insolvent*.[11] The question whether, on a death, the costs of burial enjoyed priority over the claims of creditors rested on a precedent of 1693, when Lord Chief Justice Holt had ruled that 'For strictness no funeral expenses are allowed against a creditor except for the coffin, ringing the bell, Parson, Clerk, and Bearers' fees. But not for a Pall or ornaments.' This ruling, confirmed by cases in 1830 and 1834, gave much latitude.[12]

The conduct of funerals was regulated by money and by custom; the waste of the former and the overstepping of the latter provoked censure. A utilitarian puritanism, a new Catholicism conscious of its mediaeval heritage and impatient of Caesarean imagery, an Evangelicalism with its emphasis on 'works', and a sense that proper class distinctions were being obscured to an extent where it seemed almost necessary to impose funerary sumptuary laws, all contributed to the chorus of disapproval. This disapproval preceded the social changes that were eventually to banish the old-style burial and mourning customs.

The 'sumptuary' strain occurs over and over again:

' "If", says a correspondent, "the poor were wise, their funerals would be as simple as possible; a plain coffin, borne by near male relations, and followed by the family and friends of the deceased in decent mourning, but without any of the undertaker's trappings on their persons, would be sufficient. The poor like funeral pomp because the rich like it; forgetting that during life the condition of the dead was entirely different, and that there ought to be a consistency in every thing belonging to the various ranks of society." '

The passage goes on to condemn 'the poor' for depriving their children of necessities or comforts for an 'imaginary and false pride'.

The *Quarterly Review* took up the point of funeral costs, raised by the 1843 Committee, in words later quoted or paraphrased by Mrs Stone and other writers on the subject:

'Will Christian England hear this simple statement and be still? There is a cry in the streets of towns that count their inhabitants by tens of thousands, for schools and churches; gaunt and squalid poverty, heathen ignorance, and what is worse, half-knowing infidelity, call aloud for almoners and teachers, and pastors . . . This estimate does not include the vain marble, "the storied urn and animated bust", and the emblazoned hatchment, of monumental affection and parade. To what then does it go? To silk scarfs, and brass nails—feathers for the horses—kid gloves and gin for the mutes—white satin and black cloth for the worms. And whom does it benefit? Not those in whose honour all this pomp is marshalled . . . not the cold spectator who sees its dull magnificence give the palpable lie to the preacher's equality of death—but the lowest of all low hypocrites, the hired mourner whose office it is a sin to sustain and encourage.'

The last conclusion was stressed: 'We do not hesitate to denounce the present accumulation of ceremony and outlay at funerals as not only ridiculous but sinful.'[13] Here was the final condemnation; propriety was being attacked on its own ground.

The survivors had to pay according to the rank of the deceased. The obsequies of the sixteenth Earl of Shrewsbury, in 1852, are a good example of a high-class funeral of a nobleman of advanced religious and aesthetic views; the younger Pugin and the great firm of Hardman provided the impedimenta, all of the highest quality of design and execution; the cost corresponded (Appendix C). Poor people were often hit hard by funeral expenses, especially when, although poor, they were 'gentle': 'to . . . widows of officers in the army or navy, or of the legal profession, or. . . persons of the rank of gentry who have but limited incomes, the expenses of the funerals often subject them to severe privations during the remainder of their lives'. The widows of these people often spent on funerals sufficient to have educated their children, for whom they had afterwards to beg assistance: the expenses were frequently incurred in direct disregard of the express wishes of the dying—no light matter, in a period where 'the last words' had an almost mystic significance. (One of the main reasons why people attended public executions was in order to hear the culprit *say* something before his death—it was this that caused the breathless hush beforehand.)[14] Frequently, the expenses were against the wishes of the survivors—a distracted widow would instruct the undertaker to provide what was customary and proper, and would then find herself committed to all the trimmings thought necessary to her husband's rank. An extract from the 1843 minutes shows both this strict hierarchical grading by classes, and a hint of one of the abuses—the existence of middle men (Appendix D).

The effect of the middle men was atrocious: the 'Black Jobmaster' had 'let the coaches and horses to a furnishing undertaker, who had let 'em to a haberdasher, who had let 'em to a carpenter, who let 'em to the parish-clerk, who had let 'em to a sexton, who had let 'em to the plumber painter and glazier who had got the funeral to do . . . .'[15] Mr Dix, an undertaker, described the practice in more measured terms: the lowest average expense of a poor man's funeral was £5, but that was where it was done, as it was usually, second or third hand; he frequently performed funerals 'three deep'. People generally applied to the nearest person, and since 'everybody nowadays' called himself an undertaker, including the bearers, everybody got a rake-off. 'I have known one of these men [a bearer] get a new suit of clothes out of the funeral of one decent mechanic.' Moreover, undertakers sometimes paid doctors and nurses £10 to £50 for recommending them; thence arose the polite fiction at funerals, where they often met, that the doctor and undertaker were mutual strangers. The incompetent, drunken, snuff-taking hired nurses, who specialized in both midwifery and laying-out, were exposed by Dickens in the persons of Mrs Gamp and Mrs Prig. The former lady is also recorded as getting clothes out of funerals; she always arrayed herself in dilapidated black, for 'this at once expressed a decent amount of veneration for the deceased, and invited the next of kin to present her with a fresher suit of weeds; an appeal so frequently successful, that the very fetch and ghost of Mrs Gamp might be seen hanging up . . . in at least a dozen of the second-hand clothes shops around Holborn . . . .'[16] The evil of the hired nurses continued; Mr Sadler, an undertaker, said in 1878 that 'I know one man in the suburbs of London who writes up "undertaker" and who keeps an invalid chair and a patent chair, and all the old nurses in the neighbourhood are in his pay. How am I to compete with such a man?'[17]

Mr Wild, himself an undertaker, told the 1843 Committee that funerals could be performed for fifty per cent less without any diminution of 'solemnity' (that favourite Victorian word): 'A confident opinion is expressed that interments might be performed, under general arrangements, at a rate of between £5 and £6 each funeral, instead of about £15, the present average.' Oddly enough, there were few rich undertakers; when one hears that the daily deaths in London, during the three years before 1843, had averaged 114 inclusive of workhouse deaths (which would mean parish funerals), and that there was a total of 1025 undertakers in London, to 275 of whom undertaking was the sole source of livelihood, one realizes that the trade was over subscribed.[18] There must have been little work to go around. An undertaker once remarked that 'in nine cases out of ten the undertaker who has much to do with the corpse is a person of cadaverous hue, and you may almost always tell him wherever you see him';[19] he was thinking of the noxious effect of exhalations, but undernourishment may have had as much to do with it.

A frequent agent of fraud was the burial club. Members paid a regular amount to these friendly societies, in order to cover the expenses of a decent funeral. Often, however, they were a swindle arranged on a profitable basis by the undertaker and publican; the former was usually secretary and the latter treasurer; meetings were held at public houses, and the consumption of a certain proportion of liquor was a condition of attendance. In practice, ordinary members were little consulted; dishonesty was common. One favourite trick was that when a widow, for example, asked the secretary-undertaker for money to bury her husband, he would tell her that he could not advance it until the committee met; this might be three months hence. She could not delay burial; he would offer to advance the money personally on condition that he conducted the funeral; reduced by grief and worry, the widow would consent, and the funeral would be performed at an extortionate cost.

The disorderly conduct of many clubs impelled people to join several as a multiplied insurance for their own or their relations' burial; sometimes one person was insured with as many as thirty clubs; this practice became dangerous, since the accumulated monies tempted premature collection. Children were the chief sufferers, and girls more often than boys—they were considered less useful. A grim neighbourly comment was recorded as common in the north: 'Aye, Aye, that child will not live; it is in the burial club.'[20]

One of the commonest results of attempts by relatives to raise the money for burials was that the body was kept unburied far too long; this effect touched very nearly the sanitary preoccupations that had brought the 1843 Committee into being. It is reiterated:

'There is one point which is material, the keeping of bodies in low neighbourhoods before interment; I have seen frequent proofs of the injurious consequences . . . . At present the poor bury almost entirely on the Sunday, and frequently if a person dies on the Wednesday, if they have not time to make the arrangements prior to the Sunday following, they keep that body perhaps till the Sunday next proceeding. I have frequently known a body kept on the table or the bed in a poor man's room; perhaps he is living in that room, sleeping there, and performing all the usual and necessary offices of the family with his wife and five or six children. I have often wished for an absolute power to compel the burying of those bodies . . . .'[21]

This was thought particularly dangerous at times of 'fever'; the witness was asked the longest time he had known bodies to be kept: 'Twelve or fourteen days. In this cul-de-sac, Wellington-court, there were two bodies in the house when the other children were attacked; there the stench was so horrible, the neighbours, Irish as they were, were obliged to complain; they could bear a great deal, but they went to the parochial authorities about it.'[22]

One undertaker said that he often buried for nothing after a lapse of time; poor people were too proud to let the parish bury their dead—the lowest priced coffin cost 3s 6d; it had a shroud, but no cloth, nails, name-plate, or handles, and often broke into pieces when taken to the grave.[23] Evidence was given of the 'desecration' of Sunday funerals, usual with the poorer classes and with shopkeepers since it was the only day on which they did not work. Unfortunately the public houses were open; no 'genteel funeral' was ever held on a Sunday! The Irish were amongst the worse offenders in delaying burials, since they had to collect money not only for the funeral, but also for the wakes.[24] A curious contradiction was noted: a 'benevolent clergyman' remarked that while with the upper classes a corpse excited feelings of awe and respect, with the lower orders 'it is often treated with as little respect as the carcase in a butcher's shop. Nothing can exceed their desire for an imposing funeral; nothing can surpass their efforts to obtain it; but the deceased's remains share none of the reverence . . . . ' He attributed this to the continual presence of the corpse; it was pulled about by the children, things were rested on it, it was even used as a hiding place for the beer or gin bottle. His conclusion was a moral one: 'It removes their wholesome fear of death which is the last hold upon a hardened conscience.'[25] When, as the secretary of a burial club remarked, corpses were kept for a fortnight, the modern reader can hardly believe that the 'wholesome fear' of death was not made more real than if they were swiftly and hygienically removed; the effects of dissolution are not reassuring.

Another continuing cause of scandal was the conduct of the mutes at a funeral; they offended the evangelical decorum of the times, and compromised the 'solemn-ity' for which the mourners were paying, by drunken and disorderly conduct. References to it, and jokes about it, were legion (see the coat-of-arms on the hatch-ment, plate 85). 'Mr Mould's men found it necessary to drown their grief, like a young kitten, in the morning of its existence; for which reason they generally fuddled themselves before they began to do anything . . . the whole of that strange week (before the funeral) was a round of dismal joviality and grim enjoyment.'[26] (The grimness of that particular funeral, and the irony of its elaborate and meaningless paraphernalia, is emphasized by the later realization that a parricide had arranged it for his murdered father.) An undertaker thus described the conduct of his men to the House of Commons Committee:

'They are frequently unfit to perform their duty, and have reeled in carrying the coffin. The men who stand as mutes at the door, as they stand out in the cold, are supposed to receive more drink, and receive it liberally. I have seen these men reel about in the road, and after the burial we have been obliged to put these mutes and their staves into the interior of the hearse, and drive them home, as they were incapable of walking. After the return from the funeral, the mourners commonly have drink again at the house.'[27]

By the 1840s, therefore, the case for the reform and simplification of funeral ceremonies had been recognized: it was also recognized that the desire for as grand a funeral as possible would be difficult to eradicate. The reformist *Quarterly Review* admitted that 'we cannot bear, perhaps, the thought of withholding, in the case of others, even the lacquered cherubs and French polished mahogany . . .'— it advocated that each person himself should strictly direct in his will that a certain named sum should be spent on his burial, in order to restrain his relatives.[28] Progress in reform was at first extremely slow; it was, however, discernible. A 'great movement' had been 'inaugurated by a novelist like Charles Dickens' (not strictly true) and 'subsequently accepted and recommended by the clergy';[29] the latter were active, and the attack was led by the Ecclesiologists.

The Ecclesiologists had long taken note of the deficiencies in funerary customs when, in September 1845, they declared their plans: ' We suppose that no one has ever been summoned to attend a funeral, without bitterly feeling the Paganism, the heartlessness, the atheistical character of the procession. The present race of undertakers are a most crying evil, the system is almost too corrupt to be amended. We have pleasure therefore in announcing, that arrangements are in progress as to the conducting funerals on a more Christian system.'[30] In April 1846 their full proposals were published, a strange compound of good intentions and common sense, a gothic and often gloomy 'enthusiasm', and romantic archaisms.

The intention was to correct abuses and to revive old practices; to restore the former sacred nature of the funeral act. The corpse's hands were no longer, as of old, clasped in prayer with the cross between them; it was not watched, as once it had been, by 'prayerful' friends and mourners, nor were tapers used, which once had burned 'with great significancy in the chamber of the dead'. Instead, the corpse was put by 'vulgar and heartless officials' into a coffin adorned with miserable and perhaps 'merely worldly' emblems. Horrible modern inventions had appeared, such as the 'Economic Funeral Company' and Shillibeer's 'one-horse hearse-coach' (plate 80). The 'cold Pagan cemetery', the 'Necropolis', the 'patent cast-iron tressel' with its cramps and pulleys, the chaplain 'a perfect stranger to the mourners' —all were even worse than the old kind of burials, with their kid gloves, seed cakes, feathers, and 'funeral pue'.[31]

The Ecclesiologists shared their hatred of Shillibeer's invention with the undertakers and the *Quarterly Review*; Loudon alone approved it. It was a significant invention. Shillibeer had taken out in 1841 a patent for a combined hearse and mourning coach: Loudon wrote in 1843:

'The expense of funerals has last year been considerably lessened about the metropolis by the introduction of one-horse hearses, which convey the coffin and six mourners to the place of interment. These appear to have been first suggested in 1837, by Mr J. R. Croft, in an article in the *Mechanic's Magazine*, vol. xxvii, p. 146, and the idea has subsequently, in 1842, been improved on and carried into execution by Mr Shillibeer, to whom the British public are indebted for the first introduction of the omnibus. Mr Shillibeer's funeral carriage embraces in itself a hearse and a mourning coach, is very neat, and takes little from the pomp, and nothing from the decency of the ordinary funeral obsequies, while it greatly reduces the expense; the hire of a hearse with a single horse costing only £1 1s, and with two horses, £1 11s 6d. These carriages have one division for the coffin, and another for six mourners; and when the coffin has been taken out for interment, before the mourners re-enter to return home, the front part of the carriage and the fore wheels are contracted and drawn close up to the hinder or coach part of the carriage by means of a screw, so that the part for containing the coffin disappears, and the whole, when returning from the place of interment, has the appearance of a mourning coach. The invention is ingenious and most useful.'[32]

A less favourable opinion spoke of the lately introduced '*Cruelty van*, with a long boot under the driver for the coffin, and a posse of mourners crammed into the Clarence behind, all drawn along by one poor horse at a very respectable trot.'[33]

The Ecclesiologists thought that nobody could think of such things without disgust.[34] Even worse—'indeed how infinitely *wicked*'—were paupers', or any poor man's, funerals: the priests themselves were in the habit of 'insulting CHRIST in his poor' with a mutilated and hurried service, an unsympathizing neglect of the weeping family, a soiled and torn surplice . . . add to this the extortionate undertaker's bill. It was remarked that the Cambridge Camden Society had looked unsuccessfully for a person to arrange funerals on a better basis.

The Ecclesiologists wished the parish priest to be the first agent of reform, and besought him to give the whole burial service, with equal reverence, to rich and poor: 'the poor man's corpse might even be met at the lych-gate, without any great fall to the priest's dignity'. Where two or more priests were attached to a church, both or all were exhorted to attend the funeral; where there was a choir, the service should be chanted, and the poor should not be expected to pay. People should be encouraged to have Holy Communion celebrated at funerals; the bells should be properly rung, the clergy should attempt to persuade mourners to order the funeral in the right way, and to select suitable memorials. 'Of course, the great and illustrious may have more pomp and dignity in their funerals. If there is to be any distinction . . . it should be made by something additional to the average standard in the case of the rich, not by detracting anything in the case of the poor.'

The parish priests were, most of all, encouraged to persuade burial societies and benefit clubs to become like religious confraternities; this wish to capture existing institutions, together with the ideal of the corporate religious community, were constant features of the Ecclesiologists' programme. The burial confraternity was to be organized on high principles; when a member of it—it was also called 'a guild'—fell sick, those of the 'brethren' whose turn it was to visit went on duty, and it 'may chance thus that the nobleman communicates with the dying labourer, or the artizan in the gilded bed-chamber of the prince . . .' (not such a fanciful idea then as now, since the rich often did visit the poor; it was the principle of reciprocity that was novel). The 'passing bell' would wake the fraternity to prayer for the passing soul; it was thought that this would break through 'the mere family distinction—a great present evil with us'. The officers of the guild, closely superintended in order to prevent abuses, would provide the coffin and equipment.

A pall was to be used in common; a costly one, and embroidered with a 'goodly' cross. For a young person, the pall should have a white border. The kind of pall the Ecclesiologists were thinking of is illustrated in a design by Butterfield in *Instrumenta Ecclesiastica* (first series, plate 63); it is simple, with an abstract circular design and a cross; this text says, 'Palls may be made of silk, velvet, or cloth. Their colour ought to be blue or purple; the cross is made of the same material as the ground work, and ought to be white or red; the embroidery is in gold.' The palls in Pugin's *Glossary* are austere (plate 82); the black and white pall remained by far the commonest type. By 1878 it could be said, 'Of late years the fashion of substituting violet for black palls has largely prevailed',[35] and that Anglo-Catholics used violet in place of black for funeral vestments. The full Ecclesiologist array was sumptuous and fearsome, and must have terribly shocked Low Church opinion (plate 26).

The funeral procession, with its cross, chaplain, and mourners carrying the bier, should be met at the lych gate by the clergy singing a 'solemn anthem'; it should be greeted by a triumphant peal of bells. In the open nave, with the company all around, the bier should be set down. Plate 32 of the *Instrumenta Ecclesiastica* shows a Butterfield bier; it was to be placed on a herse, and covered with a pall; it was advised that herses should be included by architects amongst the necessary fittings for new churches. Herses, as a better arrangement to carry a coffin than trestles, were revived by Pugin. The coffin having been placed on the herse, psalms should be chanted around it, the famous and moving lesson from St Paul should be read, and the procession would move to the grave.

The Ecclesiologists believed that music, banners and a full panoply were appropriate for a great man's procession; tapers should be 'burnt without scruple' while persons of rank lay in state. Feathers should be abolished from funerals; the universal custom of cloaks and hoods for mourners was a valuable remnant of ancient practice. The *Ecclesiastical Art Review*, in 1878, repeated this: 'we differ, no doubt, from many of our compeers, in saying a good word for "funeral cloaks" but these are *not* inventions of the modern undertaker, and it seems a pity that they should share the fate of hatbands and plumes'. By the time of *Jay's History of Mourning*, towards the end of the century, it could be said that 'it is only a few years since that ladies ceased wearing a scarf and hood of black silk, and gentlemen "weepers" on their hats and arms, which were black or white according to the sex of the deceased.' (Women did not, in the earlier half of the period, themselves go to funerals; but when black silk scarves were given they were so beautiful that they were often kept, until enough had been accumulated to make a dress.) Walking funerals were, to the Ecclesiologists, preferable to riding ones. Also, they objected to the shape of modern hearses, and pointed to the old gabled shape still used in some parts of the north as far better. (Again, Butterfield shows a design for a hearse of this type.) And they asserted that undertakers' men should never sit on the roofs of hearses—presumably a gabled hearse would make this difficult, as well as being more Gothic! Priests should be buried in their vestments, and the insignia of their office should be borne in procession.

Many of the ideas of the Ecclesiologists were displayed in 1852, at the funeral of the Earl of Shrewsbury (see page 114); its character was emphasized by the position of the dead earl as the most active Roman Catholic lay patron in the country. His funeral contrasted at many points with that of the Duke of Wellington slightly earlier in the same year, which had been a flagrant embodiment of the pagan, martial ritual detested by the reformers (see page 80). The two funerals shared only their magnificence. In place of regiments of soldiers, Lord Shrewsbury had flocks of clergy—four bishops, representatives of the monastic orders, and at least a hundred-and-fifty secular clergy; in place of Messrs Banting, the great Royal undertakers, and the school of design at South Kensington, Lord Shrewsbury had the firm of Hardman. (This was appropriate; Augustus Welby Pugin, despite his uncompromising temper, had been helped by Lord Shrewsbury from the beginning: the earl, although a very rich man, had lived in the utmost simplicity, that he might contribute towards Pugin's new churches.)

The Earl's funeral called upon the firm's full resources. It is remembered at Alton Towers that the head of the procession, after climbing the hill and traversing the meandering village street, had reached the doors of the church when the coffin could be seen just emerging from the lodge gates of the Towers, nearly a mile away in the valley below.[36]

The Ecclesiologists favoured the use of flowers at funerals and the grave; this use was revived in genteel society during the Victorian period, perhaps in a mediaevalizing vein. Washington Irving spoke of the custom of strewing flowers before funerals and planting them on graves as 'only to be met in the most distant and retired places of the kingdom'; he lamented that 'a custom so truly elegant and touching has disappeared from general use'; in this he seemed to include wreaths and 'chaplets'.[37] The romantic mind valued the Ophelia-like spontaneity and wildness of self-gathered 'floral tributes'—a phrase used already by Irving; Mrs Stone spoke disparagingly of 'wreaths, or rather circlets of the yellow flower, the French immortelles, of which the common English name is "everlasting". All . . . of precisely the same size, shape and colour . . . which evidenced one hand in the preparation.' She preferred simple, scented flowers, and anticipated the Spiritualists by asking 'What must flowers have been in Paradise? Unquestionably they are our most beautiful type of it', the 'pale snowdrop, meek emblem of consolation . . . the *red* rose . . . in commemoration of persons of more advanced life . . . remarkable for benevolence.' She mentioned that flowers were so little used in some places that her employment of them was once deprecated as 'papistical'.[38]
The premises of Messrs Dottridge Brothers, 'among the first funeral reformers preeminently', and a large undertaking firm, were described in some detail in 1878.[39]

The first room contained the funeral department, of which the chief feature was various palls; particularly attractive was a 'rich purple velvet, bordered with gold fringe, interset with text of Scripture, and having the sacred monogram IHS worked in gold thread in the centre'. Next came the chief wareroom, with 'metal ornaments', including breastplates, handles, lid ornaments and crosses; then the drapery department, with cloths, silks, cambrics, gloves, flannels, etc.; then a mysterious department reserved for wicker-baskets: mysterious, that is, to those not acquainted with the 'Earth to Earth' doctrines of Francis Seymour Haden. Then came the dipping room, where metals were oxidized to improve their appearance; the burnishing room, where the processes of electroplating, coppering, bronzing, were carried out; the lacquering room and the japanning shop, in both of which women worked; the Coventry-room, where women sat at sewing machines, and pinked, goffered, and embroidered the shrouds (plate 51). Then came the general metal-workers shops, where worked the draughtsmen, engravers, chasers, polishers, planishers, turners, etc.; the stamping room, where presses, of which the largest weighed three tons, embossed designs on tin and other metals (plates 2, 48).

This tremendous establishment was devoted to the maintenance of the 'solemnity' so highly valued by the Victorians. Solemnity, like Mercury, came on winged feet—Messrs Dottridge Brothers could produce a coffin 'of the most artistic finish' complete in seven minutes, at a cost of thirty shillings. The firm watched its rivals: 'Last year, when the American "Caskets" were first introduced into England, this firm immediately secured machinery whereby they could compete with the Americans, and in a short time actually received orders from America.' Also, it had just patented a new funeral car; as a 'mighty improvement' it was open and had an open 'ornamental roof supported by four elegant twisted columns, relieved in colour. The framework is of polished oak, and at each end is an appropriately carved pillar. At the sides are ornamental iron railings, and from the violet roof, relieved with gold, curtains are gracefully draped, which are especially intended for wet weather. The whole effect is exceedingly pleasing.' It had certainly departed from the black grandeur of forty years before.

That still existed. The panegyrist of Messrs Dottridge remarked that 'we really trust that our old friends—or enemies—the black studded coffin and be-plumed hearse are in a fair way of being done to death by the unrepulsive substitutes provided . . . .' He went on to say that the forms, and especially the colours, of funerals must depend upon the view of the survivors concerning the after state of the soul. Those who held that the soul slept between death and resurrection, and those who considered that death brought total extinction, alike would mourn; those who anticipated immediate paradise would rejoice, whilst those who believed in a period in purgatory (plate 95) would temper their rejoicing with grief. It would be interesting to hear this gentleman's speculations upon the theological beliefs that might have inspired the form of William Morris' funeral (plate 55).

It sounds simple enough. But neither the expense nor the problems, theological and aesthetic, ended with the funeral; when it, and its attendants, had departed from the burial ground, a corpse remained for disposal, and any aspirations towards perpetuity in stone or marble remained to be satisfied. The fiercest ire of the reformers was directed towards the sanitary and religious problems thus created.

31

3 God's Acre

'Burial places in the neighbourhood of the living are . . .
the cause, direct or indirect, of inhumanity, immorality,
and irreligion.'[1]

It is not possible to understand how passionately the Victorians concerned themselves about the decent disposal of human corpses without a hint of the theological
basis on which their solicitude rested. Even now, it is difficult to consider the subject of disposal with the comfortable materialism that obtains in other matters:
emotional illogicalities creep in. An acquaintance with Victorian beliefs makes it
easier to appreciate the fear and horror aroused, for example, by the Resurrection-
ists, or by the noxious practices of the old graveyards; it becomes easier, also, to
appreciate the truculent unorthodoxy of such a man as Jeremy Bentham, who left
his own body for scientific purposes, and who seriously proposed that the bodies
of others should be set up as varnished monuments in their own parks![2]

To the Victorians, as to their predecessors, the glory and hope of Christianity
was the doctrine of the resurrection of the body, of life everlasting, of the paradise
that ultimately awaited those who had not transgressed overmuch in this life. It
was this hope that made death a part of life; it softened the terrors of dissolution
and made possible death's celebration as a passage to perfect happiness. A contemporary hymn, one of many, put it in homely language: it was quoted on her
deathbed by the daughter of a pious nobleman:

> Sweet has been our earthly union,
> Sweet our fellowship of love;
> But more exquisite communion
> Waits us in our Home above.[3]

The *Quarterly Review* was more lofty:

'But when our Lord by His own dying had taken away the pollution, as by His
rising again He had taken away the sting of death: when life and immortality were
brought to light, and the doctrine of the Resurrection of the Body had established,
once and for ever, all touching the mystery of the grave and of the life hereafter . . .
the particular Christian doctrine of the Resurrection of the Body . . . [suggested]
a decency and comeliness in the funeral solemnities . . . it should be remembered—
what is too much forgotten—that the Resurrection of the Body is no mere abstruse
scholastic dogma . . . but a peculiar revelation of Christianity . . . it presupposes our
flesh here upon earth the abode of the Holy Spirit . . . the Christian believes that
when this corruptible shall have put on incorruption, he who was made in the
beginning after the image of God shall be restored to that image . . . each person
may speak of himself the words which Christ Himself spoke after His Resurrection,
"Behold, it is I myself." '[4]

Mrs Stone, more simply, said:

'It is difficult to understand the feelings of indifference with which some, sincerely good people too, declaim on the worthlessness of the body, and their carelessness of what becomes of it. "What matters", say they, "this old vile garment, these rags?" Oh much, very much. For are we not told that *it* shall rise again?'

She emphasized her point. 'Yes, *this body*—waiting, sleeping, changed—this human chrysalis shall waken, and soar on radiant wing to that empyrean whence its immortal spirit first emanated.'[5] Judge her feelings, had *she* been the young woman who, a few days after the burial, recognized her mother's finger among a heap of rubbish.[6] Given a literal belief in the resurrection of the body, and the consequent importance of the body, the shocking nature of the revelations of the state of public burial grounds made in the 1830s and 1840s can be understood, as can the effect of such items of information as that 'many tons of human bones every year are sent from London to the North, where they are crushed in mills constructed for the purpose, and used as manure'.[7] Hence the continuing importance of consecration as a protective measure, albeit not always an effective one, as a leader in *The Queen* pointed out in 1880, when soil from the Whitfield Tabernacle was being sold to florists in Camden Town:

'This proceeding, so opposed to public decency, is also, happily, contrary to the provisions of the Burial Act, and the offenders have been summoned by the Vestry of St Pancras . . . Can it, therefore, be a matter for wonderment that persons outside the pale of the Church of England clamour for admittance into her last sanctuary, where there is an assurance that their remains may rest in peace, and not be subject in a score of years to be sold at eighteenpence a bowl for forcing mignonette and flowering geraniums?'[8]

The inviolate nature of that sanctuary must have appeared doubtful in the 1840s, when the religious and the sanitary conscience suffered from outrageous disclosures.

It should perhaps first be said that the earlier attempts to solve the problem of overcrowded churchyards, made by shareholders with the same profit motive as that which influenced other business men, anticipated the main mass of polemical evidence on the subject—Kensal Green Cemetery, the first of the great London cemeteries, opened in 1832; Walker's *Gatherings from Grave Yards*, the obsessive work that first really opened up the subject, did not appear until 1839. Cemeteries were not a new idea; indeed, Wren had included suburban cemeteries in his designs for a new London—'since it had become the fashion to solemnize funerals by a train of coaches (even where the deceased are of moderate condition)'.[9] They had not solved the problem, it was said in 1838, because only the affluent were buried in them.[10] They were tainted with commerce, which was thought unbecoming in this context; even Walker found it necessary to declare, at the beginning of his book, that he was entirely unconnected with cemetery speculations. New burial methods were à la mode, in a curious way, in the 1830s; in 1831, for instance, when the new vaults under St Martin-in-the-Fields were opened, *The Sunday Times* reported, 'Crowds of ladies perambulated the vaults for some time, and the whole had more the appearance of a fashionable parade than a grim repository of decaying mortality.'

33

A principal reason for the investigations that led to the shocking revelations concerning graveyards was the new interest in hygiene, itself a result of cholera epidemics. Cholera, like other diseases, struck most viciously at the poor; in 1850, for example, it was reported that the Registrar General's returns demonstrated that in the poorer districts cholera mortality averaged 98 in 10,000; in the richer, 46 in 10,000—more than twice as many poor died. But rich and poor alike regarded it with particular fear.[11] The horror communicated was immense; its victims were sometimes buried within ten minutes of expiring.

Cholera first appeared in England in 1831; by January 1832 the first cases had been reported in London. In 1846–9 another, and more serious, epidemic occurred; in September 1849 two thousand died in one week. During 1853–4 over twenty thousand died; a fourth, less severe, visitation occurred in 1865–6. It was not until 1883 that the cholera germ was discovered; until the 1850s cholera had been grouped under the general heading of 'fever', an umbrella term that covered many illnesses.

Peculiar theories were current concerning fever; it was thought to be caused by atmospheric pollution, and 'air confined, heated, and deprived of its elasticity, is of itself dangerous from whatever body it proceeds, even if it results from the perspiration of persons in the best state of health'.[12] The general view was expressed in a comment of 1840 on the first *Annual Report of the Registrar of Births, Deaths, and Marriages*: the Registrar had drawn the conclusion that deaths from many causes doubled in cities: 'are cities then necessarily the graves of our race? . . . . There is no reason why health should be impaired by residence in 1 more than 100 square miles, if means can be devised for supplying . . . pure air and for removing the principal sources of poisonous exhalations.'[13]

Graveyards were considered to be one of the principal sources of poisonous exhalations. Dr Southwood Smith, reporting to the Poor Law Commissioners in 1838, was fairly cautious: the poison from putrid exhalations 'acts as a powerful predisposing cause of some of the most common and fatal maladies' even if it did not kill or produce fever directly. Mr Walker, surgeon, was more sweeping: he said that burial places were more important in producing typhus fever than either filth or poverty.[14] Dissent was uncommon, although it did exist. The *Quarterly Review* said that 'it may be a newer feature in the controversy to say that there has been a serious doubt among the medical profession whether the putrid exhalations from such masses of corruption have any injurious effect on the health of the living',[15] and a Dr Todd, of King's College, uttered the heresy that 'the gases that are generated in graveyards are generally sulphuretted hydrogen and carburetted hydrogen with ammonia. If these gases be generated in the laboratory . . . they will produce the same effect. These effects are very different from the ordinary symptoms of typhoid fever.' He added that he considered that the open burial ground next to King's College Hospital was, far from being a cause of infection, a useful source of ventilation.[16] Nevertheless, the 1843 *Supplementary Report . . . into the Practice of Interments in Towns* clearly concluded that 'putrid emanations' formed the principal 'cause of the most developed form of typhus, that is to say, the plague . . .' and the General Board of Health, in its report of 1850 drawn up with the guidance of Chadwick, included graveyards as one of the causes of cholera.

In 1842 Mr Henry Helsden, testifying before the Parliamentary Committee, was asked: 'How were the graves generally made?' He replied:

'. . . in accordance with [the plan] generally observed or adopted throughout London: this is, the opening, what is called a public grave, thirty feet deep, perhaps; the first corpse interred was succeeded by another, and up to sixteen or eighteen, and all the openings between the coffin boards were filled with smaller coffins of children. When this grave was crammed as full as it could be, so that the topmost coffin was within two feet of the surface that was . . . considered as occupied.'[17]

Walker said that paupers at Aldgate were buried seventeen or eighteen to a grave with no earth whatsoever between the coffins.[18] Such overcrowding (plate 59) meant that the old churchyards became exceedingly offensive; it was said that flies were generated from them.[19] A typical metropolitan church, St Martin-in-the-Fields, had a burial ground 200 feet square, which was estimated to contain 60,000 to 70,000 bodies.[20] In 1843 the new Bunhill General Burial Ground was receiving 2323 bodies per acre.[21]

It was widely believed that the gases given off by decaying bodies were *directly* noxious, as well as being the cause of lingering illnesses and fever; Loudon's opinion was typical: 'To inhale this gas, undiluted with atmospheric air, is instant death; and, even when much diluted, it is productive of disease which commonly ends in death . . . .'[22] There are many circumstantial accounts of the deaths of grave-diggers from the effects of the corruption they unearthed; one of the most famous and widely quoted was related by Walker—the case of two grave-diggers who died at Aldgate in 1838, one 'as if struck with a cannon-ball', when engaged in digging a pauper's grave. It was directly stated at the inquest that they died from the effects of carbonic acid gas; it is quite clear that Walker and others thought this explanation only a partial one. Walker said in 1840 that a man employed in removing bodies from the vaults of St Dunstan's,

'complained of a nauseous taste in his mouth and throat, severe pain in the chest, accompanied with a cough: his skin subsequently became of a deep yellow tinge, and extremely harsh and dry. This man was at times so affected with the effluvia, that he was compelled to support himself against the wall of the vault. In removing the body of a man who had committed suicide, the gaseous exhalation was so powerful that he was rendered unconscious for a considerable period. He invariably declared that this was the cause of his death—"Do you think it was?"—"I should think it more than likely."'[23]

Other accounts spoke of ulcerated throats (lasting two years) and skin eruptions. When asked about the practice of leaving graves open in order to save time, Walker said of one grave:

'I examined [it] the other day . . . [it] was dug twenty-two feet deep; it is within a few feet of the windows of the house; there were ten or a dozen coffins projecting into the grave; I have no doubt some of them had been cut through. My opinion is, that the lighter gases pass off; the heavy gases, the carbonic oxide and carbonated

35

hydrogen, will fall down to the bottom of the grave. It is generally supposed a candle will not burn in a place of that kind . . . I tried a candle; it was extinguished at a depth of twelve feet from the surface.'[24]

Open graves were a common complaint. Walker recorded a grim comment concerning one from a man who lived in Clement's Lane, an area devastated by the prevalent and triumphant 'fever': 'Ah, that grave is just made for a poor fellow who died in this house, in the room above me: *he died of typhus fever . . . they have kept him twelve days*, and now they are going to put him under my nose, by way of warning to me.'[25]

Walker attempted to obtain samples of the gas for analysis, employing to this purpose Mr George Whittaker, an undertaker. Whittaker related how he had tapped a leaden coffin, and collected an india-rubber bottleful of gas; unfortunately some escaped, and being 'of deadly quality' laid him up for a fortnight.[26] Grave-diggers and undertakers had a technique for overcoming the Borgia-like energy of this gas; when they observed the upper lid of a leaden coffin growing convex, through the pressure from inside, they bored a hole, put a pipe in, and set it alight; 'I have been informed that it will burn for twenty minutes'.[27]

One rather beautiful theory was advanced in 1848 by Dr Sir James Murray, of Dublin. He shone the 'Light of Science' upon 'selfish and slovenly officials'. 'Let any of the advocates of intramural grave-yards employ accurate Electricians with delicate instruments, to measure the terrible Galvanic derangements of fermenting churchyards—then, they must be convinced of their fatal practices. Every decomposing human body deposited there, is *hourly altering and disordering the electric fluid of that locality*.'

To Sir James, a disabling influence was exerted by electric agencies disturbed by 'the continuous cauldron of dissolving graves'; an 'effervescing Golgotha' in Belfast had taught him that epidemics were caused by its proximity. Also, 'I had many proofs demonstrating that persons in these tenements *could not be efficiently electrified;* because the best machines *could seldom produce sparks of any intensity.*' This and other observations had convinced him 'that *Negative Electricity pervaded this vast swamp, and drew away the Positive Electricity from the living creatures* in immediate contact with the damp earth and air of that fatal and extended trough, or Galvanic pile'. The consequences could be lethal; England's climate already made for 'a *broken* balance of Electricity'; Sir James broke into agitated capitals to denounce '*evils enough,* without adding vast *troughs* of FERMENTING CEMETERIES IN THE HEART OF TOWNS, to decompose and *deprive us of that living principle* and *true vital fluid or agent . . . .*'

The best solution was to close the cemeteries, but, lacking that, Sir James proposed an eccentric remedy:

'The EQUILIBRIUM of Galvanism will be best *restored and preserved* by the erection of numerous COPPER PIPES, or WIDE TUBES, reaching *high into the air* . . . these Pipes are intended to convey *Positive* Electricity from the air above, where it *abounds,* to the earth below, where it is *deficient.* They are easily affixed perpendicularly to walls, posts, or monuments, like spouts to houses.'[28]

36

Had this proposal found favour, and the Light of Science shone successfully upon Victorian cemeteries, how piquant an element would have been added to their composition!

The unpleasant nature of the grave-diggers' work encouraged them to drink—they were as drunken a set of men as were the mutes, and with far more excuse: 'driven from extreme necessity to an almost unusual use of ardent spirits'.[29] In this they were at times urged on by their employers: 'Several of the labourers . . . refused to continue the work. They were well supplied with brandy, and under the influence of a half-drunken excitement . . . .'[30] For this work they were generally paid from fifteen to eighteen shillings a week, a sum that might be increased by tips from nineteen to twenty-three shillings.[31] The trade attracted and bred a brutalized type; it 'has in fact educated a race of men too frequently the most degraded and abandoned; with but few exceptions, they drink to excess, and indeed too frequently they are compelled to stimulate'. They did not, apparently, always plead the unhealthiness and unpleasantness of their work: 'Men with shrunken figures and the appearance of premature age, and a particular cadaverous aspect, have attended as witness to attest their own perfectly sound condition, as evidence of the salubrity of their particular occupations.'[32] The philosophic sexton so frequently encountered in the verse and prose of the period rarely appeared in real life; he was perhaps a Romantic extension of Hamlet's grave-digger.

Overcrowded churchyards meant that recently interred corpses were constantly disturbed; it was this that made the system of interment a 'gross indecency towards the dead'.[33] In order to make room, corpses not a week buried were chopped up and burnt; choppers and saws for the purpose were kept in the graveyards. There was frequently a charnel house or 'bone house' in the churchyard. (Walker said, 'I believe that bones, independently of their tegumentary appendages, may prove injurious to health'.)[34] A grave-digger told the 1842 Select Committee a hair-raising story of how the corpse of a woman, from which the head had been chopped, fell on him in the dark from the side of a grave he was digging. The grave-diggers stole lead from the coffins, and sold the bodies to surgeons; sextons were impelled to dispose of as many bodies as possible, since the more that were buried, the greater the profit.

Coffins were occasionally sold to undertakers for re-use, but far more commonly were sold as firewood. Walker told the Committee,

'. . . it is extensively burnt all over London; that (producing it) is a portion of a coffin I have brought; that poor creature died in Charing Cross Hospital; she had frequently burnt large quantities of it herself; this wood was drying with a large quantity which the police seized, and the fire was made of this wood when we entered the room. There was a large quantity I brought away, and sent it to the head police officer in Scotland Yard, with my compliments, that they had better look into the matter; they sent it to the parish, and they said, "Oh, it must be got rid of; the poor are quite welcome to it." This I produce was part of a pauper's coffin. I know a parish in which the grave-digger burnt it as common fuel. I asked him whether he felt any stench from it; he said, "Oh, the people say it smells now and then", but he was a drinking man . . . .'[35]

Walker added that a sack of coffin wood in a house would produce most injurious effects, but that people could not see 'those active poisons evolved in their houses'. He said also that unblushing men had made enormous profits from the disposal of the dead, and that speculators had long known that a 'free-hold grave was infinitely preferable as a source of profit to any other.'[36]

Both undertakers and clergymen speculated in burial grounds. For instance, a 'burial ground' in the parish of St John's, Southwark, belonged not to the church, but to an undertaker: he had bought a cellar or 'vault' that ran under four houses, and filled it with wooden (not lead, as was customary in 'vaults') coffins; the undertaker's man, who was of course not ordained, regularly donned a surplice and read the service 'profanely'. The deception was carried as far as the establishment of a 'minister's house'.[37] The 1842 Committee asked an undertaker whether it was the custom of dissenting ministers to speculate in burial grounds in the town. His answer was, 'Yes. It has been remarked to me that they get more money by the dead than by the living.'

The most notorious case of a speculation of the latter type was that of Enon Street Chapel in Clement's Lane. Built in 1823, it had a cellar measuring fifty-nine by twenty-nine feet. Between the cellar and the chapel above was a boarded floor, without lath or plaster. Within the cellar, which contained a sewer, it was estimated that, by 1842, 12,000 bodies had been placed. The average interment rate was thirty a week. Besides being used as a chapel, the place was used as a Sunday School.

Intolerable smells arose through the planks of the floor into the chapel. Frequently, four or five women fainted during the services: 'Was the congregation a crowded one?'—'Not latterly; it fell off.'[38]

This was purely and simply a speculation, although originally the fear of resurrection-men may have played a part in the chapel's foundation. The burial fees were low, and members of the Church of England were often buried there for economy. The 1842 Committee, members of which were refused admittance by the minister, Mr Hawse, were told that he and his wife burned bodies 'under the copper, and frequently in their own fire place'.[39] Corpses were 'slipped into the sewer'[40] into which admission was possible from the cellar; the opening was bricked up after investigation. A report compiled in 1847 mentioned that dead bodies were conveyed from the vaults through holes made in the kitchen wall, '*for the purpose of sale and dissection!*'[41] It was observed that the preacher must have profited considerably from providing anatomical schools with subjects.

The upper rooms had, by 1847, been let to 'the lovers of Terpsichore'[42]—the chapel had become a dancing assembly room, a place where 'the *dead are buried*, and the *living dance, under one and the same roof*' (plate 60). The two uses of the place consort oddly enough to have been yielded by the diseased art of Edgar Allan Poe, or some gothic morality.

A reporter descended into the vaults with the persistent Walker; coffins lay strewn all about: 'Most of them, although in a high state of preservation, (having the date of 1838 on them,) were empty . . . some with entire skeletons . . . others with skeletons in an imperfect state, bearing on them the evident marks of great violence, from the rude hand of the grave-digger,—acting under the orders of his *mammon-worshipping* employer . . . '.[43] Such accounts abound.

38

Burial in vaults was attacked mainly on two grounds. One, that it was a continuation of class distinction after death, is dealt with in the next chapter; the other, that it was a gross offence against hygiene, was expounded by Sir John Simon: 'It is a very serious matter . . . that close beneath the feet of those who attend the services of their church, there often lies an almost solid pile of decomposing human remains . . . heaped as high as the vaulting will permit, and generally but very partially confined.' He mentioned that many supposed bodies in vaults, from the sealing of the coffins, to remain unchanged through ages 'like the embalmed bodies of Egypt and Peru'. Or at least they thought the coffins were left intact. They were wrong. If the coffins were not tapped by the sexton, in order to avoid detonations, the decay of the outer wooden case led to the yielding, bulging, and bursting of the inner leaden coffin 'as surely as would a paper hat-box under the weight of a laden portmanteau'.[44]

Loudon shared these views, and proposed, in the pursuit of hygiene, to deny even to his Sovereign the right to the ancestral graveyard:

'We may, perhaps, be thought unreasonable in wishing to prevent interments in Westminster Abbey and St Paul's, or in the royal vault at Windsor, but we consider that the memory of the great men of the nation, including even our sovereigns, would be quite as much honoured by having their bodies buried in the free soil in the country, and appropriate monumental cenotaphs erected . . . as by having their bodies buried under their monuments, or preserved in wooden or leaden cases in vaults or catacombs. Surely it is pleasanter in idea, when looking on the statue of Dr Johnson in St Paul's, to think of his remains being covered by the green turf in the open ground . . . than to think of them lying in black earth, saturated with putrescent moisture, under the damp paved floor of the crypt of a cathedral.'[45]

Burial fees were another expense that had to be met; they were legitimate, although they caused ill-feeling. They quite often formed no inconsiderable part of a clergyman's income, and therefore were a barrier to reform. The response of the Rector of St Giles-in-the-Fields, who, when asked whether any pecuniary loss would be incurred if legislation prohibited future interments in towns, replied 'A very great pecuniary loss',[46] was that of most of his brethren. The Bishop of London declared that the establishment of Kensal Green Cemetery had deprived the incumbent of Paddington of over £200 a year in burial fees.[47] The figures are remarkably high; the fees for St George's, Hanover Square, were £397 in 1838, £423 in 1839, and £438 in 1840: the average income from fees at St James', Westminster, during the six years before the establishment of cemeteries in 1838, was £405; it then dwindled to £128 in 1838, £130 in 1839, and £81 in 1840.[48] Double fees were often charged for dead who had been inhabitants of another parish.

Taken as a whole, the evils discovered and revealed, whether new, or newly obnoxious, or even exaggerated, provided enough ground for reform to be generally accepted as a social necessity; the investigation had been characteristically thorough, and perhaps it is correct to allow the 1842 Committee to draw the conclusions:

'. . . Your Committee have received evidence from persons in every class of life. That of some of the sextons and grave-diggers in this Metropolis exhibits a loathsome picture of the unseemly and demoralizing practices which result from the crowded condition of the existing graveyards—practices which could scarcely have been thought possible in the present state of society. Your Committee have also obtained the evidence of men of a superior education and acknowledged ability: of gentlemen at the head of the medical and surgical professions; of Clergymen and high Dignitaries of the Church and, after a long and patient investigation, Your Committee cannot arrive at any other conclusion than, that the nuisance of Interments in large Towns, and the injury arising to the Health of the Community from the practice, are fully proved.'

4 Cemeteries

'How can a halo be cast over the departed, or "sweetness and light" be reflected on the grave?'[1]

The detested Poor Law Commission produced in 1838 a report that demonstrated the huge and growing demand on the rate caused by epidemics and sickness, themselves the result of the appalling lack of proper sanitation. This concern to keep the rates down was manipulated by Edwin Chadwick to produce the 1842 Report which mentioned in passing that 'since the legislature has been reported to be contemplating the removal of burial from populous places, it has been commonly suspected of having been led to entertain the measure through the influence of joint-stock cemetery proprietors'.

The joint-stock companies had begun to build the new cemeteries long before the reformers won any victories. The cemetery cause perhaps gained from the cemeteries' association with the rich; to be buried in a cemetery became a sign of some affluence. But joint-stock companies were regarded generally with suspicion, partly perhaps because they represented the now total predominance of money over land—Dickens and Trollope were only two out of many who voiced their dislike. There was, especially, a steady expression of distaste for the companies that invested in death, and for their exorbitant profits:

'The joint-stock establishments at present existing, objectionable on many grounds, are wholly unavailable to the mass of the people, by reason of their expense. They are nothing more than the exclusive luxury of the indulgent few .... The high profits realized by the existing companies clearly show, that even with very great reductions in the fees of the rich, and gratuitous interment to the poor, a considerable surplus would remain above the ordinary interest on the original outlay.'[2]

The £400,000 invested by 1843 in the eight chief metropolitan cemeteries was not invested without return.[3] The Church was strongly urged itself to found new cemeteries, partly because of the impossibility of persuading Churchman and Dissenter to occupy the same ground, and partly because any government that attempted to devote public money to 'an object trenching upon religion' would have to sacrifice either the Church or its plan.[4] The Church did not attempt to found cemeteries and this can be seen as a symptom of incipient decline, a refusal to participate in a significant social/ecclesiastical development. It had a strong, if at times a negative, interest in them—the matter of burial fees has been mentioned above. The result of all this was that 'most people's idea of a Cemetery is a something associated with great Egyptian lodges and little shabby flower-beds, joint-stock companies and *immortelles*, dissent, infidelity, and speculation, the irreverences of Abney Park, or the fripperies and frigidities of Père la Chaise'.[5]

The cost of cemetery burial was high. In one cemetery the sale of graves was at the rate of £17,000 per acre; a calculation made for another gave the rate of £45,375

FIG 3 Heading of an undertaker's invoice 1887. *Worthing Art Gallery and Museum*

per acre, not counting the fees charged for monuments. These are extraordinary figures. A later source gives some actual prices charged. The most expensive type of interment of all, that in a brick vault, 'only suited for those in comfortable circumstances', cost from £51 7s at Abney Park to £35 17s 6d at the Great Northern; a vault to contain six coffins cost from £40 at Abney Park to £27 14s 6d at the Great Northern; burial in the public vault cost from £8 8s at Highgate, Nunhead, and Kensal Green to £6 6s at Brompton.[6]

The commercialism associated with cemeteries offended the sense of romantic spontaneity:

'The scattered flowers . . . infinitely touching in the old and rustic churchyards of Wales, fail to move us in the suburban cemetery, where we suspect them to have been bought of 'Harding, marchand des bouquets' . . . the trim grave-gardens cease to please when we read the company's charge for maintaining them 'with or without flowers, per annum, 5s' . . . the whole spirit of the present establishments is necessarily mercenary, and smacks strongly of half-yearly dividends and Copthal Court.'[7]

To some, that flavour added piquancy. The accents of a kind of post-mortem gossip column pervade an account of Kensal Green published in *Ainsworth's Magazine* of 1842. It first compares the cemetery (figs 4, 5 and 6) with the old London churchyards: 'What an escape . . . from the choked charnel house to that verdant wide

42

expanse, studded with white tombs of infinite shapes, and stone marked graves covered with flowers of every brilliant dye!' The writer then records at tedious length the epitaphs of the titled, the rich and the famous buried there. The first mentioned achieves a standard from which the others do not deviate: 'an elegant column, on which is chiselled a withered lily; and on the top, white as snow, is a young lamb, bound and dying. *Julia Lamb* is the inscription below. Pitying and sad is the sentiment with which the beholder turns aside . . . .' Such an apposite pun is fortunately rare, but most of the epitaphs recorded are of wearying banality. Typical of the rest is 'a niece's intensity of love struggling to express itself in a tribute':

> The loss of an aunt I deplore,
> A dear and affectionate friend;
> To me she will never return,
> To her I hope to ascend.
> Her love that of aunts surpass'd
> Can nature do less than weep?
> Oh, no, for my tears flow so fast,
> No bounds my poor nature can keep.

The writer's wonder is always strongly expressed before expensive monuments; the 'magnificent catacomb mausoleum' of Mr Huth, which cost £1500, and could hold forty coffins, aroused his 'mute surprise and admiration'. This stood in the 'Circle' before the church, where were many of the 'more splendid and spacious mausoleums'. In the South Walk a column touched his sentiment: 'Sacred to the memory of Francis, the *only* child . . .'—'What a depth of meaning—what a gush of agony—what a sense of loneliness and bereavement, are in that word *only* . . . .'

The inscriptions range from the heretical:

> Death! like an irresistible King,
> Reigns over us all; he holds in his hand
> An iron sceptre; and when he smites
> None can escape!

and the ineptly romantic:

> In the dismal night-air dress'd,
> I will creep into her breast,
> Flush her cheek and blanch her skin,
> And feed on the vital fire within.
> Lover, do not trust her eyes,
> When they sparkle most, she dies;
> Mother, do not trust her breath,
> Comfort she will breathe in death;
>
> Father, do not strive to save her,
> She is mine and I must have her;
> The coffin must be her bridal bed,
> The winding sheet must wrap her head;

The whisp'ring winds must o'er her sigh,
For soon in the grave the maid must lie;
The worm it will riot on heavenly diet,
When death has deflowered her eye.

to the bathetic:

Death found strange beauty in that cherub brow,
He touched the veins with ice, and the rose faded.

One 'startling' yet 'impressive and sweet' epitaph in the Dissenters' area ran:

'She was a pattern of good works, and though her faith was weak, it triumphed over
the gates of Hell on the very threshold of death, and she began the Hallelujahs of
Heaven before she left the earth!'

The writer gave a list of some of the eminent buried in the Catacombs, which
could hold ten thousand coffins; it is indeed a 'Long array of noble and honourable
names'.

The snobbery, triviality, and lack of taste to be found in the early cemeteries
(and in the later ones, plates 74, 83) explain the ire and austerity of the Ecclesiologists; one begins to forgive the latter's eccentricities and embarrassing archaisms.
The early cemeteries have been ennobled by time, by association, and above all by
decay; some (plates 77, 78) are now beautiful. In the early days they must have
displeased many of discriminating sensibility. Pugin's denunciations conjure up a
picture that to our eyes is delightful: classical tombs and weeping willows, urns and
cypresses, make up a picture romantic in the extreme. But when he got down to
details, and illustrated the details with one of his magnificently hard and literal
engravings, one can see what he meant (plate 80):

'... the entrance gateway is usually selected for the grand display of the company's
enterprise and taste, as being well calculated from its position to induce persons to
patronize the undertaking by the purchase of shares or graves. This is generally
Egyptian, probably from some associations between the word catacombs, which
occurs in the prospectus of the company, and the discoveries of Belzoni on the
banks of the Nile; and nearly opposite the Green Man and Dog public-house, in
the centre of a dead wall (which serves as a cheap medium of advertisement for
blacking and shaving-strop manufacturers), a cement caricature of the entrance to
an Egyptian temple, $2\frac{1}{2}$ inches to the foot, is erected, with convenient lodges for the
policeman and his wife, and a neat pair of cast iron hieroglyphical gates, which
would puzzle the most learned to decipher; while to prevent any mistake, some such
words as "New Economical Compressed Grave Cemetery Company" are inscribed
in Grecian capitals along the frieze, interspersed with hawk-headed divinities, and
surmounted by a huge representation of the winged Osiris bearing a gas lamp.'[8]

In such a description is enshrined the hatred of a devoted mediaevalist, not only
for the aesthetic style of the community in which he found himself, but for its style
of life as a whole. The mediaevalists based their attitude on the Romantic idea that
'God is the eternal law; his origin, and whatever relates to his worship, ought to be
enveloped in the night of time'.[9] They detested that vile and pagan upstart,

44

sepulchral Baroque; their ideas for the ideal cemetery, set out in some detail in 1845,[10] illustrated this (see page 54).

The lineaments of their cemetery are Gothic. It should have a fence, lychgate, Cross, and the yew trees appropriate to any place of Christian burial. The lychgate, if unusually large and elaborate, would plainly symbolize the purpose of the cemetery; it should be built of stone, with sculptured figures and a groined roof, perhaps with a chamber or 'parvise' over it, to accommodate an 'ostiarius'.

Much attention was given to the purpose and status of the cemetery chapel; there was no thought of its being an almost secular or, at best, all-denominational building. A series of arguments concluded that it must be a building in which Holy Communion could be celebrated—a kind of religious college was envisaged (the Ecclesiologists gave an institutional character to everything remotely susceptible). The college would be made up of priest, clerks, choir, bell ringer, sacristan, and so on.

The bier would be placed west of the rood-screen. A rich pall (plate 82) would be essential; purple or violet with a red or scarlet cross, or black with a white cross, would combine well. A *herse* or wooden frame, covered with a drapery ornamented with heraldic banners and devices, and surrounded by lights, would carry the coffin (this was a revival of an old device, although *The Ecclesiologist* says defiantly that herses *were* used after 1688. Pugin illustrated one in his *Glossary*, and a Pugin example survives at Oscott).

The chapel should have a large western doorway, for processions, and perhaps a porch. Bells must be rung (LXVII Canon) and a bell tower would therefore be needed; it should lie north or south of the nave, so that the ringers could see the procession approaching. 'Private munificence may be indulged in the erection of aisles to hold monuments, or mortuary chapels.' The resolution of all these details would be a chapel of which the character as a whole would be,

'grave—sombre, for the portion of humanity is sorrow; but not dismal, for the sorrow of a Christian is full of hope. The windows, save the one over the Altar, will be small and few, and all will be filled with stained glass. The glare of day will be thus excluded, and a more fitting light will be created internally by the employment of solemn tapers. Round the walls will be hung pieces of dark-coloured tapestry, worked in suitable patterns, and frescoes will be painted above these. The subject for the stained glass, in the east window, may be the Resurrection, or the Final Doom. Memorials to the departed may occupy the side lights. These, and Brasses, will be the only monuments allowed in the public parts of the chapel.'[11]

The writer concluded by saying that cemeteries were new to Churchmen, and hoped that architects, having no vicious precedents, would choose the right road. Some did, or approximated to it (plate 79). Some remained defiantly classicist (plate 81).

Many of those who wrote about cemeteries were influenced by the great Parisian cemetery of Père-la-Chaise. It was generally felt that in the matter of interments France was far ahead of England; the former had regulated burials as early as 1765. Père-la-Chaise had been consecrated in 1804; in 1811 a precedent had been set by the regulation of undertakers' tariffs. Père-la-Chaise was praised by all save the Ecclesiologists, who detested its pagan assemblages. It was a cemetery designed to appeal to the romantic and to the snob—George Blair, for instance, stated that the Glasgow Necropolis may be 'justly regarded as the Westminster Abbey of Glasgow. It is to this City what the beautiful cemetery of "Père-la-Chaise" is to Paris.'[12] Loudon was more interested in its picturesque than in its social qualities:

'The greenhouse myrtle flourishes in the parterre dedicated to affection and love; the chaste forget-me-not blooms over the ashes of a faithful friend; the green laurel shades the cenotaph of the hero; and the drooping willow, planted by the hand of the orphan weeps over the grave of the parent. Everything is there tasteful, classical, poetical and eloquent.'[13]

Another romantic influence, that of the great cemetery at Constantinople, hovered as an ideal before those interested in cemetery reform. Its effect is more hard to discern; Loudon, especially, seems to have paid more lip-service to it than actually to have used it as a model.

Loudon's book on *The Laying Out, Planting, and Managing of Cemeteries, and on the Improvement of Churchyards,* was published towards the end of his life, in 1843. The discussion of the subject was then at its height; it would have been an untypical failure of his encyclopaedic career had he not had his say on the subject. And not only his say—one of his last professional acts was to survey the cemetery he had designed at Southampton. The book is a curious work; 'modern' in its more utilitarian attitudes, but old fashioned in its time in that it took little note of the more 'advanced' theories of the Ecclesiologists, which to his contemporaries would probably have seemed to hold the promise of the future. The utilitarianism gave great offence; the *Quarterly Review* confessed that had the grave, which he had so lately discussed, not closed over him so recently, it had 'mended a hard pen' to deal with the work; it was impossible for a 'mere utilitarian mind rightly to embrace a subject which hangs so closely on the confines of another world': the book fell altogether short of what a guide to a Christian cemetery ought to be.[14]

This utilitarianism becomes at time almost comic, as when Loudon discussed the advisability of hastening the destruction of the corpse. There was a general prejudice against quicklime, revealed both by the repeated questionings of the House of Commons' committees and by reviewers' reactions to the 'revolting nature of the question'. Loudon's solution attempted to combine reverence and efficiency:

'If the bones were to be destroyed in the case of a single grave, a hint might be taken from the following passage in Fellowes's Asia Minor. "The outward marks of respect are scarcely visible in their burial-grounds, little more being left to mark the place of interment than a row of stones indicating the oblong form of the grave; but a pipe or chimney, generally formed of wood or earthenware, rises a few inches above the ground, and communicates with the corpse beneath; and down this tube libations are poured by the friends of the deceased to the attendant spirit of the dead." (Vol. xi, p. 16.) Were the libations withheld for five or six years, till the muscular part of the body was completely destroyed, and then diluted nuriatic acid employed as a libation, the result would probably be obtained in the course of a year or two.'

46

Loudon was of the new age in his interest in the use of machinery: he mentioned with approval that used at Kensal Green to lower the coffin into the vaults. Invented by 'Mr Smith, Engineer, Princes St, Leicester Square', it was obtainable at a cost of £400. The reaction of the *Quarterly Review* to this and to other such suggestions was typical of its conservatism and of the general concern for the maintenance of 'solemnity'—

'We should be very scrupulous as to the admission of every new-fangled and patented contrivance into the sepulchral pale. King Death's is a very ancient monarchy, and quite of the old régime. The lowering therefore of the coffin from the chapel into the crypt by means of Bramah's hydraulic press, so highly extolled for its solemnity in some of the cemeteries, has too much of the trick of the theatre about it for the stern realities of the grave. Nor is there anything much better in Mr Loudon's cast-iron tallies for gravestones, temporary railroad cemeteries, and "co-operative railroad hearses"'.

At times Loudon became inconsistent, divided between the demands of sensibility and utilitarianism. He waxed hot concerning the perpetuation of class distinctions beyond the grave:

'By the cemetery bill brought into parliament in 1842, both in the consecrated and unconsecrated ground, portions are to be set apart for the poor, a hard-hearted and unchristian proposal, worthy only of barbarous times . . . . He who has had familiar intercourse with the poor must have observed their sensitiveness with regard to their treatment after death, a subject often of more painful interest than the good or bad in store for them while living.'

After such high-mindedness, the following comes as a surprise:

'The following suggestions are made with a view to the interment of the poor, of paupers, and of such persons as desire no monuments to their graves . . . let each district, besides its permanent cemetery, have a temporary one . . . . This temporary cemetery may be merely a field rented on a 21 years' lease, of such an extent as to be filled with graves in 14 years. At the end of seven years more it may revert to the landlord, and be cultivated, planted, or laid down in grass, in any manner that may be thought proper; the landlord binding himself . . . that the field should never again be let for the same purpose, or for building on.'

He also suggested that workhouses should use part of their gardens as a cemetery, which would revert to its former use after the lapse of sufficient time. The reviewers were quick to seize upon this; 'Finding Mr Loudon justly indignant at this cheap burial cry, what shall we say when he himself proposes to convert paupers into manure?' The atrocities of the communal burial pits at Leghorn and Naples were less revolting than such nice calculations of the best way of disposing of the greatest number of troublesome bodies at the least possible expense and to the greatest possible advantage. This was not altogether fair to Loudon, who did not always follow the most utilitarian way:

'Though levelling the surface of ground filled with graves having no stone monuments, instead of finishing the grave with a raised grass mound, renders the grass

47

much easier mown, yet, as it confounds all distinction between ground filled with graves and ground not so filled, we would not on any account follow this practice . . . because it exhibits nothing characteristic of a place of interment. As it destroys the distinctive feature of a graveyard, it cannot be considered in just taste . . . . Technically, the appearance of the turf mound over the grave is the expression of purpose or use, and this expression is essential to every work of art.'

However, in a way, this very interesting passage smacks of functionalism, which is half way toward utilitarianism.

Loudon defined the main object of a burial ground as the disposal of the dead in such a way that their decomposition would not injure the living, either by affecting their health or by shocking their feelings, opinions, or prejudices. He thought the latter very important; 'Adorn the sepulchre, and the frightful visions which visit the midnight pillow will disappear.' Could this be regarded as an evasion of the principal issue, an evasion which is the essence of modern funeral practice?

The secondary object of the burial ground was the improvement of the 'moral sentiments and general taste of all classes, and more especially of the great masses of society'. The moral effect of the cemetery was a Victorian preoccupation; there 'vice looks terrible, virtue lovely; selfishness a sin, patriotism a duty'; the cemetery was 'the tenderest and most uncompromising monitor of man'. Not only was the cemetery moral; it was educational; 'the tomb has, in fact, been the great chronicler of taste throughout the world'. The cemetery should take up all the past functions of the churchyard:

'To the local resident poor, uncultivated by reading, the churchyard is their book of history, their biography, their instructor in architecture and sculpture, their model of taste, and an important source of moral improvement . . . . The intellectual and moral influence which churchyards are calculated to have on the rural population will not, we think, be disputed.'

Churchyards and cemeteries could educate taste; Loudon acknowledged that such an effect had been hitherto slight, but declared that their potential influence was great, since they were visited by 'every individual more frequently than any other scene, except that of his daily occupation'. The possibilities were of encyclopaedic proportions:

'A church and churchyard in the country, or a general cemetery in the neighbourhood of a town, properly designed, laid out, ornamented with tombs, planted with trees, shrubs, and herbaceous plants, all named, and the whole properly kept, might become a school of instruction in architecture, sculpture, landscape-gardening, arboriculture, botany, and in those important parts of general gardening, neatness, order and high keeping. Some of the new London cemeteries, might be referred to as answering to some degree these various purposes, and more particularly the Abney Park Cemetery; which contains a grand entrance in Egyptian architecture; a handsome Gothic chapel; a number, daily increasing, of sculptural monuments; and one of the most complete arboretums in the neighbourhood of London, all the trees and shrubs being named.'

Others shared these preoccupations. The author of *The Glasgow Necropolis* declared that sermons in monuments were 'one of the high and holy uses of an ornamental cemetery'. Markland insisted on legibility; 'A monument ought to be a book, open for the perusal of the multitude. Unless it declare its meaning fully, plainly, and sensibly, the object, for which it was raised, has failed.'[15]

The *Quarterly Review* placed a different emphasis on the 'moral effect' of cemeteries, an emphasis in which the sentiment was everything; the gulf between this attitude and Loudon's is wide. It asserted that the moral effect came better recommended in the language of Wordsworth, as published by Coleridge; the language is that of Romanticism:

'. . . when death is in our thoughts, nothing can make amends for the want of the soothing influences of nature, and for the absence of those types of renovation and decay, which the fields and woods offer to the notice of the serious and contemplative mind. To feel the force of this sentiment let a man only compare, in imagination, the unsightly manner in which our monuments are crowded together in the busy noisy, unclean, and almost grassless churchyard of a large town, with the still seclusion of a Turkish cemetery in some remote place, and yet further sanctified by the grove of cypress in which it is embosomed.'[16]

Loudon listed about five hundred trees, shrubs and flowers suitable for cemeteries and churchyards. For the former, he preferred to have no flowers: 'a state of quiet and repose is an important ingredient in the passive sublime'—the phrase betrays how far he was thinking in the Picturesque terms of his youth. If flower beds were thought essential, they should be shaped to resemble graves or coffins. In churchyards, the decoration of graves with flowers might be encouraged: 'In Britain, respect for the dead is not generally shown by the introduction of flowers over their graves, but the practice prevails in some places throughout the country, more especially in Wales, and is not infrequent in the metropolitan and other cemeteries . . . .' The *Quarterly Review* objected to his list as more suitable for a select arboretum and flora than for cemeteries and churchyards—Loudon himself had complained that modern cemeteries bore too great a resemblance to pleasure-grounds. It gave its own horticultural view; many clergymen were beginning sadly to overplant their churchyards. Appropriate trees were limited; yews, hemlock-spruces, the cedar of Lebanon, the vine, fig-tree, rose of Sharon, and Scots pine were suitable; evergreens were best. The oak was dismissed with ignominy—'Too Erastian as well as too utilitarian a symbol'—as was the weeping willow, 'a modern sentimentalism, false as a Christian type, and its name . . . a mere pious fraud of the botanists'.[17]

Loudon was full of practical and moderating suggestions. Cemeteries should have a solemn and soothing character 'equally remote from fanatical gloom and conceited affectation'; one hears in this a distant echo of the eighteenth-century distrust of enthusiasm, the excesses of which Loudon would most probably have detected in the Ecclesiologists. Cemeteries should be conspicuous from a distance, because their buildings and tombs would make them an 'ornament' to the surrounding country, and an 'impressive memento of our mortality'. Order was necessary: dogs, improper persons, smoking, eating, drinking, running, laughing and whistling

49

should not be allowed. The roads within should be straight, not winding, to give solemnity and grandeur; the best system for the graves would be to lay them out in double beds, with green paths between. It was necessary to admit sun and air; the trees, therefore, were to be planted not in belts, but singly. Loudon's plan of a cemetery (plate 84) has a curious fascination, a logical inevitability that approaches poetry.

A great deal of attention must be paid to surface drainage, which at Kensal Green was as lacking as were foundations for monuments—monuments must have foundations. Catacombs should always be sealed, and not by gratings: brick graves, used as substitutes for vaults, should be covered with a ledge stone. Loudon went into much detail on necessary tools; he also made the intriguing recommendation that a 'handsome open structure' in harmony with its surroundings, might be erected for strangers to watch the performance of a funeral. Practical as always, he did not shrink from institutionalizing the funereal curiosity of strangers; no doubt it would have been easy for a Victorian to justify it on moral grounds, and it is possible that the erection of one funeral grand-stand alone would have led to the institution becoming popular and common. The iron-work bandstands that yet survive here and there in our public parks might have found their equivalent in our public cemeteries!

By 1850 the reports of the Parliamentary Committees and the various exposures of scandals connected with burials had prepared public opinion for an attempt at solution. It was generally accepted that the exclusion of burials from churches and churchyards, the construction of cemeteries, and the burial in cemeteries of the famous, would be a return to primitive practice. Moreover, it had been discovered that cemeteries did not necessarily depress the status of a neighbourhood; for example, the establishment of a cemetery at Highgate (plate 76) had at first been strongly opposed by the inhabitants, but its flowers and trees, its quietness and seclusion, made so favourable an impression that people who lived nearby purchased keys which enabled them to walk within the cemetery at whatever time they wished.[18] On the other hand, by 1850 it had become apparent that some cemeteries had suffered the same fate that afflicted churchyards (plate 59); the need for action was urgent.

The Metropolitan Interments Act of 1850 provided that a Board of Health should have power to provide cemeteries; the Queen in Council could, on the advice of the Board, forbid further interments in churchyards (from 1852 to 1862, 500 Orders in Council closed 4000 old burial grounds); certain rights in vaults were reserved. No body was to be buried within two hundred yards of any house— save that of the keeper of the cemetery!—or within any cemetery chapel. The Board could provide mortuaries. Complicated clauses compensated incumbents for burial fees. Two chapels were to serve each cemetery; one would be consecrated, for Anglicans, the other unconsecrated, for other denominations. The forms of many cemetery entrances, with their twin chapels on either side, embody this bigotry in stone (plate 79).

There were two other interesting provisions. The first regulated the carrying of corpses on the railways, a subject that had been aired by Loudon. The second allowed the Board to provide for funerals at fixed charges; this had been advocated for many years. The Board could receive tenders for contracts for the undertaking of funerals 'according to Classes arranged with reference to the Nature and Amount of the Matters and Services to be furnished and rendered, but so that in respect of the lowest of such Classes the Funeral may be conducted with Decency and Solemnity . . . .' The Board could, if it so wished, contract separately for different services for each funeral—obviously an attempt to stop sub-contracting—and was to publish the scale of charges for funerals.

The undertakers were aghast: 'Here's a bill . . . this General Interment! What's to become of my old hands who haven't been what you may call rightly sober these twenty years? Ain't there any religious feeling in the country?'[19] The popular Press seized delightedly on their discomfiture, and on the amalgam of hostility and pathos with which they greeted the Act (plate 85). The truth was that the times were changing; although the palmy days of the great funeral were by no means over—the greatest of all, that of the Duke of Wellington, was to be celebrated two years later—for the undertakers themselves the knell had begun to toll; the 1850 Act, coming so neatly in the middle of the century, marks the beginning of the great change.

5 Sepulture and Commemoration

'National sepulture is a part, and a most important part, of national religion.'[1]

The whole domain of ecclesiastical art—and in that, despite their often non-sectarian character, the new cemeteries must be included—was greatly affected by the High Church movement associated with such names as Pusey, Newman, Keble —and Pugin. Within the movement, religion and aesthetics seem to be inextricably mixed; when the latter became dominant as it did with such later devotees as Pater, preciosity replaced religion. Ronald Firbank pushed this exquisiteness to a comic extreme, and High Church aestheticism has hardly been taken seriously since. But in the early days the moral tone was both high and ascetic, fierce rather than self-indulgent; it surveyed the whole of life and of death, and its gorgeous visual manifestations should not obscure this fact. The views of *The Ecclesiologist*, in an article of September 1844, on epitaphs, illustrate this asceticism.

The article denounced the 'paganism' of modern epitaphs: it recommended that an enormous amount of irrelevant information such as the age, trade, or craft (plate 60) of the deceased should be omitted; such references were rare before the 'more worldly age of the House of Lancaster'! The ideal epitaph for persons of 'humble life' would consist merely of the words '+ Jesu mercy!'—there was no need to record a name. The occupation of ecclesiastics should be mentioned, an exception necessary as 'a testimony to the more exceeding reward which will be the lot of every faithful steward in That Day . . . Hic jacet C.P. *clericus.*'

The word 'died' and the formula *'requiescat in pace'* were pagan, and the former was inappropriate: 'No whisper of despair shall wrong our holy religion. We will sign our brother's tomb with the mighty Cross in token that he has a share in the victory over Death.' The words *'obiit'* or, in English, 'deceased' or 'here resteth' should be used. (This, incidentally, aroused dissent; a correspondent objected to the objections to the word 'died' but the reply cited the paucity of people who 'died' in the New Testament; St Stephen, the first martyr, 'fell asleep' and St Paul declared 'the time of my *departure* is at hand'.[2])

Heresy in epitaphs was to be avoided—anything that indicated confidence in the blessedness of the deceased was heretical! Humility was necessary; there were few mediaeval instances of any eulogy. Such phrases as 'during the course of a long and painful illness, she exhibited the greatest resignation and fortitude'; 'who exchanged this life for a better'; 'they shall hunger no more' were objectionable. No epitaph was 'Catholick' unless it contained a distinct prayer for mercy. Epitaphs were to be brief, not more than twenty words; for ecclesiastics, Latin only was to be used. Capitals were appropriate only for the initial letters of the names of the people commemorated; all lines were to be of uniform length without breaks. *No* epitaphs should be constructed in the shape of urns or altars, as with:

In
memory of
Sir Richard Roe, Bart
many years an
active magis-
trate
of this county[3]

But 'The Cross . . . the symbol both of peace in the grave and of triumph over death, will find its place in every correct memorial' (plate 64).[4]

A Tract upon Tomb Stones by a member of the Lichfield Society for the Encouragement of Ecclesiastical Architecture (1843) repeated these injunctions and added that genealogies, in such a context, were sickening and disgusting. The urge to turn everything into a verse was responsible for such meaningless jingles as:

Requiesce
Cat in pace!

and the inclusion of irrelevant detail led to epitaphs such as:

To the Memory of K.L.
etc. etc. etc.
Who departed this life, May——, 18——

This design of a STONE represents the size of one that was taken from the above K.L., which weighed $4\frac{1}{2}$ ounces.

Reform was desired not only of epitaphs; the form of the sepulchral monument itself, as developed during the Renaissance and beyond it, was hotly attacked. Ridicule was the chosen weapon, of both the aesthetic forms used and of the symbolism that lay behind them—or of the lack of symbolism, or its misapplication. The movement of opinion was with the reformers; there was a general wistful longing for the old days, in which Gothic Romanticism played a large part as in this picture of an ancient churchyard '. . . a great stone Cross reared high amongst the graves, a venerable weather-beaten yew tree, a wooden lich-gate over the entrance, and, it may be, a spring rising within the precinct or a brook running through it. Probably, too, beautiful foliage grew thick around, making the abode of the departed peaceful and secluded . . . . Was there not a feeling in all this— a sentiment?'[5] Indeed there was.

The panegyrist of *The Glasgow Necropolis* praised the variety of monument available within the early Victorian cemetery; memorials embraced 'every variety of order and style, from the simple grandeur of the Doric to the exquisite elegance of the Corinthian—from the massive Egyptian obelisk to the picturesque Gothic, the graceful Italian, and the formal yet fanciful Elizabethan'. But even he had doubts, doubts that an age fascinated by symbolic and sentimental allusion was increasingly to express: 'They are elegant as works of art, but they express nothing . . . erect them in any other locality . . . and their object . . . would be somewhat difficult to divine.'[6] Pugin was amongst the first to condemn the obscurities and inconsistencies; he did so with his customary insanely logical vigour:

'If we worshipped Jupiter, or were votaries of Juggernaut, we should raise a temple

FIG 4 An urn. From 'A Visit to the General Cemetery at Kensal Green' illustrated by
W. Alfred Delamotte, *Ainsworth's Magazine* 1842. *Collection Mrs Betty O'Looney*

[plate 63] or erect a pagoda. If we believed in Mahomet, we should mount the
crescent, and raise a mosque. If we burnt our dead, and offered animals to gods,
we should use cinerary urns [fig 4] and carve sacrificial friezes of bulls and goats.'

He viciously attacked cemetery monuments, concluding:

'Surely the Cross must be the most appropriate emblem on the tombs of those
who profess to believe in God crucified for the redemption of man; and it is almost
incredible, that . . . the types of all modern sepulchral monuments should be
essentially pagan; and urns, broken pillars, extinguished lamps, inverted torches
(plate 63), and sarcophagi, should have been substituted for recumbent effigies,
angels, and emblems of mercy and redemption.'[7]

The theme of the Cross was taken up by many writers, and many echoed the words
of the two most important and influential, Pugin and Markland—the work of the
latter, *On the Expediency of Rendering Sepulchral Monuments subservient to Pious
and Christian Uses*, had appeared in 1842. Much effort was put into proving that
the Cross was not a papistical emblem; those who accepted the Cross sometimes
asserted their orthodoxy by denouncing the Crucifix.

In an article of 1845 these views were applied to cemeteries; it declared that
although a cemetery gave more liberty for monuments than a churchyard, 'influenced as such display may be by the different feelings and worldly position of the
survivors', nevertheless scrupulous care should be taken to exclude all allusions
to 'heathen rites or heathen notions, and all the emblematical devices of despair . . .
to the Faithful death is no death at all, but a very deliverance from death . . .'[8]

Within this limit every variety could be allowed, from the humble wooden cross and the flowers planted beside a mound of turf, to the 'high coped tomb, or the more sumptuous erection of a Mortuary chapel'.

The reformers thoroughly enjoyed themselves in their strictures on post-Renaissance monuments. They usually included an historical sketch of the gradual 'degradation' in design that had occurred from the High Middle Ages onwards, a decline that was associated with the loss of true religion:

'But when the so called dark ages were passing away, first the words of prayer disappeared, and then prayer's attitude. This change appeared in the reign of Elizabeth, when pride of birth, pride of mental or corporeal qualities, or even utterly baseless pride, began to raise up the Effigies of the dead; next to support them lollingly on their elbows, dressed out in flowing wigs and court suits; and, finally, to ensconce them in chairs, whilst the pompous Epitaphs below were quite in accordance with the sculpture above—an evil which, though abated by the improved and improving taste and feeling of the present century, in many cases still breaks forth but too apparently, in the struggle to claim relationship in the grave, with the comparatively great, or to clutch as eagerly at the titles of Esquire, or even Gent, as when life animated the slumbering dust below.'[9]

This succinct account is a comparatively late (1858) condensation of a circumstantial account by Markland, who complained also that 'for more than a century, mural monuments with cherubs, skulls, lamps, and twisted columns, with little variety, were permitted to deform our churches. In later days we have had the urn or the sarcophagus—strange ornaments in a Christian temple!—or a female figure, veiled with drapery, sitting under a willow [fig 3], bending over a tomb, or leaning upon an extinguished torch!'[10] The *Quarterly Review* took up his point concerning the national monuments in Westminster Abbey and St Paul's; in this account Victorian prudery enters the precincts of the church:

'. . . when the government of a great and Christian nation could find no better mode of commemorating the dead than by re-erecting images of Neptune, and Mars, and Fame, and Victory, mixed up with dragoons and drummers, catapults and cannons, men without clothes in a field of battle, or English generals in Roman togas, and all the trash of the poorest pedant; and when a Christian church in a Christian metropolis is selected as the fittest depository for these outrages . . . there must have been something most unsound in the tone and manners of the age.'[11]

This review objected strongly to one of the most 'monstrous innovations upon the pure principles of Christian art—we mean the studied and elaborate representation of the naked human figure'. Actually, despite a modern shift in taste, the neo-classic monuments in St Paul's do, as a whole, remain empty, ugly and offensive.

One of those who most relished the controversy was the Reverend John Armstrong, who lectured to the Exeter Diocesan Architectural Society in 1844; he sounded a trumpet call to action: 'the age of lath and plaster maintains a fight with the age of stone and oak'. He praised Chantrey's 'Sisters' at Lichfield as a return to the ancient model of the recumbent figure, a 'prostrate, dependent being'; a praise repeated by other writers, and substantiated by Victorian reproductions of the monument in parian ware. He employed satire, writing: 'The most *comfortable* looking monuments are those which represent a gentleman sitting in an easy chair in a toga-like dressing gown with a book or a paint-brush in his hand; but the most popular device, and assuredly the most unintelligible, is the employment of little boys, a race of disconsolate cupids.' Cupids or putti came in for a good many side swipes; 'the large uninteresting head of some Justice Shallow of the day, supported by a couple of fat lugubrious boys, who are so much wrapped up in their grief as to be negligent of all other apparel . . . .' To Armstrong the worst effect was that these monuments very often deformed the whole church; original features were chiselled away or entirely removed to make way for them, they were completely— Egyptian or Grecian—out of style (a subtly different argument, in its archaeological approach, to the objection on grounds of inappropriate symbolism), and, at times, their insertion undermined the stability of the building.

More ordinary monuments were equally condemned—mural tablets, or, as Markland called them, '—marble excrescences: —sepulchral fungi: —stone tumours'. To Thackeray these 'braggart heathen allegories' were appurtenances of Vanity Fair. The most numerous class of mural monuments consisted simply of 'White Slabs, more or less deeply surrounded by black borders perhaps simply washed in. There they are, in full array!—Greek tablets, Roman tablets, perhaps Egyptian tablets—but all in one garb of black and white, and almost all destitute of any Christian character, or of artistic feeling; whilst the general repose of the sacred edifice is utterly destroyed . . . by this medley of sepulchral placards.'[12] Moreover, these tablets were attached to the fabric of the church in a purely arbitrary way, and in almost any town church one would find 'the figure of a lady embracing a heathen urn, partly covered by an unmeaning cloth . . . affixed to the wall by the mean expedient of cramps!'[13]

The Ecclesiologist condemned the 'list of deformities' in more sober fashion; 'strange and uncouth varieties of monumental piles . . . the ponderous high-tomb, standing like an altar, on four or six legs; the square pedestal, surmounted with an urn and gilt flame; the spacious railed enclosure; the broken column; the mural marble . . .'[14] By that time (1845) many improvements could be recorded; churches were beginning to be cleared of their seventeenth- and eighteenth-century features. 'The half-naked marble effigy, the . . . pediment and the pilaster, the cupid and the cherub, have given place, in many a church, to the Catholic symbol of the blessed Cross, the glowing Memorial window, or the consoling and inspiring portraitures of Saint and Angel.'[15] The swept and garnished mid-Victorian church, with its scraped and restored fabric, its pious Gothic detail, and its richly coloured windows, was in course of creation. And the dead were not now dead, extinct, annihilated, and entombed in pagan pomp, but lay in expectant slumber.

In regard to churchyards, such optimism was impossible; even the Ecclesiologists found the problem almost beyond solution. To introduce correct designs amongst the anomalies was almost the only avenue to reformation, but its end was not in sight. All that could be done was to lay the headstones flat, to minimize their offensiveness. And slate, unfortunately, was so durable; the calligraphic doves found so meaningless by the author of *A Tract upon Tomb Stones* were likely to last until the end of time. *The Ecclesiologist* found it all deplorable:

FIG 5 A broken column. From 'A Visit to the General Cemetery at Kensal Green'.

'What a truly singular . . . aspect does a modern church-yard present . . . almost every mound having at its head a tall slab of painted stone . . . at the top a "SACRED TO THE MEMORY" in immense black letters of fanciful device . . . hackneyed verses, often of the most wretched, vulgar, and unmeaning, if not heretical description . . . . The top affords space for an angel's cheeks in relief, blowing a gilded trumpet . . . . Sometimes these slabs are rendered still more offensive by a miserable imitation of Gothic tracery . . . .'[16]

It is not generally realized that many Victorian churchyard monuments were painted. If they were painted in the same palette as coffin plates—many of which have survived in their original colour as 'old stock' (plate 2)—they were garish indeed. They do not sound enticing:

'I suppose there are persons who admire those conventional forms of ugliness, with puffy faces of pink and white, black (often squinting) eyes, gilt hair and wings . . . certainly if tawdriness or colour can attract, these things look *smart* enough when they come out of the stonemason's yard—but let a few months pass, and what a change has taken place! The summer's sun has faded the red of the cheeks, and the damps of autumn have covered, perhaps, one half of the face with a mouldy green . . . .'[17]

The symbol of the broken column (fig 5) aroused particular hostility: 'What design . . . could have been conceived in worse taste than the *broken pagan pillar* erected, or about to be erected, to the memory of Grace Darling?'[18] The choice of such a symbol for the dead heroine would have been warmly approved by the eulogist of Kensal Green (fig 6) '. . . a beautiful conception, to illustrate, by a broken shaft, a column, rising in strength and sapped midway—the sudden cessation of life in its prime and vigour—cut off where its ties were strongest, and the pride of health gave promise of length of days'.[19]

The Ecclesiologist conveniently summarized the various available forms of monument. It remarked on the probable pre-Reformation use of low and simple wooden crosses; 'this kind of monument we have always recommended for the graves of the poor, as well as of the humble in spirit, who desire not the parade of costly funerals, and the pretension of magnificent monuments'.[20] The most suitable models for imitation were the small headstones, embodying an heraldic form of the cross, of which examples had been dug up; others were the flat stones in the shape of coffin lids, often incised with a cross and a marginal legend, or, coped, carved in relief with a floriated cross. Designs for such monuments appeared in the *Instrumenta Ecclesiastica*—in the first series, an oak grave cross by Butterfield and a coped tomb (first plate), floor crosses (third plate), and pierced and solid head stones (fifth plate) were illustrated. All had undergone a subtle transmutation into an indefinably High Victorian idiom, and all occur ubiquitously in Victorian cemeteries.

The Ecclesiologist dealt tactfully with the tomb recess. There was no reason why a limited number of strongly arched recesses should not be made deep in the foundation walls of a *new* church for benefactors, or for those who approved of privileged sepulture. For a founder, especially one of rank or consequence, nothing could be more correct 'provided the style be not later than Decorated'.[21] A recumbent effigy, a coffin stone with a bold carved floriated cross, a slab of native marble and an incised cross—all were suitable, but not if inserted into an ancient church. Recumbent effigies were 'most touching and interesting'[22] but artists who attempted them would be on dangerous ground.

Memorial brasses were the most fitting kind of monument; *The Ecclesiologist* had 'no hesitation in urging our artists to recover so fine and effective a department of Catholick art'.[23] At this time brasses were difficult to obtain, but their cost was less than that of a mural tablet. A footnote gave the price of 'excellent' ones from Messrs Waller of London: large double brasses, with canopies and a legend, cost £60; a floriated cross, with a calvary and a legend, £15. How 'to adopt our modern brasses to the severe and plain lines of the ancient graves, would readily be learned from the suggestions thrown out by Mr Pugin on this subject'; Pugin, in addition to throwing out suggestions, produced brasses in large quantities through the Hardman firm. He drew up certain propositions on the type of costume to be depicted on modern brasses: he declared the principal reason advanced by sculptors who used classical costumes, that modern dress was unsightly and ludicrous, was fallacious. This would have been perfectly true, he said, if it were necessary or correct to use 'the ordinary costume of domestic life', but most people sufficiently dignified to warrant an effigy held an ecclesiastical, civil or military office, the robes and insignia of which, 'if properly and severely represented, would produce effigies little inferior in solemn effect to the ancient ones'. Pugin did not favour archaism; to represent persons of the present century in the costume of the fourteenth 'is little less inconsistent' than to swathe them in the toga. He included the recommendation that the Sovereign should be depicted in coronation robes, with a 'more beautiful form of crown than that actually in use'; adding that the 'present female costume is by no means ill-adapted for sepulchral brasses', and that 'for private gentlemen, even, a long cloak, disposed in severe folds, would produce a solemn effect'[24] (plate 71).

FIG 6 Kensal Green. From 'A Visit to the General Cemetery at Kensal Green'.

The brass was revived, and in 1878 the *Ecclesiastical Art Review* expressed the common disfavour such revivals suffer in the period that follows them. Modern brasses, it said, were disappointing; this was not because of the way in which modern costume was rendered (which was tasteful in most cases), nor was it because of the sheen of modern brasses, to which objections had been made. But the filling of the lines with black made the brasses 'harsh and obtrusive'; it was wrong to place the brasses on polished marble, 'one thinks with regret of the old dull brasses on their unpolished stones, which, if not so smart, are at least pleasant for the eye to rest upon'. It was, anyhow, questionable whether it really was desirable to revive the brass; it could not compete as decoration with that 'most beautiful of all monuments'—the altar tomb with a recumbent figure.[25]

The Ecclesiologist commended the canopied tomb, the most costly and beautiful of all monuments. Where room was limited, as in a parish church, this was almost always mural, but it could stand isolated in its magnificence, like a shrine (plate 67). Effigies were the usual and appropriate complement, and it should have 'crockets, pinnacles, finials, shafts, buttresses, panels, and tracery, with under-groinings, colour, gilding, and diapers, according to the style and design'.[26] This Tennysonian richness of ornament makes up an assemblage that sounds, to our ears, like the High Victorian Church visible.

The Ecclesiologists stressed academic correctness; they castigated that 'favourite modern deformity, a *Gothic mural tablet* [plate 70]. We object to these altogether as most faulty on the grounds both of principle and effect. It is just like trying to make galleries look tolerable by panelled Gothic fronts. A white marble slab, enclosed between two buttressed pinnacles, and recessed some few inches behind a crocketted canopy . . . often erected, at a very great cost, under the mistaken idea that because its details are Gothic, it is therefore consistent with Gothic principles.'[27] These remarks could well be applied to many Gothic memorial cards (plate 66).

The reformers were anxious not to go too far; to exclude monuments entirely from the church would diminish the religious effect, since they were part of the 'moral' of church architecture; (this preoccupation of Alice's Duchess was shared by the reformers and the unreformed; all scanned every nook for the moral). Monuments should remain within the church; burials should take place outside it.

Sepulchral vaults were hotly criticized by the reformers; they symbolized lay dominion and extended the pew system, also under attack, into death. It was perhaps impossible to prevent the use of vaults inside a church, a use so long sanctified by custom, although the construction of vaults opening into a church was now (1844) illegal. The construction of sepulchral vaults of brick and stone in church-yards was a 'monstrous abuse'; they took up all the room, and were 'driving the poor out to some distant corner . . . attempting with still more daring presumption, to continue in the presence of THAT GREAT BEING, who is no respector of persons, the conventional distinction of riches or of rank'. The tomb, because it was more durable, was a more extravagant appropriation than the pew; 'Vaults, therefore, are pues for dead men, as pues are vaults for living sleepers'; moreover, 'we ascribe vaults to the state of mind engendered by pues . . . the natural effects of the same anti-Christian spirit . . . a fraud upon posterity . . . an illegal occupation of the property of others . . . .'[28] This fraud had been perpetuated by our immediate ancestors since the 'Dutch Usurpation'; the act was illegal, since the churchyard was the perpetual property of the parish. And such wanton misuse encouraged the appropriation of portions of the churchyard for secular purposes. The reformers descended to the last detail, castigating the common indication above of the vault below: 'we candidly admit that if there be one material, which from our hearts we hate, it is cast-iron. The sameness, tameness, stiffness of cast-iron rails make them an expecial abomination to us.' The reason, no doubt, was the fashionable use of cast-iron on secular buildings during the Regency.

Loudon also objected to vaults, in terms slightly different from those of the Ecclesiologists, who were always concerned to maintain the honour of the priestly caste:

As to public vaults in churches, their origin is security, and they are continued partly owing to the crowded state of the churchyards, but principally on account of the higher fees obtained from those who bury in them by the clergyman and the undertaker. Hence, on account of the expense, burying in vaults becomes a mark of wealth or distinction, and for that reason is adopted by many of the London tradesmen, even in the new cemeteries.[29]

The proposed solution to the problems of unsightly pagan monuments, and space-consuming vaults, was the same. The money spent on them should be diverted to purposes which would equally commemorate the dead, at the same time bene-fitting the church and the community—'Surely by the rebuilding and restoration of *the old waste places* of our Zion, we should render far more homage to the dead, than by a continuance of our present practice.'[30] In this ingenious way the reformers hoped at the same time to rid themselves of a nuisance and to subsidize the building, restoring, decorating and furnishing activities that occupied so much of their attention. They had much success.

Rather than erect proud and ugly monuments, a person of rank and wealth was advised to build or restore a parish church, a chapel, school, alms house, or hospital. When such large-scale works were too expensive, an altar, rood-screen, font, lectern, window (plate 29), roof, or item of church furniture, ornament, or plate (plate 75) should be provided or restored: the cost of the plainest marble tablet, £40, would buy a beautiful font and cover. Or part of a church—a pillar, a transept, a choir, or a section of a window—could be given; or the old custom of building by degrees could be revived. Laymen possessing advowsons of a church might well return them to the church as a memorial to themselves or to another; the same could be done where tithes belonged to a lay-impropriator.

By the end of the 1850s Edward Trollope could refer to the 'now widely adopted expedient of filling a window with stained glass'. He suggested an expedient of arcade or niche work with inscriptions within: 'These inscriptions might be cut on white marble slabs of uniform size; but as this material never contrasts well with ordinary free-stone, the shafts of the arcades should be of Purbeck, or some dark marble, or else a small border of red or green marble, should be interposed, between the slabs and their stone frame-work.' So easy it was to depart from strict Ecclesio-logical principles! A less costly substitute sounds even more idiomatically Victorian, 'a single row of Minton's wall tiles, of a green and buff, or blue and gold colour'.

61

Markland guarded against a possible objection to his suggestions—that they would lead to the neglect of sculpture, and the transfer of the commemoration of the dead from sculpture to architecture—by counselling instead that statues, reliefs, and busts, should be multiplied, but that their destinations should be changed. The statues and busts of literary men could be placed in institutions connected with them—those of lawyers in the Halls of the Inns of Court, those of medical men in their colleges or hospitals, those of ecclesiastics in their college libraries or halls (not in their churches), those of politicians in the Houses of Parliament.

The ideas of the reformers influenced and altered the designs of buildings and monuments, but they never ousted the obnoxious 'pagan' elements entirely. Airy Gothic shapes appeared all over England; the cross gradually took over the new cemeteries, but the old ideas persisted. Not a single Gothic motif appeared on the title page of the new memorial to Nelson (plates 72, 73), royal and state funerals and commemorations (see pages 80 to 90) remained obstinately un-Gothic, and the latter end of the century saw some of the most outlandish eclecticism that had yet appeared (plate 65). Heathen emblems had taken too firm a hold on the minds of the people (plate 74) to be easily eliminated, and the confident mediaevalizing of such a man as Pugin would have recoiled had a whisper reached him of the great future that lay before the urn.

6 Mourning Dress and Etiquette

'. . . a breathless smell of warm black crape—I did
not know what the smell was then, but I know now.'[1]

'Blessed are they that mourn': the injunction of religion fortified the custom of a
society in which every class, every occupation, had its own style of dress which it
was more than a mistake of taste to abandon. It is not surprising that the state of
mind called 'mourning' had also its peculiar costume, nor is it strange that, since
the persons of women bore the signs of wealth or of servitude, it was on them that
the external signs of grief were hung.

Mayhew, in 1865, said that a 'gentleman of the present nineteenth century,
attired for the gayest evening party, would, apart from his jewellery, be equally
presentable at the most sorrowful funeral'.[2] Women, especially later in the century,
when their increasing activity made restraint increasingly irksome, and when a
greater freedom of manners made it possible to speak, noted their position with
resentment: '. . . the custom of mourning presses far more heavily on women than
on men. In fact, so trifling are the alterations made in a man's dress . . . that practically the whole burden of mourning wrappings would seem to have fallen on women
. . . they [men] positively manage to mourn by proxy . . .!'[3] This writer complained
that wives often stayed at home while husbands—although it was *their* blood relation who had died—could go to a party; the same practice obtained with sisters
and brothers. The idea was heathen; it was, explicitly, 'a survival of the outward
expression of the inferiority of women' since 'the inferior always expresses grief
for the superior . . . .'[4]

Despite such complaints, the force of custom must have appeared to the majority
immutable; attempts at change were desperately resisted, and the usual riposte,
even late in the period, was a charge of indelicacy, or worse. A working man
recounted to the National Funeral and Mourning Reform Association (founded
1875) the trials endured by a family that, choosing not to go into mourning, with-
stood an extraordinary amount of ill will and anger from its neighbourhood: *The
Englishwoman's Domestic Magazine* attacked the Association's contention that
mourning was expensive and ostentatious by accusing it of undermining the
fabric of society; it recalled the 'often quoted' fact that French aristocrats had,
before the catastrophe of the Revolution, in increasing numbers abandoned
mourning dress, and wondered 'with a shudder whether these, too, are signs of the
times to be followed by as awful a retribution'.[5]

The desired optical effect of mourning was the abolition of reflection. 'Deep'
is the adjective used most commonly of it; it describes accurately the profound
drabness and the impenetrable darkness of first mourning. Plainness of form
was the corollary: this is consistent, since any decoration that called attention to
itself, that distinguished itself from its background, would dissipate the 'deep'

impression. It is remarkable how sombre and intimidating is the effect of Victorian full mourning dress, as surviving costumes show; the description of the effect of Mrs Pipchin's gown, the gown of a widow who had, like many, remained in black for forty years, is exact enough—'black bombazeen, of such a lustreless, deep, dead, sombre shade, that gas itself couldn't light her up after dark, and her presence was a quencher to any number of candles'.[6] It was reported that the immense multitude in mourning absorbed the newly installed gas light in St Paul's Cathedral, on the occasion of the Duke of Wellington's funeral. This deadness of attire was the outward expression of a spiritual state; the blackness of garb spoke desolation within—'Atramental and all other lugubrious Attire', as an advertisement of 1847 put it.[7] Only a Duchess of Omnium, to the question 'Was she weeping?' could make the light answer, 'Not actual tears. But her gown, and her cap, and her strings were weeping.'[8] Perhaps, in that answer, we hear the suggested tones of a great Whig lady, strayed into the nineteenth century, and faced with the mourning pretensions of the middle class.

The material that, more than any, symbolized mourning, that imposed on its wearer and on all who encountered her a rigid convention, was crape (plates 86, 92). From the presence of crape more frivolous materials withdrew, or ventured only at the peril of social impropriety: 'Many do not realize that crape, symbol of the deepest mourning, cannot be worn with non-deep mourning materials. Thus, crape is inadmissible with velvet, satin, lace, bright or glacé silks, embroidery, fringe—excepting the special "crape fringe"—or, indeed, with anything but mourning silk, paramatta, merino, cashmere, woollen barège or grenadine, or barathea.'[9] The materials last mentioned were of the required 'dead' quality; by the 1880s paramatta was as synonymous with mourning as crape, and was 'now used only for mourning.'[10]

Crape, a silk fabric, had a peculiar crisped or crimpy appearance produced by heat. The less important variety, 'soft' crape, known as 'Canton' crape, had an undulating and graceful line; the more typical and important 'hard' crape was tightly crimped; its aspect is harsh and repellent. A type of crape made at Norwich, of mixed silk and cotton, eventually became bombazine; this was a cheaper material —on the vicar's death, 'the farmers' wives brought out their black bombasines'.[11]

Crape had been associated with mourning for three hundred years before 1850; it was not until then that it became associated solely with it—it had been a fashionable fabric in eighteenth-century Italy. There is poetry in the way its fortunes as a mourning material waxed and declined with 'Victorianism'; its story is almost exactly coincident with the nineteenth century; it, more than any other material, dominated Victorian England, and the Queen herself became a kind of Crape Deity, withdrawn in inconsolable grief from the gaze of her people—the 'Widow of Windsor' (plate 106). Its manufacture became virtually monopolized by the firm of Courtauld (plate 91); that family, long concerned with silk textiles in a small way, founded its modern giant finances on crape.

At the turn of the eighteenth and nineteenth centuries a Mr Francis introduced 'Norwich crape'; this was taken up and given official sanction in the 'Orders for court mourning for Queen Charlotte' (1818); included were crape hoods, crape fans, and 'Undress—Dark Norwich crape'. Other manufactories felt encouraged to compete, and in 1822 the Grout brothers took out a patent for embossed crape—mourning crape or 'crêpe Anglais'; Courtauld's probably succeeded in making crape between 1820 and 1822. In 1826 imported wrought silks were allowed for the first time since 1773; the native silk manufacturies were ruined. Only the black crimped crape could compete with the foreigner's products, and secrecy alone would preserve the monopoly on which prosperity so heavily leaned. Employees were sworn to silence; the different stages of manufacture were carried on in different towns. The financial gains increased; by 1838 Courtauld's was using power-driven looms in its factory at Halstead; by 1841 it employed over 1500 workpeople; by the 1850s its agents were travelling on the Continent and in the USA; in 1855 its crape was awarded a gold medal at the Paris International Exhibition. The production figures reflect the growing obsession; from 1829–41, 69,191 packets of crape were produced; from 1842–51, 224,171; from 1852–61, 279,605.[12]

The 1870s saw the climax of the crape trade; the Franco-Prussian war created an unprecedented demand on the Continent; in 1872 *The Queen* reported that 'the demand for [crape] in this Country is so great that the supply does not always equal the requirement'. But a disconcerting change in fashion was soon to threaten the industry that depended on a lucrative show of grief. In 1888–9 the upper-class demand for crape was seen to be reduced, and Courtauld's, despite a vastly expanded advertising campaign, began to feel the pinch. In 1893 a reconstruction reduced the capital of the Company from £400,000 to £200,000. By 1900 the sale of coloured fabrics equalled that of crape; the use of the latter fell sharply after 1912.

Crape changed little during the period, although in 1870 a 'spot' (plate 92) appeared in the texture. 'Albert' crape, which contained cotton, was introduced in the 1870s; it was cheaper than real crape, the cost of which was mentioned with a continual sigh, and was therefore despised—'the common kind of crape is called The Albert which is an inferior and coarser material . . . and therefore not suitable for really good mourning'.[13]

The effect of rainwater upon crape gave cause for distress; a recipe of 1856 to remove water stains from black crape commented, 'When a drop of water falls upon a black crape veil or collar it leaves a conspicuous white mark.'[14] To obliterate it, 'place underneath the stain a piece of old black silk. With a camel's hair brush dipped in common ink go over the stain; wipe off the ink with a little bit of old soft silk. It will dry immediately and the white mark will be seen no more.'[15] The remedy sounds amateur, and could help to explain another recipe, 'To Remove Black Stains from the Skin', which mentions that 'Ladies that wear mourning in warm weather are much incommoded by the blackness it leaves on the arms and neck which cannot easily be removed even by soap and warm water . . . .'[16] The ladies were to have always at hand a box containing equal proportions of cream of tartar and oxalic acid to remove the stains. The mixture, if swallowed, was poisonous, and no doubt general relief was felt when crape was waterproofed. This had been achieved by 1897; the *Drapery World* said, 'Hitherto one dare hardly venture out in wet weather while wearing crape for the effect of a shower was simply ruinous But, happily, all that is done away with, owing to the very general use of Courtauld's Crape, which will withstand any amount of rain.' In 1900 this crape was given the Grand Prix at the Paris Exhibition, an honour promptly advertised with the crape.

65

It was thought unlucky to keep crape in the house after mourning had ended; this may account somewhat for the enormous sales, and for the present rarity of Victorian mourning wear, which must once have been so common.

The other material that, with crape, formed the staple of mourning, was jet. 'It should be borne in mind that, with crape, only jet ornaments are permissible; neither gold, silver, nor precious stones can be worn, nor can lace be worn with crape.'[17]

Jet (plates 89, 90, 93) is a kind of hard coal, an anthracite or lignite, probably formed from driftwood; the best and hardest natural jet came from the neighbourhood of Whitby, where the major industry arose. Spanish jet, from Galicia, was too soft for fine work; it was imported after about 1870, when standards began generally to fall. 'French' jet is cut black glass (plates 87, 88, 96).

Jet had been worked into ornaments for hundreds of years before the nineteenth century, but it was not until after 1800 that two Whitby jet workers abandoned the primitive knife, file, and rubbing stone technique in favour of a lathe—a great advance. Progress in the nascent industry at first was slow; in 1820 only a few workers were regularly employed. By 1832 two jet shops employed twenty-five workmen. Jet was prescribed in the 'Orders for court mourning for William IV'; the demand grew, and by 1850 seven firms employed several hundred workmen. It became high fashion in the 1850s—'The recent revival of the old fashion of employing jet trimmings adds greatly to the elegance of mourning.'[18] On the advice of the editor of the *Art Journal*, jet was shown in the Great Exhibition of 1851. By 1856, sales were valued at £20,000 a year; by 1870, they had reached £70,000. Between 1870 and 1872 the highest number of workers was recorded, some 1400 people. But from about 1870 soft Whitby jet began also to be used; its unsuitability eventually gave Whitby jet a bad name; the chief imitation jet, vulcanite, an early plastic, began seriously to compete with it—vulcanite could be cheaply moulded, and was, when new, virtually undistinguishable from jet. The years of high prosperity rapidly receded; many workers were forced to find other employment, until by 1884 less than three hundred were left; by this time a man earned only 25s a week, compared to about £3 4s at the height of the boom.

The best pieces of Whitby jet have often a massive dignity; by a happy coincidence, the years of prosperity coincided largely with a broad style well suited to its nature. It was carved into all the allusive shapes recognized with joy by Victorian feeling. It could be worked both matt and shiny; the two surfaces often being combined in one piece with fine decorative effect. 'French' jet, by its character, was cut more in the manner of a precious stone, and inserted into elaborate settings; it has a bright hard glitter, very effective in artificial light. Jet is rich combined with gold, with mosaic, with pearls and with diamonds, all admitted into mourning jewelry, although not in the first stages of mourning.

The jewelry of sentiment *par excellence*, in which symbolic allusions were supplemented by the use of an actual part of the body of a friend or relation, was that made from hair (plates 50, 91, 93). Much of the surviving hair jewelry, especially that in which the hair alone was used, has a dead and unlovely look, but when new it would have shone like fine wire. It was made both at home and professionally; an advertisement of 1852 for 'Hair Mementos' runs 'Book of

66

specimens sent by Bewdney to Ladies resident in any part of the Kingdom for 2 postage stamps';[19] they were then made up to approved designs. The 1840s and 1850s, the apogee of the Romantic period, produced the finest hair work. In 1888 *La Belle Assemblée* said,

'The sentimental jewellery of Limonnier is of another character from that all the world is acquainted with, and which gives the locket, or brooch, or ring, in which some beloved tress or precious curl is enshrined, the appearance of having been designed from a mortuary tablet. Have we not all met ladies wearing as a brooch, by way of loving remembrance, a tomb between two willow trees formed of the hair of the individual for whom their crape was worn, and which from its very nature must be laid aside with it?'[20]

The magazine then described the extended scope of modern hair work, which made it suitable as 'an ornament for all times and places'. Another publication, of 1864, was *The Jewellers' Book of Patterns in Hair Work, containing a great variety of Copper-Plate Engravings of Devices and Patterns in Hair: suitable for Mourning Jewellery, Brooches, Rings, Guards, Alberts, Necklets, Lockets, Bracelets, Miniatures, Studs, Links, Earrings etc, etc.*; it was issued by William Halford and Charles Young, Manufacturing Jewellers of Clerkenwell. The illustrations probably had, even to the ladies of 1864, an archaic air; all the old weapons of the symbolic armoury were brought forth—willows (plate 50), urns, scythes, setting suns, anchors, hearts, padlocks, ostrich plumes (plate 93), roses, forget-me-nots, wreaths, yews, the snake swallowing its own tail (eternity) and wheat ears; the last probably referred to the full ear reaped in maturity.

In the later stages of mourning, gold and diamonds, pearls (plate 56) and other stones, such as amethysts (appropriately mauve) could be worn; the rules, again, were strict. In 1856 Flora, whose father-in-law had died, rejected a Cairngorm brooch 'of dark pebble, with a silver fern-leaf lying across it, the dots of small Cairngorm stones'; it sounds sober enough, but '. . . you must wear it now. I shall not wear coloured brooches for a year', she says to her sister Edith. The latter, in complimentary black, was uneasy, since 'she felt as if her black dress ought, perhaps, to be worn for a nearer cause'[21]—an early allusion to the unmeaning formality of much mourning etiquette.

The etiquette of mourning was strict, and the rules intricate; it was easy to make a mistake. The women's journals of the period are full of anxious requests for clarification, often prompted by an attempt to combine economy with correctness. Sometimes a general reply, giving general guidance, appeared, summing up the collective female wisdom on mourning for a decade. They had very much the aura of mysteries delivered to the ears of the elect only—the elect being those rich enough to be able to follow the minutiae: 'We must of course be understood as speaking only of the *strictly orthodox* periods and degrees of mourning. There must be many who cannot afford to dress correctly, either in mourning or out of it, and it is to those who lack the knowledge, rather than the means that our remarks apply.' [*The Queen* 1880] By 1880 there was a 'decided inclination on the part of fashion to shorten some of the periods of mourning';[22] nonetheless the magazine added that 'some may object to the periods mentioned as insufficient. This must be a matter of individual feeling; we only indicate the conventional periods required by custom, and everyone naturally is at liberty to lengthen them at pleasure.' Despite reform, *The Queen* did not suggest that everyone could *shorten* the conventional periods at pleasure!

It is worthwhile to quote *The Queen* of 1880 at some length; this period displayed the *plenitudo potestatis* of Victorian mourning, an ultramontane rigidity and intensity of mourning, when even a bride could appear in black (plate 102). The figure of the widow embodied the convention in its most exaggerated form: she was self-consciously set apart in grief (plates 105, 106); the victim of 'a mild form of suttee',[23] she might possibly never emerge fully from her eclipse (plate 31). Her dress was regulated to the extent of being a uniform. For the first twelve months, she should wear a paramatta dress and mantle, with crape applied to the skirt, in one piece, to within an inch of the waist. Her sleeves should be tight to the arm, with lawn cuffs and collar; her body should be covered entirely with crape. Her bonnet also should be covered entirely with crape; inside should be a widow's cap, with a crape veil with a deep hem (plates 90, 93). When the crape on her dress needed renewing, it was to be put on exactly as before; after nine months it could be renewed in two deep tucks with the space of one inch between them. A year after the death 'widows' silk' could replace paramatta; it should be still heavily trimmed with crape; after six months of this the crape could, during the next three months, be lightened, and jet and fringe (plate 87) be introduced. Twenty-one months after bereavement crape could be left off entirely—this was known as 'slighting' the mourning—and plain black worn; two years after the bereavement the widow could go into half mourning for six months. The colours worn in half mourning (plates 44, 91, 95) were grey, lavender, mauve, violet, or black, grey, and white stripes; the change should be gradual.

The widow's dress was uncomfortable. The streamers on the cap, because of their weight and roughness (they caught on the dress) made it difficult to turn the head. The dress was said also to be 'unhygienic', and exercise was 'impossible'.[24] With the dress went a social ostracism; for the first year no invitations could be accepted, and it was 'in the worst taste to be seen in places of public resort'.[25] After the first year, the widow could, gradually, resume her place in society.

The etiquette for the mourning of a child for a parent was the same as that of a parent for a child; twelve months in all was required. For the first three paramatta, merino, and such dull cloths were worn, with a good deal of crape; the latter was usually arranged in two very deep tucks. For the next three months mourning silk was worn, with less crape, the crape ornamentally arranged in folds, plaits, or bouillonnés (our age, accustomed for many years to plain surfaces in dress, perhaps finds it difficult to realize how deprived the Victorian woman would feel robbed of the elaborate trimmings that helped to mark her status). The bonnet was trimmed with jet, and had a net veil with a deep crape hem: 'Linen collars and cuffs cannot be worn with crape; crêpe lisse frills are de *rigueur*. Sable or any coloured fur must be left off; sealskin is admissible, but it never looks well in really deep mourning.' After six months, crape could be abandoned for plain black, with jet ornaments and black gloves. This, after another two months, could be augmented with gold and silver, pearl and diamond jewelry; grey gloves, sewn with black, could replace

68

black gloves. Then half mourning could be worn. Society was to be relinquished totally for two months.

For grandparents 'the mourning was formerly nine months, but six is now generally considered sufficient'. Two could be spent in silk, with moderate crape, two in black without crape, and two in half mourning.

For brothers and sisters, six months was sufficient; three in crape, two in black, and one in half mourning. 'For an uncle or aunt the period was formerly three months; but two is now considered ample, and some reduce it to six weeks.' No crape was necessary: black was to be worn the whole time, for the first month with jet but afterwards with gold, silver or diamonds. For a great-uncle or aunt the time was cut to six weeks, three in black and three in half mourning. For a first cousin, four weeks only were spent in black. 'It is very uncommon now to wear mourning for a second cousin, but if it is done three weeks is sufficient.'

Relations by marriage were mourned exactly in the same degree as blood relations, with some exceptions. For instance, a lady 'would mourn for her uncle by marriage for two months, if his wife [her aunt] were alive; but if she were dead, the mourning for the uncle might be curtailed to one month.' And there was the strange institution of 'complimentary' mourning—the second wife of a man (second wives were common, because of the number of deaths in childbed) must wear slight mourning for three months for the death of his first wife's parents, or two months for his first wife's brothers or sisters; 'this is not *de rigueur* like real mourning for absolute relatives, but is in good taste, and is usual in good society.' This observation points a curious feature of the highly formalized mourning of Victorian society; with some exceptions—the Sovereign, the vicar, etc.—it founded its rules firmly on the institution of the family, that sacred focus of Victorian life. Complimentary mourning was, after the funeral, rarely extended to friends, although they might be the friends of a lifetime; no such strict hierarchy of rules existed to deal with them. Complimentary black was sometimes worn when making the first visit to a house of mourning; it was not absolutely necessary.

The correspondence of the Stanleys of Alderley, from the first half of the period, contains many references to the demands of etiquette. In February, 1844, Lady Stanley wrote to her daughter-in-law, Mrs Stanley, 'I suppose the Court Mourning still continues or if not I hope you will put it on for Sir Gregory Way he is my first cousin and there are several of the family in town who might observe and be hurt if you did not.' In 1846 she wrote 'You have perhaps heard of the death of Mrs William Way (I am quite tired of mourning but I think it need not eclipse Alice at all and you very little, except, for the sake of the additional Way connexion a little black may be necessary).' Then in 1846, 'I ought to be in mourning, for George Way, but I think I shall only mourn in *black wax*, which you shall see *next* time not to *alarm* you now'—the 'black wax' refers to the practice of sealing a letter in black wax during the mourning period (plate 96, see page 71); to see it unexpectedly might well unnerve the recipient.

An amusing letter of 1841 shows some of the mortifications of mourning: 'What a stupid woman Mlle Alyse is—I wrote today I liked my caps very much but I wanted one for evening rather more dressy—with a few white flowers—but did not I suppose say anything of mourning . . . . Yesterday arrived as pretty a cap as I ever saw, but any one I had would do just as well—blonde and flowers with coloured leaves . . . I could have saved the present expense and done without it for a long time to come, as I have a good stock of smart caps out of mourning.' There is an interesting letter of June 1850: 'Mrs Whitby was my first cousin . . . but she has lived so long out of the world that I never thought of your mourning for her, or doing so myself though I did seal with black to Emmy.'[26] It seems that the dead woman had lived so long out of Society that social mourning might be discarded.

Many Victorian novels have chronicled the effect of etiquette on the widow; it is sometimes not easy for the modern reader to grasp the complexities of the situation. A widow who did not follow etiquette was liable to have her conduct misinterpreted. In *Cranford* (1851) Mrs FitzAdam appears 'as bold as a lion' and dressed in 'rustling black silk' so soon after her husband's death that 'poor Miss Jenkyns was justified in the remark she made, that "bombazine would have shown a deeper sense of her loss".'[27] Even the way in which garments were worn carried its implications. Mrs Nickleby (1839) an impeccably respectable widow, had become affected by the attentions of the mad gentleman, and 'even her black dress assumed something of a deadly-lively air from the jaunty style in which it was worn . . . her mourning garments assumed quite a new character. From being the outward tokens of respect and sorrow for the dead, they became converted into signals of very slaughterous and killing designs upon the living.'[28] It was not only Dickens who could hardly use the term 'widow' without comic implications; they existed even when one was infatuated with a pure, high thinking, irreproachable widow:

' "You know what they say about widows generally, my boy."

"That is all very well when one talks about widows in general. It is easy to chaff about women when one hasn't got any woman in one's mind." '

Emily, this particular widow, the heroine of Trollope's *The Prime Minister* [1875–6], illustrates a widow entangled and confused by custom. Her scamp of a husband has committed suicide; a better man waits to marry her; out of delicacy he will not even speak until twelve months have passed by since 'that wretched man perished'. Emily, whose 'very face and limbs had so adapted themselves to her crape, that she looked like a monument of bereaved woe', has to return gradually to the world. The first trial comes:

'She had never as yet packed up her widow's weeds. She had never as yet even contemplated the necessity of coming down to dinner in them before other eyes than those of her father and brother. She had as yet made none of those struggles with which widows seek to lessen the deformity of their costume. It was incumbent on her now to get a ribbon or two less ghastly than those weepers which had for the last five months, hung about her face and shoulders.'

Having moved again into society, she finds it difficult to be lively; her brother remonstrates about her effect on others; she asks him what she can do about it. He counsels her to be more cheerful, and to 'drop something of the heaviness of your mourning'. 'Do you mean that I am a hypocrite?' This is a fascinating question; she obviously is not; nonetheless she did not love her husband, she is not sorry that he has died, and her true love wants to marry her. She has, in assuming the dress of widowhood, put on with it the state of mind it embodied, and this conventional state has taken complete possession. She has *become* THE WIDOW. Her moral struggle was real, although self-induced. Her brother knows she is not a hypocrite, but he is less conventional; he repeats that she should 'make a struggle'. 'She did make a struggle, and she did do something. No one, not well versed in the mysteries of feminine dress, could say very accurately what it was that she had done, but every one felt that something of the weight was reduced.'

A year after her husband's death, her friends discuss her eventual remarriage: 'Of course the marriage ought not to be until March twelvemonths. But if it is understood that it is to be, she might alter her dress by degrees—and alter her manner of living. *These things should always be done by degrees* [my italics].'

Another trial faces the widow—her brother's wedding, a year after her husband's death. She feels she cannot go: 'I could not stand at your marriage in black clothes,—nor should I have the courage even if I had the will to dress myself in others.' Like most Victorian women, however, she could not withstand the stronger sex; she eventually buys a dress for the wedding—an indelicate business:

'Then she went forth and chose her dress,—a grey silk, light enough not to throw quite a gloom on the brightness of the day, and yet dark enough to declare that she was not as other women are. The very act of purchasing this, almost blushing at her own request as she sat at the corner in her widow's weeds, was a pain to her. But she had no one whom she could employ . . . . And then there was the fitting on of the dress,—very grievous to her, as it was the first time since the heavy black mourning came home that she had clothed herself in other garments.'

At the wedding, she 'appeared for the first time in her grey silk dress, and without a widow's cap. Everything was very plain, but the alteration was so great that it was impossible not to look at her.' Afterwards, she immediately resumed her mourning; convention could no longer be outraged, despite the persuasions of her family.

Most women in mourning attempted also to remain in fashion (plate 98). Some queer incongruities resulted; to name a widow's dress 'The Houri' (plate 97) is blatant, and even 'The Aesthetic' betrays too close an interest in the world. These contradictions seem commoner towards the end of the period. A half mourning costume of 1890 (a year in which, following a winter influenza epidemic, semi-mourning colours such as black, grey and heliotrope were fashionable) was described as being 'of a woollen velvet; violet ground striped with thick lines of grey, white and black; sleeves of violet looking-glass velvet; the consoling influence of such a costume could not fail to be great.'[29] The nuances of the last comment would have been unthinkable in such a context during the Romantic period.

An essential appurtenance was a lady's writing paper and cards; they shared in her mourning (plate 96), and had an etiquette of their own. 'Black edged paper and envelopes must be used; the width known as "extra-broad" is the deepest that should ever be used, the "double-broad" being too much.'[30] The simple 'broad' was considered the most correct taste, even for widows; how easy it must have been inadvertently to reveal vulgarity, even in grief! 'Middle' was the width used in mourning for a parent or child; 'narrow', for brothers and sisters; 'Italian', for all other relatives. It was equally easy to slip into a tasteless excess with cards: 'Cards are only edged with black when crape is worn: therefore black-edged visiting cards are not etiquette for an uncle or aunt. Cards returning thanks . . . for kind enquiries . . . should not be sent out till the mourners feel equal to receiving visitors . . . .' The complimentary principle was extended to correspondence: 'letters of condolence should be written on paper with a slight black edge, and offence should never be taken if they are left unanswered.'[31]

Children's mourning (plate 100) was, in the early Victorian period, almost as etiquette bound as that of their elders. Instances in fiction are numerous. In Charlotte M. Yonge's *The Daisy Chain* (1856) the children wear crape for their mother; the younger child wears 'black ribbons' for her brother—the underclothes of both adults and children were often threaded with black ribbon. Instances in real life were also common; Queen Victoria thus clarified her attitude: 'I think it is quite wrong that the nursery are not in mourning, at any rate I should make them wear grey or white or drab and baby wear white and lilac, not colours. That I think shocking.'[32] White was a mourning colour, and was regarded as deeper mourning than grey, or grey and white mixed; it was often used for children (plate 86) and for the young. Mrs Gaskell (1859) advised that 'pure entire white is mourning for girls in an evening'[33] and in *North and South* (1854) Edith Lennox, in mourning for her uncle, is contrasted with her black-clad cousin, 'dancing in her white crepe mourning, and long floating golden hair, all softness and glitter' (the hair was, as far as possible, concealed in deep mourning). In 1901 it was stated that 'The Duchess of Cornwall and York has always put her children into white for mourning.'[34] White mourning was accepted for a wedding; in 1881 the Ladies' Treasury recommended for a bride, 'The wreath wholly white, not a tinge of colour, no green leaves. The veil white with a deep hem. The gloves white sewed down the back with black.'[35]

It has been pointed out that the relaxation of etiquette for children was often the precursor of that for adults. By the 1880s, 'It is desirable that children should be put into mourning dress as seldom as possible; only in fact for the very nearest relatives. The little children do not understand it and it is absurd to invest them with the signs of grief they cannot feel. Absence of a positive colour is quite sufficient mourning for children.'[36]

The family servants were thought as much an extension of the family as the house and its contents; consequently, the servants were put into mourning when a member of the family died. In *The Daisy Chain* the family engages a servant shortly after the mother's death, and 'there was no more to be done but settle that she should come on Saturday, and to let nurse take her into the town to invest her with the universal blackness of the household . . . .'[37] in favour of a woman she had never seen. *Sylvia's Home Journal* said in 1879 that 'All servants should have black dresses, black shawls, and black bonnets. It is customary to give servants mourning when an important member of the family dies.'[38] The reformers denounced this habit as 'the innate vulgarity of mind which leads to people putting their servants into mourning',[39] and the *Woman's World* in 1889 strongly inveighed against it as

72

'self-glorification'; it pointed out that the ritual was not confined to the bereaved household, but frequently included near relations, and helped to make domestic service undignified and unattractive.

Such customs explain the propriety of shops like Peter Robinson's dressing their coachmen in black from head to foot, with crape hat bands and arm bands, and whips with crape bows; also clad completely in black were the lady fitters inside the broughams, with their patterns and designs.[40] This was merely an extension of complimentary mourning and, indeed, anything else within the bereaved house would have appeared sorely out of place.

The growing demand for mourning clothes prompted a mushroom growth of 'mourning warehouses' or '*magasins de deuil*', retail shops for the sale of mourning. The first and most famous, Jay's Mourning Warehouse (plate 97) opened in 1841 at Numbers 247, 248 and 249 Regent Street; it was followed by Pugh's Mourning Warehouse in 1849. By 1853 Peter Robinson's 'Court and General Mourning Warehouse' ['black Peter Robinson's'] and Nicholson's 'Argyle General Mourning and Mantle Warehouse' made a total of four such large shops on Regent Street alone.[41]

Before the establishment of these shops women who wished to equip themselves with mourning were obliged to rush to different places to buy separate articles of dress: their houses were invaded by milliners and dressmakers, and 'the quietude of the chamber of grief [was] disturbed by the everlasting rustle of silks and satins, and the crackle of bombazine and paramatta'. The warehouses shortened and lightened the chore; the old rule that full mourning was not put on until eight days after bereavement no longer obtained. The general manufacture of the sewing machine after 1850 mechanized the dressmaking industry, and assisted the rapid production of mourning orders. The mourning houses emphasized the speed and ubiquity of their deliveries; Peter Robinson's, for example, sent mourning out at once, upon receiving a letter or telegram; in 1881 they advertised 'A large staff of very competent Dressmakers and ASSISTANTS are kept purposely to TRAVEL to all parts of the country—no matter the distance—(free of any extra charge whatever to the customer) with a full assortment of Made-up Goods . . . .'[42] And 'for a Family Mourning, and also Mourning for Servants, Orders, however large, can be completed at very short notice by Dressmakers of the greatest proficiency (either French, German, or English).'[43] Prices varied from £3 15s 6d for a widow's dress, to 13s 9d for a bonnet (*Myra's Journal of Dress and Fashion*, 1881).

Mourning warehouses also conducted funerals, in town or country. They did not enjoy any monopoly of fashion; the smaller dressmakers continued to flourish as can be gathered from multifarious advertisements: 'ROYAL MOURNING—BLACK TRAIN SKIRTS of fine flexible steel . . . Mesdames Marion & Maitland, 238 Oxford-street' or, offered at Mrs Creaton's Showrooms at Oxford Street ' "Second Widows' " Mourning Caps, so difficult to be met with at other establishments . . .' (both advertisements of 1861).[44]

The *magasin de deuil* was one of the most idiosyncratic institutions of Victorian England. Mayhew's description of Jay's is vivid:[45]

'Let us walk upstairs into the spacious show-rooms. Here we can lounge about on the most comfortable of sofas and easy chairs; we can look at ourselves in the most dazzling of mirrors; and should we wish to purchase mourning for our wife—who may have just lost her uncle, and remembered us in his will—we have only to intimate our wish, and we shall have a bevy of bright-eyed fair damsels, clad in black silk, who will "do their spiriting gently", and in a few minutes will lay before us every description of mourning we may require.

Mantles all a-bristle with bugles and beads, and trimmed with every variety of gimp ornamentation — marvels of design and workmanship — are exhibited to our wondering eyes; white silk Zouave jackets, whose sheen is dazzling, and whose braiding is a mathematical puzzle [plate 86]. Putting aside those massive curtains which drape the doorway . . . we see a wonderful assemblage of caps, which seem to range in density from the frosted spider-web to the petrified "trifle". We observed one widow's cap which was a marvel: this wonder was under a glass-case; for it was as light in texture as thistle-down, and might have been easily blown away, with long streamers like fairies' wings; so that we, at first, took it for some new kind of bridal veil — in fact, it seemed the kind of head-dress that the fair Imogene might have worn when she married somebody else in Alonzo's absence [plate 104].

Bonnets of the most subtle design and most ornate specimens of sable floriculture nod at us from every table . . . collars of white crape, of black crape, of *tulle* and of muslin, collars dotted with black and edged with black; also the clearest muslin Garibaldis, which, with a *ruche* of the faintest mauve-coloured ribbon, will constitute slight mourning.

Would ye see more, O stranger? If so, wander in the silk department — look tenderly on the massive black silks and satins — glance carefully at the delicate shades of slate-colour, grey, mauve and purple, and go not hence till you have seen a certain delicate robe of the palest violet tint fairily frosted with crystal spots.'

Mayhew also quotes, from *Hoods Magazine*, a satirical sketch that is more enlightening than pages of more sober description:[46]

' "Shopman.—. . . How deep would you choose to go, ma'am? Do you wish to be very poignant?

"Lady.—Why, I suppose, crape and bombazine, unless they're gone out of fashion . . . .

"Shopman.—. . . We have a very extensive assortment, whether for family, court, or complimentary mourning; including the last novelties from the Continent.

"Lady.—Yes; I should like to see them.

"Shopman.—Certainly. Here is one, ma'am, just imported—a widow's silk—watered, as you perceive, to match the sentiment. It is called the 'Inconsolable', and is very much in vogue, in Paris, for matrimonial bereavements.

"Squire.—Looks rather flimsy though. Not likely to last long; eh, sir? . . .

"Shopman.—. . . several new fabrics have been introduced to meet the demand for fashionable tribulation.

"Lady.—And all in the French style?

"Shopman.—Certainly—of course, ma'am. They excel in the *funèbre*. Here, for instance, is an article for the deeply afflicted. A black crape, expressly adapted to the proposed style of mourning—makes up very sombre and interesting . . . .

Or, if you would prefer a velvet, ma'am—

"Lady.—Is it proper, sir, to mourn in velvet?

"Shopman.—O quite!—certainly. Just coming in. Now here is a very rich one—real Genoa—and a splendid black. We call it 'The Luxury of Woe.'

"Lady.—Very expensive, of course?

"Shopman.—Only eighteen shillings a yard, and a superb quality—in short, fit for the handsomest style of domestic calamity . . . . The mourning of the poor people is very coarse—very; quite different from that of persons of quality—canvas to crape . . . .

"Lady.—To be sure it is! And as to the change of dress, sir; I suppose you have a great variety of half-mourning?

"Shopman.—Oh! infinite—the largest stock in town. Full, and half, and quarter, and half-quarter, shaded off, if I may say so, like an India-ink drawing, from a grief *prononcé* to the slightest *nuance* of regret."'

Jay's, at this time, employed a hundred hands at Regent Street, and, in their auxiliary premises in Prince's Street, a 'miniature railway-station',[47] about 150 girls. Their official *History of Mourning*[48] speaks grandly of the benefits to civilization brought by the ingenious idea of the *magasins de deuil*. It asserts, significantly, that of late years business had enormously increased, and that not only was everything necessary for mourning sold, but also dresses of a 'more general description'; the colours of the latter were, however, only those suitable for half or full mourning. Black silks were, pre-eminently, still a speciality, and 'Continental journals frequently announce that "le maison Jay de Londres a fait de forts achats".' To keep down prices, the firm bought directly from manufacturers, and its agents went to Lyons, Genoa and Milan, the principal silk markets of Europe. The *Illustrated London News* reported, in December 1861, that

'The distressed state of the Lyons manufacturers, and the consequently low scale of prices, caused English wholesale houses to purchase silks so largely that it was believed at one time the stocks would scarcely ever be disposed of. But the death of the lamented Prince Consort brought about an extraordinary change . . . . In whichever direction one moved—east, west, south, or north—the shops, particularly at the West-end, were crowded to inconvenience . . . .'

But this prosperity was not to last. Mourning, like life itself, had a term set to its existence. Its cost, its magisterial formality, its meaningless etiquette, aroused growing opposition; as society and its habits changed, its restraints became unbearably irksome. The attacks gradually mounted; that made in 1858, by Mrs Stone, on the *magasins de deuil* is typical:

'They have the "melancholy-pleasure-of-showing-you" every degree of sorrow, from the deepest widowhood through the various "mitigated affliction" departments, "small by degrees and beautifully less" to the lightest wreath of complimentary violets and love ribbon . . . in each department . . . an attendant is stationed, a sort of living lay figure, dressed in costume suitably assimilated to the bereavement that room is intended to exemplify; a sort of "glass of fashion" in which you are instructed as to the degree of grief you ought to exhibit . . . .'[49]

Such an artificial etiquette was bound, with the increasing freedom of society, eventually to retreat, but the struggle was lengthy. In 1875 the 'National Funeral and Mourning Reform Association' was founded; in the same year the Church of England sponsored the 'Funeral and Mourning Reform Association'. Both were accused of concentrating on funeral reform at the expense of mourning reform.

The opinion grew that mourning had become intensified to a degree unsanctioned by scripture; Lady Wharton in 1875 could say to Emily, 'excessive grief is wicked, especially in the young'.[50] Dottridge's introduced, in 1878, an 'armlet' of crape to replace full mourning.[51] In 1889 an article on 'Mourning Clothes and Customs' declared that the customs were neither good in themselves, nor did they command general approval. Mourning made its demands at the worst possible time, when money was short and when grief had enervated the mourners. Relatives met and discussed dress, and sought the shopkeeper's advice (plate 99) in a manner that could only be distasteful; how much crape should be worn, whether it should be worn in that shape or this, whether an edging, rather than a whole width, would do, and so on. Sometimes an illness in a family would, in a very unpleasant, calculating way, restrain relations from buying new clothes. Armbands would be better; perhaps edged with white or grey for widows and widowers, and red or blue for others. They would exclude the embarrassment of chance allusions.[52]

The fashion journals in many cases stoutly defended the old order. *The English-woman's Domestic Magazine* in 1876 denied that mourning was 'ostentatious' or 'expensive' as the Mourning Reform Association would have it, and quoted *The Queen* of 1875:

'The expense of mourning is much exaggerated, and is very far from being necessarily as great as those who dislike it would fain have the world believe; but it would surely be more sensible if those who cannot afford it would give up the notion that seems to prevail that in mourning, though at no other time, must they wear the magnificent attire suitable to the very rich, and to use their common sense and discretion . . . a plain black dress is by no means inordinately costly.'

The richness of materials probably compensated for the sobriety of hue.

Notes on Fashionable Mourning, a genteel little pamphlet banded in pale mauve, published in 1902, sufficiently indicates that the reformers did not prevail, although they had some success, even in high places—the Princess of Wales had, in 1894, repudiated crape while mourning for her eldest son, the Duke of Clarence. In the pamphlet is mentioned an 'important novelty'; the production of crape retaining its characteristic figure, but 'of a soft drooping character', to be used with the 'soft clinging fabrics now so largely worn'. To clinch the matter, 'in Paris soft finished Crape is now worn much more largely than Crape of firm crisp finish'.

Most of the pamphlet yet again reiterates the 'Correct Periods of Mourning' as given by the 'Leading Authorities', including *The Queen*, *The Lady*, *Gentle-woman*, *Lady's Pictorial*, and the *Ladies' Year Book*. The discrepancies in advice must have sadly puzzled the hyper-correct; no guidance is given, and the reader is left to judge for herself; the journals agreed only over the widow. For a daughter mourning her parents, *The Queen* advised twelve months in all, the *Gentlewoman* fifteen months; for a mother mourning a child *The Queen* advised six months in crape, *The Lady* only three months; for a grandparent *The Lady* advised nine months, the *Ladies' Year Book* only six;—and so on. The propriety of mourning itself was still taken for granted. An old lady recounted recently that on her marriage, in the first decade of this century, she showed a great aunt her trousseau; the response was 'Very nice, my dear, but *where are the mourning clothes*?'

The last great and universal demonstration of mourning happened when Queen Victoria died (plate 57); even in Dublin, commented the *Lady's Pictorial*, its correspondent saw only two people not in black.[53] Black was everywhere in London on even the first day after her death; this speedy assumption was assisted by the fashionable ubiquity of black that season. Nonetheless, there was an unprecedented rush at Peter Robinson's; the firm apologized via the Press for late deliveries. The London Glove Clinic saw a 'phenomenal' demand for black gloves.

The Earl Marshal's Orders for general mourning at first specified no set time for mourning, following in this the precedents for William IV and the Prince Consort. The only difference was that 'deepest' was substituted in place of 'decent' mourning. The King eventually instructed that mourning was not to be worn after the middle of April; this relieved the fashionable world, since a longer period would have meant that the London Season could not have taken place. The magazines advised ladies to be moderate, and that crape was not absolutely necessary for general mourning, although 'many wear a rosette or two'. One significant comment was that although 'in the strictest sense velvet is not admissible for mourning, the rule will be hardly adhered to so stringently in the case of the young folks . . . .'[54]

Pearls and diamonds were forbidden only to the Court, which was restricted to jet. The usual attempts to follow fashion were made: 'if you want to follow the latest Paris fashion you may choose white lace, where a striped effect is secured by narrow bands of black velvet ribbon threaded in and out of the lace from décolleté to hem, while to still further add to the decorative effect, medallions of black Chantilly lace lightly broidered in jet are appliqué on the white lace at intervals.'[55] Spence's *National Mourning Display* illustrated a hat called 'The Tempest' at 16s 9d; described as a 'very Stylish Black Hat, brim of Glace silk tucked at intervals. Two Pairs Angel Wings, and large Silk Rosettes, finished with Jet Ornament. Very stylish.'[56]

Black Chantilly lace and angel wings did not reconcile smart women to the disadvantages of mourning. '. . . what a city of mournful spectres London has seemed during the last two weeks. For black—unmitigated black—takes the roses out of all but the youngest and freshest faces, throws up hollows in the cheeks, and attenuates the long, thin figure of the average Englishwoman.'[57] It seems that despair had brought an uncommon realism into fashion magazines. A conclusion was drawn that would grievously have startled opinion of thirty years earlier:

'The King . . . would be doing the nation a service if he would deign to make violet, not black, the tint which all who mourn for friends and relatives should wear . . . violet has much in its favour as the garb of tears . . . as dignified as black, and well nigh as sombre, and yet what a difference to the eye and to the mind if everyone were clothed in the colour of pansies or of violets instead of in lustreless black . . .'[58]

In 1889 the Court had been criticized for absurd regulations concerning mourning dress, and for its other 'funereal vagaries'; these were unworthy of the nation, setting a bad example. The new Queen was of a different character.

'Queen Alexandra, too, it is well known, is no stickler for the outward wearing of mourning, of the expression of mental woe by the symbols of crape and bombazine . . . . The fact is that for the last decade or so, the time of mourning for private persons has been considerably shortened, and the mourning garb itself shorn of much of its distinctiveness. Young widows no longer are constrained to parade their loss in long crape veils, caps, and streamers, and such an accumulation of sombre crape as made a widow in former times just what she would wish not to be, the cynosure of all eyes . . . . Good taste and common sense . . . are alike concerned in the new order of things. Living in a somewhat pessimistic age, we do not feel that death is the unmitigated evil which it was held to be, strangely enough, in more pious times . . .'[59]

We may, however, think the claim of the last sentence ignorant or disingenuous. Mitigations of the evil of death had been enumerated *ad nauseam* in the earlier period; they now became increasingly rare. Death had begun to be ignored.

Despite its inevitability and her advanced age, the death of Victoria threw her Court into a flurry. It searched for appropriate precedents. The confusion is apparent in a telegram sent to Lady Lytton, a Lady of the Bedchamber, by the Lord Chamberlain, obviously in reply to a question on the etiquette of Court mourning: 'St James St. 4.30 received 5. Lady Lytton 29 Bloomsbury Sqre. No orders for ladies at present that a terrible national calamity Clarendon.'[60] Lady Lytton was called to Osborne in another telegram that gave the essential information 'Am desired ask you come here on Wednesday remain over the funeral we wear I believe deep band of crape on stuff or woollen dresses long crape veil back of bonnet quite high dresses for dinner white lawn cuffs and collar. Harriet.'[61] Eventually a year of Court mourning was declared; the ladies of the Court had to wear black whilst the Royal Family was in mourning. Some must have sighed at this last, departing penance inflicted by the Queen; because she had worn no colours, the ladies of the Court had been confined for forty years to black, white, grey, or mauve.

Princess Marie Louise (plate 40), a grand-daughter of Queen Victoria, wrote in 1956 an account of the uncertainties created by the lack of knowledge of the proper etiquette at the Queen's death:[62]

'When Queen Victoria died, there was great consternation and bewilderment in the Lord Chamberlain's Office, as well as in the Royal Family, as to what was the correct mourning for the Sovereign. Please remember it was sixty-four years since such a tragic event had taken place. No one knew what should be worn; old prints and pictures of long ago were studied to see how to bring up to date and modernize the cumbersome trappings of mourning.

. . . I was appealed to as knowing what was de rigueur on such sad occasions abroad . . . . I advised that the headdress should be similar to that worn in Germany; namely, a Mary Stuart cap coming to a peak on the forehead, to which was attached at the back a long flowing crêpe veil. This cap and veil, it was decreed, must be worn indoors as well as outside the house.

78

For the trimming of the cashmere dresses, dull crêpe [not the bright crinkly kind] took the place of bombazine. This crêpe had to measure twelve inches in front and twenty inches at the back. Round the neck were folds of white chiffon—décolletage, of course, was not allowed—and deep cuffs of the same material reaching half-way up to the elbow. When all the Princesses were assembled together they were really rather imposing, being all dressed alike, and, quite honestly, this mourning uniform was most becoming.'

The details concerning the 'Mary Stuart' cap illustrate the peregrinations of a fashion. An earlier source states 'When Her Majesty became a widow, she slightly modified the conventional English widow's cap, by indenting it over the forehead à la Marie Stuart [plate 106], thereby imparting to it a certain picturesqueness which was quite lacking in the former head-dress. This *coiffure* had been not only adopted by her subjects, but also by royal widows abroad.'

The depreciation and eventual disappearance of the entire apparatus of mourning reflected the disappearance of the values and life that we call 'Victorian'. The process was not sealed until the coming of the Great War. Then, mourning succumbed before the vast numbers of dead; faced with this, family mourning and its conventions were an insufficient comment. The stage had become too wide for propriety.

7 State Occasion—the Funeral of the Duke of Wellington

'Lead out the pageant; sad and slow,
    As fits an universal woe,
Let the long, long procession go . . .'[1]

The grandest public spectacles of the nineteenth century, from the Coronation of King George IV to the Jubilee of Queen Victoria, were alike touched with a degree of eccentric romanticism. None exceeded in a certain strange wildness the funeral of the Duke of Wellington; the theme of Death and the Hero (plate 107) was celebrated with extravagant pomp and a sublime lack of proportion.

'This was not madness. It was an act of soberness and truth', said *The Times*. 'I cannot say what a *deep* and *wehmuthige* impression it made on me', said Queen Victoria.[2] 'Sure there never were such a *wake* as this! Oh, now, if there wor the whisky and tobacco, and the snuff on his coffin that an Irishman should have, it would be a real, right good wake as ever was seen,' said an Irishman to the *Illustrated London News*. All classes and types of people had united to play their part in this scene, 'the most memorable in our annals', the greatness of which would make certain that 'a century hence there will still be some score old people in this country who will talk to incredulous hearers of the Duke of Wellington's funeral . . . .' In 1940, Mr Frederick Mead, who had seen the funeral as a boy from a shop-window near Temple Bar, recorded his memories of it for the BBC.

Death and the Hero had long been separately cherished; Carlylean romanticism found its fulfilment in Wellington's funeral, and the prodigalities were justified by scripture: 'Let the memory of that great man be cherished and honoured, for by him the LORD hath wrought our deliverance.' Fortunately the Duke had left no instructions for his funeral; the analogy with Nelson, present from the beginning, determined the character of the obsequies; they were felt as a national need that must be satisfied: 'England owes this great funeral, not so much to Wellington . . . as to itself.' Cost was held a light matter; as the Chancellor of the Exchequer said, an economical nation had rejected all thoughts of expense; or, as *Indépendance Belge* remarked, in a tart report, 'it is a serious thing for this business-like nation to have suspended all occupation for a whole day'. The House of Lords had resolved, at the request of merchants, that all bills due to fall on the day of the funeral should be paid the day before or the day after. Politics were suspended—or almost; certainly, a great political question 'lately held sufficient to cause a dissolution of Parliament . . . had been almost indefinitely postponed'. The entire population appeared 'bent on feasting its eyes with a funeral pageant, of no extraordinary beauty, the subject of which was a man whose death had long been a matter of constant expectation'.

The Queen led her people in acts of homage to the memory of the great man; she and her household, hearing of his death, immediately went into mourning for a week; all invitations to Balmoral were countermanded. This was a tribute of some significance from the Sovereign to a subject; perhaps even more significant from Victoria, with her jealous and active suzerainty of the army, was the edict that it should mourn for the Duke as for a member of the Royal Family.[3] But then she believed, after all, that the Duke was 'the GREATEST man this country ever produced . . . .'[4] His funeral far surpassed the modest obsequies of Albert (plate 115).

Victoria ordered that the body of the Duke should be formally taken into the possession of the Crown, and retrospectively sanctioned a guard of honour to be placed around the coffin at Walmer. The Queen and Prime Minister agreed that the funeral must be public; it could not take place before the November meeting of Parliament, for the Queen was anxious that nothing should deprive the funeral of its national character—the formal approval of Parliament was necessary in order that the ducal relics might 'at the public expense, and with all the solemnity due to the greatness of the occasion, be deposited in the cathedral church of St Paul's'. The Queen and Prince Consort kept a close watch on progress; on 22 September she wrote:

'The Queen has just received Mr Walpole's letter of the 20th, informing her of the difficulty of having the Funeral Service, *according* to the *Liturgy*, performed twice: she trusts, however, that means may be found to enable the Queen's intentions to be carried out . . . by leaving the body for two months without the Funeral Service being read over it, or by reading the Funeral Service now in the presence of the family, and treating the *Public Funeral* more as a translation of the remains to their final place of rest . . . . An impressive religious ceremony might certainly be made of it at St Paul's, even if the actual Funeral Service should not be read on that occasion.'[5]

The delay occasioned criticism, for it was said that it had been engineered for a party purpose by the Derby Ministry: 'Parliament ought to have been called earlier, and Derby and Disraeli were attempting to postpone the inevitable hour when their policy must be explained.'

The Duke's body lay meanwhile at Walmer Castle, enclosed in four coffins of lead, oak, mahogany and pine; these, sumptuous enough, would have been even more so had Messrs Dowbiggin and Holland, the undertakers, known of the intention to hold a public funeral. The tributes had begun already, with the anticipation that:

> Mid pomp and show, and blazonry and pride—
> And slow funereal march, and gorgeous bier,
> The sorrow shall have vent for him who died—

Sorrow was to provide a market that was to be well supplied with goods. Already 'The Flag is Half Mast High: A ballad of the Walmer Watch by Sam. Lover' was on sale at two shillings. And already people hastened to view the coffin; ten thousand people, all 'in mourning, and of very respectable appearance' saw it before its removal to Chelsea. The floor of the little chamber in which the Duke

81

died had been covered with black cloth, from which arose groups of feathers between tall candlesticks; the coffin, placed upon a frame, was draped with a pall, drawn back in order to give people a better view. Its evening journey from the Castle to Deal station was accompanied dramatically by torches; the family and mourners followed in coaches, and the two-mile journey from the Castle to Deal station took one and a half hours. At the station, the coffin and hearse were together hoisted upon a railway truck. In London, a delay occurred whilst 'the funeral part of the cavalcade' was fitted with black velvet and feathers; it then moved towards Chelsea Hospital, to be met by the Lord Chamberlain and his staff with a hundred Grenadier Guards.

The results of the frenetic activity that had possessed those entrusted with the funeral were seen for the first time publicly by those who thronged Chelsea Hospital during the three days' lying-in-state. The Queen and Prince Albert went on Thursday 11 November; on Friday the 12th, Private View day, a two-mile-long line of carriages blocked the streets—when the doors closed at four p.m., thousands of disappointed ticket holders still waited outside. The scene on the 13th, when the public was admitted, was confused and dangerous. There was at this time no notion of queueing, a system that came in the 1870s from the Continent; people were formed into 'foetid'[6] groups of fifty, at ten yard intervals. But the multitude, which 'actually smoked like a heated haystack',[7] was too much for the police, who themselves hardly seemed to know what they were doing; two women were killed in the press, and many more injured. Such disorder excited lively apprehension that the funeral itself would witness further human sacrifices to the memory of the great Duke: the propriety actually shown was greeted with relief and surprise by the newspapers.

The lying-in-state was, perhaps, worth a crush to see (plate 21); the 'dazzling brilliancy of the catafalque' could 'hardly be described in plain prose'. It, and the approach to it, had been constructed to the design of Cockerell, assisted by 'the practical experience of Mr Holland'. The Queen and Prince had approved the designs.

The Vestibule to the Hall, approached by a covered way hung in black cloth, was itself hung in black cloth; from the centre of the ceiling descended a chandelier that caught and held the fabric. The chandelier, worthy of some phantasmagoria of Edgar Allan Poe, took the shape of a gigantic plume of black feathers, like an enormous hanging spider. The light, supplied from a few candelabra, was purposely kept dim in order to prepare for the gorgeous blaze of the hall where the coffin stood.

There, black cloth again draped the walls and ceiling, intercepted by niches in which pairs of soldiers from the Duke's regiment, arms reversed, stood like statues; the black cloth was everywhere trellised with silver cords. Light blazed from eighty-three enormous candelabra. A dais, forty-five feet wide by thirty-five feet deep, held the coffin; ten columns, representing bundles of spears tied with laurel, and studded with hatchments, carried the canopy; hollow columns lighted the dais —they carried inside them reflectors designed to throw all the light upon it whilst they themselves remained black and sombre. The dais was completely covered with cloth-of-gold of the most costly description; the canopy, of black velvet scattered with silver stars, bore on its front an heraldic mantle with the family arms emblazoned in gold; it was lined with silver tissue decorated with black spangles. The medals and orders of the Duke lay at the foot of the coffin; at its head stood three chairs, for the chief and two assistant mourners. From the top of the columns sprang gigantic plumes of black feathers. The whole effect was theatrical, eccentric, powerful and imperially pagan; it compelled admiration.

The other great *pièce de résistance* of the funeral festivities was the 'Funeral Car' that carried the coffin. After a false start—the task was first given to Messrs Banting of St James's Street, the Royal Undertakers who, having received 'imperfect' instructions, produced unsuitable designs—the new 'Governmental Department of Practical Art' at Marlborough House undertook the design. From the first sketch by Redgrave (plate 108) to completion (plate 109), the making of the car took only three weeks, although it was said that it would normally have taken twelve months. The Lord Chamberlain, the Marquess of Exeter, was indefatigable in smoothing its path. The design was by Redgrave; the construction and detail was organized by Professor Semper, the fabrics and heraldry by Professor Octavius Hudson; seven great establishments were concerned in the manufacture of the car. Prince Albert saw and approved the project.

It was determined that the car that carried the mortal remains of the Great Duke to their grave should be as immortal as men could make it. It was to be preserved as a national heirloom. No tinsel or gimcrack was to be permitted; all materials were to be as they appeared. Sir Henry Cole later dilated on the difficulties. One manufacturer sent helmets differing from the model carefully provided, and painted papier mâché versions had to be used instead of bronze; these were the only shams. A 'sort of pug-dog's head' in place of lions' heads was rejected in time to allow a real substitute. Sir Henry commented, in an interesting aside, that although the car was essentially a 'reality in its materials, it was perhaps, less a reality viewed on true aesthetic principles than a simple bier borne by soldiers would have been, and less impressive than the Duke's horse with the empty dangling boots . . . . Triumphal cars belong to a past age . . . .'[8] This particular relic from a past age cost £11,000, and materially assisted in creating the 'moral grandeur' of the funeral. Cole also said that until the morning of the funeral it was not intended that the canopy should be used; the coffin would then have been pre-eminent. Something of the antique splendour would have been lost. The silver and gold canopy, woven at Spitalfields, was of 'rich Indian kinkhol', an exotic material of Eastern splendour.

The Times' description of the car as it appeared at the funeral, although tinged with hyperbole, is an accurate enough description of its effect on most people— few shared the sour opinion of *Indépendance Belge*: 'we will not speak of it out of respect to him it carried'. The car, said *The Times*, at the funeral,

'formed by far the most magnificent and interesting feature of the procession . . . the whole lower part is of bronze . . . elaborated with an amount of skill and artistic feeling which deserve unqualified praise. Above this metallic framework rises a rich pediment of gilding, in the panels of which the following list of victories is inscribed . . . . On the sides . . . lofty trophies of arms . . . surmounted by the Ducal coronets and batons. Over the bier and its bearers, the gilded handles of which protruded from beneath, was arranged the sumptuous velvet pall, powdered with silver embroidery, bordered with laurels in silver, and showing the legend round it, "Blessed are the dead that die in the Lord" and terminated by a magnificent canopy, with pendant cords and tassels of the richest and most costly description. To this gigantic vehicle, twenty-seven feet long, ten feet broad, seventeen feet high, and weighing from ten to eleven tons, twelve of the largest and finest black horses that could be procured were harnessed three abreast. They were completely covered with velvet hangings, having the arms of the deceased splendidly embroidered on them, and with heads surmounted by nodding plumes they looked quite elephantine. Such was the funeral car as it fell into the line of procession followed by a swarm of undertakers' men.'

Typical of the ingenious Victorians was that the canopy incorporated machinery that made it possible to lower it as it passed underneath Temple Bar; the dais was constructed to turn on a central axis so that, on arriving at St Paul's, the bier could be manoeuvred easily into the cathedral.

Today the funeral car, dusty, with its corner pillars and draperies missing, shorn of its height and papier mâché helmets, stands in the crypt of St Paul's. It bears not a single ecclesiastical symbol (although the Victories with palms could at a first glance be mistaken for angels). It is worthy of some Victorian Pandemonium; certainly, had the Duke been the archetypal Tyrant depicted by Spiritualist literature, no more appropriate funeral car could possibly have been found.

Temple Bar, the monument that traditionally marked the entrance to the City, where the Lord Mayor of London held sway, underwent an extraordinary investiture for the funeral. At the hands of Messrs Herring and Son, Fleet Street, Upholsterers to the City, it became a 'vast, Roman decorated funeral arch' (plate 110). Draped in black cloth and velvet curtains, each of which had a sweep of thirty feet, with a spread of cloth-of-gold, twenty-four feet by fifteen, in the centre; enriched with silver urns, arms, and trophies, all in papier mâché, with a heavy silver fringe showing up against the black; bearing on the top 'gigantic flambeaux and silvered urns' that gave out 'huge volumes of gas-flame' the night before the funeral; it must have looked astonishing. Contemporaries did not altogether approve: Sir John le Couteur wrote in his diary, 'The Temple Bar was gaudily and critically decorated for the occasion, but without taste or solemn grandeur';[9] *The Times* told the public that 'whatever may be thought of the taste which characterized' the decorations, 'they undoubtedly showed the respect which the City entertains for the memory of the Great Duke'. The room above the arch was occupied by the Countess of Jersey (whose banker grandfather had long rented it) and her party.

Temple Bar presented difficulties to the organizers of the funeral. Its dimensions dictated limitatons to the funeral car—which otherwise might have been gargantuan; the awkward operation of lowering the car's halberds and canopy was performed without difficulty, but *The Times* nonetheless urged the Bar's removal. It also created a situation where great personages might contend; the Lord Mayor of London, within the City, had the right of precedence over all save the Sovereign and the Archbishop of Canterbury; hope was expressed that the 'good sense and good taste' of the City would waive the precedence, and that the Lord Mayor's carriage, after joining the procession at Temple Bar, would fall behind that of the Prince Consort. This, in the event, occurred, but in return the Lord Mayor was given precedence over the Archbishop of Canterbury!

The appearance of St Paul's was given much thought. 'Messrs Banting', said *The Times*, must be given credit for the arrangements made 'amid divided counsels and competing authorities'. The floor of the nave was covered in black baize, from which ascended tiers of seats; the Duke's escutcheons, in black and white satin, punctuated the scene, and the 'lower parts' of the monuments to Nelson and Cromwell were swathed in black drapery. Orders were given that ladies in the cathedral should wear mourning, and gentlemen also, the latter with white cravats; these black clothes and black cloth would necessitate gas light to 'impart an air of solemn and chastened magnificence to the scene'. Three large gas mains were laid down and gas lights, variously estimated to number from 5000 to 7000, appeared; the effect was stunning. The *Illustrated London News* said: 'The memory of those [gas lights] in the interior of St Paul's will ever be dear to those who have, with artistic eyes, drunk in the beauty of the *chiaroscuro*.'

Others prepared for the funeral by selling and preparing seats and rooms along the route. Extensive preparations were made to bring spectators from the country; special boats and trains were put on from Dublin to London. These people had to be accommodated. Advertisements for seats began to appear in October: 'Funeral, with Beds the night previous'; a drawing room 'suitable only for a family of distinction'. A rumour that the Queen was to watch from Somerset House put up the price of seats in that quarter. 'Wellington Funeral Agency Offices' were opened; plans, models and drawings of seats were exhibited in shops. Seats in churchyards were let in favour of parochial charities—St Martin-in-the-Fields made £200. The prices asked were high: 'Covered and Numbered SEATS around ST MARY-LE-STRAND CHURCH. The proceeds devoted to Parochial Charities. Some few seats still left . . . one Guinea.' The clubs issued tickets (plate 48) and prepared to open their doors to the ladies, save for the Carlton, which, as the Duke's club—he was a founder-member—remained austerely without visitors and without a public breakfast.

The lowest priced seats publicly advertised were in the Strand; 'Shop seats 8s 6d; rooms, well warmed, up stairs, from 7s . . . roof seats, 4s 6d.' (Surprisingly enough, considering the packed roofs, only one fatal fall occurred, from Drummond's Bank at Charing Cross.) The Strand's average was £20 for a first floor, £10 for a second, £8 for a third, and £4 for a roof. Near Somerset House, a furnished room for twenty with an 'ample cold collation' cost £25; at Ludgate Hill a large dining room that held fifty people cost fifty guineas. A first floor in Piccadilly cost £60; some with bay windows cost a hundred guineas. The *Observer* calculated—and this was thought a low estimate—that £80,000 changed hands for seats.

The day before the funeral, the Duke's coffin was removed to the Horse Guards; on the same day the car was drawn the whole length of the route, as a rehearsal; its performance was perfect. All was prepared; London was full of country people; more than 200,000 seats had been constructed and sold, and 1,500,000 people were prepared to witness the great ceremony. The day of the funeral was to be observed as a 'close holiday'; the Bank of England, the Stock Exchange and all places of public resort were to be shut.

The day dawned stormy; uncomfortable weather for those who had waited through the November night. During the night sounds of workmen had proceeded from the tent containing the funeral car; before daybreak, troops had gathered in St James' Park and in Horse Guards Parade, the infantry with its standards covered with crape. At seven o'clock the hangings of the tent were unfurled; the guns fired, the troops saluted, a roll of muffled drums preceded the 'Dead March in Saul' and the bronze wheels of the stupendous vehicle began to roll; 'the effect of it will long be remembered by the multitudes . . . .' Those multitudes have long since joined the Duke, but their experience lives in the superlatives of those who saw the pageant; 'never probably has the sublimity which is expressed by the presence of the masses been so transcendently displayed . . . .'

The Order of the procession gives some idea of its magnificence, as do contemporary illustrations (plate III), especially that most extraordinary memento of it, the sixty-seven foot long aquatint published by Ackermann. All the great of the land were there, save only the Queen, who could not attend the funeral of a subject, however eminent; she watched from Buckingham Palace and St James' Palace; the car halted before her so that she could take in the scene. Prince Albert, dressed in Field Marshal's uniform and a mourning scarf, followed; there were, in all, at least forty mourning coaches, covered with black velvet and powdered with silver ornaments. The domestics of the Duke preceded those appointed to public office, thence the order of precedence rose to the greatest names. The Lord Mayor was overshadowed—'the ponderous vehicle which bears the burden of civic majesty had its gilded glories eclipsed by the superior attractions of the military pageant'. It was remarked that the gay carriages of the sheriffs were hardly in keeping; they required some sign of mourning. After the car came the most affecting sight, the Duke's horse, without its rider, and after it, the family mourning coaches. They struck the spectators by their antique appearance. One gathers, through the haze of adulation, that the dead man had had a mean streak; he certainly bought no new carriages after 1815, when he had equipped his Paris embassy.

The length of the procession awed the spectators; it seemed endless to those waiting to see the hearse: 'though the Rifles led the way, at eight o'clock, it was twenty-five minutes past nine before the car started, and half an hour before the extreme rear was in motion.' The route had, for contemporaries, a 'dramatic unity and completeness', because the processions passed from the wealthy regions of palaces and great mansions, through middle-class areas, to the poorer districts, before finally reaching the metropolitan cathedral. Everywhere, people pressed to see the spectacle. The orderly crowd impressed spectators, although one incident remembered by an eye-witness was not recorded in the press—beside St Clement Dane's a crowd that had formed to follow the procession was belaboured by the police with truncheons; it melted away. On Constitution Hill, the trees were filled with spectators; in Piccadilly, windows and balconies were completely occupied. At St James' Street 30,000 saw the procession; the clubs there and on Pall Mall, their balconies draped with black, contained 'immense numbers of ladies provided

86

with places by the courtesy and gallantry of the members'. The roof of the National Gallery was full; it acquired 'a grace and animation which it never knew before'. The crowds uncovered, and fell silent, as the procession passed. It was remarked that the shop windows in the Strand were full of people compressing themselves 'for the occasion into the dimensions of charity-school children, and looking perfectly placid and resigned'. Only one hitch occurred, when the wheels of the car stuck in the mud opposite the Duke of York's column; they were extricated by the police.

The doors of St Paul's had opened, later than scheduled, at eight a.m. The earliest mourners to arrive there were the old generals and admirals; they were succeeded at ten o'clock by some foreign royalty and the House of Commons. There was no seating plan in the cathedral, which led to confusion and competition. Also, it was intensely cold; many put on their hats. At eleven thirty-five the bands outside moved slowly into a dead march; at twelve ten the car arrived before the cathedral; a large area of the railings had been removed to allow its ingress. But a delay of over an hour now occurred. It must have been agonizing for those of impatient temperaments, and exceedingly uncomfortable; the cold wind blew through the immense doors, and the 'distinguished foreigners withdrew before it . . . the clergy . . . vainly sheltered their faces in their robes.' This draught continued; a diarist wrote that during the ceremony 'the breeze coming up the nave from the west caused the feathers in the chieftain's hat that lay on his coffin to wave about, giving it a singular life-like appearance'.[10]

The service finally started, watched from a distant gallery by the new Duchess of Wellington. The scene was singularly impressive, with the 'sable of Peers and Commons, the red and purple gowns of the corporations, the black robes and white and red hoods of the university deputation, and the immense array of faces rising pile after pile, and diminishing into mere specks in the distance, beneath the arches of the upper galleries.' The Burial Service was performed in a version made by Dr Croft during the reign of George I; the *Nunc dimittis* was accompanied by a theme adapted from the slow movement of Beethoven's Seventh Symphony. It was most affecting; the Chief Mourner (whose long mourning cloak necessitated the use of train bearers), Prince Albert and the Duke of Cambridge, were observed to weep; the handkerchiefs and sobs of the 'heroic generals . . . witnessed their love for their great commander'.[11] At three o'clock all the parish churches in England tolled their bells; the coffin descended to the sublime music of the Dead March in Saul, and the Tower guns marked the end of the ceremonies. The great Duke was dead and buried. After the ceremonial, the realities supervened; one man who came up 'and looked into the tomb . . . turned speedily away, for the sepulchral faintness which arose was very sickening . . . .'[12] It remained only to produce the monument (plate 113).

Although it was counted as remarkable that no cases of theft were brought before the police after the funeral, a lot of money was made (in addition to that from the sale of seats) from the demand for mourning and souvenirs. Many shops that did not normally sell mourning clothes hastily brought them into stock. Advertisements describe mourning articles by the score: 'WELLINGTON DIED SEPT. 14, 1852. These words, encircled by a device of cypress and laurel entwined, are formed into, and appear on, the surface of a HATBAND . . . a desirable and convenient medium for national mourning at the approaching grand public obsequies . . . .' Armlets of crape, with the same device, were also obtainable, both from Nicholl's of Regent Street; it was 'probable that both Armlet and Hatband may be preserved as a relic . . . .' One could buy 'cypress hatbands', or 'a mourning head-dress, suitable for wearing in the Cathedral'—this latter was especially designed not to impede the view, as would a bonnet. Accessories were not limited to mourning wear; a tailor's firm recommended a life preserver for everybody on the 18th, and an optician his 'portable perspective glasses, for viewing objects within the distance of a mile, so extensively patronised on this occasion'. Another optician offered the 'Best View of the Funeral for 12s 6d', since his glass would bring out the 'features of the great men and the most minute objects present on that memorable occasion'. The 'Duke of Wellington's funeral wine' was in immediate demand, as was that 'delicious article, the Wellington Funeral Cake', and the 'celebrated lemon biscuits'. And, after the ceremonies, a bath establishment pointed out that 'the luxury of a warm bath will be appreciated by those who have witnessed the Duke's funeral'.

Souvenirs and relics were popular; some people produced their own (plate 114). A great variety appeared for sale. A fine mould of the Duke in parian ware (plate 112) appeared just before his death; the monogram is encircled by an ambiguous wreath; the model was assiduously advertised after his death. The public's participation was asked for in some ventures; on October 2nd the Art Union of London offered £150 for the winning model of a bas-relief; it was to be twenty-nine inches long, to represent an event in the Duke's military life, it was not to be allegorical, and it was to be cast in bronze. Other three-dimensional souvenirs available were life-size busts in artificial stone; equestrian bronze statuettes cast from D'Orsay's *Wellington*; bronze medals by Pinches, the head jointly painted by D'Orsay and Landseer serving as a model for one side, with a laurel wreath and the Duke's dates on the other. Portraits were a prolific alternative. The 'best portrait' published by Ackermann sold at 7s 6d, 10s 6d or 21s 1d; or one could have the two volumes of the illustrated Life by J. H. Strocqueler, at 12s. The pithy character of the late Duke was expounded in many collections; 'Wellington Anecdotes. A Collection of Sayings and Doings of the Great Duke. Addey and Company, Bond Street 1s' or 'Wellingtoniana: Anecdotes, Maxims and Opinions collected by John Timbs 1s'. Of one such collection, the *Illustrated London News* acidly commented, 'We do not precisely understand the principle on which this collection is made; although the editor tells us that for offering it "no apology is required". There may be more than one opinion on this point, especially as acknowledgment is very sparingly made of the sources whence the anecdotes have been obtained. Thus the anecdotes "A Musical Amateur" . . . are taken, verbatim, from the *Illustrated London News*.'

Poetry poured in profusion into the ears of the public. As early as October 2nd the second edition of 'A Dirge for Wellington' by Martin Tupper was advertised at 6d; or one could buy 'His Pilgrimage is Ended' for 2s, or 'A Great Man Fallen' for 6d, the latter a sermon preached in St Peter's Church, Yoxell. The 'National Song'—'The Death of Wellington'—'to the memory of the Prince of Waterloo' by G. A. Macfarren sold at 2s. Some ludicrous eulogies appeared; as the *Illustrated*

London News said, 'some scores if not hundreds of individuals, who seem to think that by the Duke of Wellington's death they have in some mysterious manner been gifted with the "fine frenzy" ' had ventured into verse:

> I see the Martial Pier by his Sovereign's side
> With noble Form supporting the Sword of State,
>   Graced with honours England's pride,
> Titles of his fame too many to numerate

or

> In the Councils of State of old England's fate
> Our Queen he did oft call upon her;
> He is gone, we may see, aged near 83,
> Full of age, full of glory and honour.

Unfortunately the king of such poets, William McGonagall (died 1902), had not yet appeared on the scene; the writer of the matchless odes on Gladstone's and Victoria's funerals was not available.

Music was not lacking—'Mourn for the Mighty Dead' by Sir H. K. Bishop. Nor were more ambitious commemorations; by October 16th a diorama of Walmer and the Duke's room had been added to the 'Gallery of Illustration' at 14 Regent Street, the 'only complete Illustration of his Grace's career ever exhibited'.

But the most extraordinary traffic was in personal relics. A forewarning of this had occurred in 1825 when the Duke's Waterloo charger, Copenhagen, which had 'furnished so many bequests from his mane and tail to enthusiastic young ladies, who had his hair set in brooches and rings', was dug up, despite the solemn cypresses and railings that encircled his grave, and bereft of a hoof by souvenir hunters. And now 'the Orphan Daughter of a Military Officer is desirous of disposing of the Autographs of His Grace the Duke of Wellington . . .'; *The Times* of November 10th contained thirteen such advertisements, at prices ranging from twenty guineas to thirty shillings. *The Times* of November 12th advertised for sale fragments of an 'Ode on the Death of Napoleon' by Manzoni, torn up by the Duke and thrown out of his carriage window, whence they were picked up by a gentleman who had witnessed the incident. Hair abounded; 'a genuine and unique relic of the late Duke of Wellington—a lady will dispose of a Lock of his Grace's Hair, which can be guaranteed . . . the owner would not like to part with it under fifty guineas, but is open to a liberal offer'. Many such 'unique' relics were offered including some from the son of the Duke's barber at Stratfieldsaye, which must have rather spoiled the market. Copenhagen entered this field again: 'The Greatest Relic of the Age—a lock of the Mane of the Horse the late Duke rode in the Battle of Waterloo. Cut off by the Duchess . . . .' A waistcoat was included in other offers. Such advertisements did not cease with the funeral; they provided a kind of diminuendo to its grand climax.

The funeral, as an affair of state, involved the greatest in the land, and it is remarkable that such a precedent-bedevilled affair did not arouse more squabbles. Few unhappy incidents marred it; there were murmurings against the clergy of St Paul's, and complaints from the Order of Baronets that no place in the procession or cathedral had been assigned to it by the Earl Marshal. There was little else.

But Disraeli, that most modern of Victorian politicians, did get into a delightful scrape, caused by an excess of cynicism in composing the eulogy given before the House of Commons: 'The speech which Mr Disraeli thought fit to deliver was only his own in those passages of it which were marked with bad taste.' Word for word, the statesman had transcribed a eulogy given by Thiers in 1828 on the Marshal Gourion de St Cyr; the Hero of Waterloo, the Iron Duke, the saviour of the people, had been subjected to a second-hand eulogy written for a 'second-rate French Marshal'. Disraeli, even before he was found out, could not have been unconscious of the ironies.

8 Means of Disposal

'Coffins are not recognized by any authority whatsoever . . .
generally, their use can only be regarded as an encroachment
on the rights of the living.'[1]

The reaction of the Committee of 1842 to Walker's opinion that 'I think that the
old Roman plan of burning would be preferable' is not recorded, but possibly it
found that opinion almost as upsetting as the revelations of graveyard horrors·
There is plenty of evidence that his contemporaries thought that 'consuming the
bodies of the dead on the funeral pile' was 'repugnant to the feelings and the
usages of all Christian countries'; half of the objections of Ecclesiologists and
others to symbols such as urns was that they were 'memorials of the abominable
usage which the heathens, in their ignorance, inflicted on the bodies of the dead'.[2]

To burn or not to burn became a great question; the long time that elapsed
before cremation became acceptable to ordinary people indicates how firm a
prejudice had first to be conquered. In 1885, three cremations took place; in 1886,
ten; in 1887, thirteen; in 1912 there were over a thousand, but by 1936 there
were still only ten thousand, and it was not until 1968 that over half of those who
died were cremated. It is not surprising that such a fundamental change in social
habits took time to be accepted, for it indicated a profound shift in belief. The
complete revolution in the method of disposing of the dead that cremation consti-
tuted, and the decline in formalized mourning, were obviously closely connected;
both, as obviously, were connected with the decay of institutionalized religion.
Open doubt and infidelity, the frank disbelief that could say only

> That faiths by which my comrades stand
> Seem fantasies to me,
> And mirage-mists their
> Shining Land,[3]

was uncommon. But even devout Churchmen began to display unease when their
more fundamentalist persuasions appeared to oppose the progress of science and
sanitation.

Victorian beliefs, and especially Victorian religious beliefs, were corporeal;
religion had little of the abstract quality of modern religious thought. The attitude
to angels, and the Victorians' belief in palpable angelic presences, is touched upon
in the following chapter: the same literal and straightforward fundamentalism
informed their attitude to their dead. It was the religious equivalent of the materialism that, in the presence of nobler strains, was so prominent a part of their way of
life. The exhortations of enlightened religious leaders bring to light the largely
unnamed apprehensions aroused by the thought of cremation; for instance Bishop
Fraser, at the height of the first controversy in 1874, said in the sermon that opened
the cemetery at Bolton:

'The ancient Romans believed in immortality, and yet they believed in burning the bodies of their dead. Urn-burial was certainly as decent as the practice of interment . . . and urns containing the ashes of the dead were more picturesque than coffins. Could they suppose that it would be more impossible for God to raise up a body at the Resurrection, if needs be, out of elementary particles which had been liberated by the burning, than it would be to raise up a body from dust, and from the elements of bodies which had passed into the structure of worms? The omnipotence of God is not limited, and He would raise the dead whether He had to raise our bodies out of churchyards, or . . . out of an urn in which they were deposited 2000 years ago.'

He also said—and one wonders how large a proportion of his hearers disbelieved him,

'I feel convinced that before long we shall have to face this problem, "How to bury our dead out of sight" more practically and more seriously than we have hitherto done. In the same sense in which the "Sabbath was made for man, not man for the Sabbath", I hold that the earth was made not for the dead, but for the living. *No intelligent faith can suppose that any Christian doctrine is affected by the manner in which, or the time in which, this mortal body of ours crumbles into dust and sees corruption.*'

Even he had to add, 'I admit that my instincts and sentiments—the result, however, probably of association more than of anything else—are somewhat revolted by the idea of cremation.'[4]

The advocates of cremation were at constant pains to destroy that association, and to deny that cremation was an intrinsically pagan idea: Sir Henry Thompson, in his famous article in the *Contemporary Review* of January 1874, said that nothing could be more appropriate to the religious interpretation of 'ashes to ashes, dust to dust' than cremation, and that the metaphor of the dissipation of the body in the 'ethereal form of gaseous matter' was far more suggestive than the prison of the tomb —perhaps he was influenced by subconscious memories of Elijah's Chariot of Fire! William Eassie, the first secretary of the Cremation Society, represented that it was nonsensical to suppose that cremation could hinder resurrection by quoting the question of the Earl of Shaftesbury: 'What would in such a case become of the blessed martyrs?'[5] The mind of the Victorian was perhaps materialist, but it found it difficult to conceive of divine injustice.

As early as 1857 a work entitled *Burning the Dead, or Urn Sepulture*, by Charles Cobb, Surgeon, appeared, but it seems to have made no impression and it was not until the 1869 International Medical Congress, held at Florence, discussed the subject that interest in cremation was revived. The Italians were for a long time the pioneers of cremation; it is strange that the idea was canvassed in such a strongly Roman Catholic country before being adopted elsewhere; is it possible that the antique ideals of the Risorgimento revived also an interest in Roman funeral customs? In 1873, a model of a new Italian-designed cremating apparatus was shown at the Vienna Exposition; there it was studied by Sir Henry Thompson, Bart., FRCS, Surgeon to Queen Victoria. It was fortunate for the cremation movement that its most active protagonist and supporter came from within the inner circle of the medical establishment.

Sir Henry's article in the *Contemporary Review* brought into existence the cremation movement in Britain. He began, soberly enough, by reiterating the certainties of the sanitary reformers over the past thirty years, that thousands of human lives had been cut short by the poison of 'slowly decaying, and often diseased, animal matter', and that the 'grave-yard pollution of air and water' was one of the most potent threats to human happiness. This was not new; the division that he made between the two ways in which the matter could be regarded— from the standpoints of utility and of sentiment—was; the Victorian age was changing when retrograde attitudes could be so boldly labelled 'sentiment'. It was quite plain that to Sir James the arguments of utility should prevail.

It seemed to him inevitable that the growing population would eventually demand that every waste spot should be utilized for food and shelter; the country could not afford that the land should be polluted with dead bodies. Also, the matter should be looked at from the economic point of view: sentiment might deny that it was an economic question, but in reality it was so, inescapably. In 1871, for example, 80,430 deaths occurred in London; these represented 206,820 lbs of ashes and bone earth; 'the pecuniary value of this highly concentrated form of animal solids is very considerable'. Britain spent more than half a million pounds annually in importing foreign bones; 'Few persons, I believe, have any notion that these importations of foreign bones are rendered absolutely necessary by the hoarding of our own some six feet below the surface.' One can imagine the sharp intake of breath at this passage. Sir Henry adopted the familiar tactic of arrogating propriety to his own view; such a waste was, he said, an absurd, 'if not wicked' result, rendered more ridiculous by the lavish funeral expenditure necessary to bury these assets. The answer was cremation; to burn was, in effect, to achieve far more rapidly the same chemical processes accomplished by a slow and dangerous putrefaction. Sir Henry continuously emphasized the naturalness of cremation: 'follow Nature's indication, and do the work she does, but do it better and more rapidly'. In short, to 'treat our dead after this fashion would return millions of capital without delay to the bosom of mother earth, who would give us back large returns at compound interest for the deposit'. Nobody could accuse Sir Henry of failing to be explicit.

The public reception of this uncompromising stance was surprisingly favourable; Sir Henry received over eight hundred concurring letters; the Press almost wholly supported him. Sir Henry put 'the undertaker's' attitude to his proposals in these words: 'I only desire to serve the public's want; as long as the public demands funeral cars, magnificent horses, display of feathers, and a host of attendants in black, I must furnish them; but I am equally ready to perform cremation tomorrow if the public demand it . . . .' On 13 January 1874, a group of friends met at 35 Wimpole Street, Sir Henry's house, and signed a declaration urging the adoption of cremation; this was the beginning of the Cremation Society of England. Those who signed included Tenniel, Millais, Trollope, Charles Voysey, and Spencer Wells—all indisputably respectable.

The counterblast came quickly—a reply in the February 1874 issue of the

Contemporary Review by Philip Holland, MRCS, Medical Inspector of Burials in England and Wales. The article is curious: it bears all the signs of having been written in a great hurry, its sequence of thought is strange, and it contains inconsistencies upon which Sir Henry pounced with delight. Perhaps the author's faculties were benumbed by shock.

Holland began by saying that had not the advocate of cremation been of such eminence as Sir Henry, he would not have bothered to reply. He went on to declare that a well managed cemetery need be no more dangerous than a well managed railway. Sir Henry had argued that cremation would avoid the horrors of premature burial, an ever present nineteenth-century bogey—to Holland, to be burnt alive was as unpleasant as to be buried alive. Also, the practice of cremation would be difficult; it would scarcely be possible to obtain sufficient men to superintend 'that kind of work' and, badly done, cremation would be 'inexpressibly shocking'— and this event would not be rare. It is clear that Holland had not bothered to inform himself about possible methods of cremation. As for the economic side of the question, Holland could hardly believe that Sir Henry was serious in his contention that 'we should use our father's ashes as turnip-dressing'. Only the most savage and insensitive barbarians could adopt such methods; it would be better to sink our dead in the ocean, which 'need be attended with nothing revolting to our feelings'. It is clear that, to Holland, out of sight meant out of mind.

The next issue of the *Contemporary Review* produced Sir Henry's answer. He expressed astonishment, and pleasure, at this unexpected protest from a member of the medical profession—pleasure at being given the opportunity of demolishing the most formidable possible opposition. He brought up all the old spectres evoked by the 1843 Enquiry; he repeated the estimate of Dr Lyon Playfair (now HM's Postmaster General) that in 1849, 2,572,580 cubic feet of noxious gases were emitted from 52,000 metropolitan burials; these latter numbered 80,000 in 1873. And the cemeteries were being surrounded by an increasing population. He went into the precise technical details of which Holland was ignorant: a powerful reverberating furnace would reduce a body 'of more than average size and weight, leaving only a few white and fragile portions of earthly material, in less than one hour'. He went on 'I challenge my opponent to produce so fair a result from all the costly and carefully managed cemeteries in the kingdom, and I offer him twenty years in which to elaborate the process.'

He denied that he was joking concerning the 'economic' aspect, and observed, apropos of Mr Holland's sea proposals, that bodies in the sea would merely be devoured by fish and crustaceans: 'no animal multiplies more rapidly than fish, and the "economic" question would be determined in a manner more complete and more direct, and with a more remunerative result than any which I ever dared, or still should dare, to suggest!' In a way, it is a pity that Sir Henry did not find a worthier opponent. One verdict on this initial phase of the controversy was given in May of the same year, when the Cambridge Union voted in favour of cremation by a hundred and one votes to forty-two.

The Cremation Society's theories were expanded in the publication in 1875 of *Cremation of the Dead*; the author, William Eassie, was Secretary of the Society. There was little new in the book. It contained several grisly stories of the effects

FIG 7 'Sketch of Family Columbarium, or Niche in Private Chapel' from *Cremation of the Dead* by William Eassie 1875.

of disinterring the bodies of people who died from infectious diseases. Eassie made the pious point that cremation would, once more, enable the dead to be buried within churches; in discussing the destination of the ashes, he remarked that it would be unseemly for the *poorer* classes to keep them in their homes. He mentioned the patents taken out, from 1825–71, in search of the ideal coffin—coffins made of stone, marble, granite, slate, porcelain, earthenware, bitumen, asphalt, paper, peat, indiarubber, iron and glass—all in the vain search for hygiene and preservation. His statement that the cost of a cremation would not necessarily exceed that of a 'seventh-class funeral' in London is interesting. There was a good deal about the styles of urns; he suggested that those in Gothic churches might well be designed in reliquary style (fig 7). This was obviously an attempt to get away from pagan associations.

95

In 1875 another theory was advanced to complicate matters; it was hostile both to the current mode of burial and to cremation. It appeared in three letters to *The Times* from Francis Seymour Haden, FRCS; these were later printed as a pamphlet, with additions, by the Earth to Earth Society that sprang from them.

Haden declared that the earth was the natural destiny of all bodies. Coffins, vaults, brick graves, and all attempts at preservation were vain resistance to an inevitable dispensation. The earth was the 'most potent disinfectant' known; in it, resolution replaced the putrefaction that was made permanent by the use of a coffin. Coffins, a pernicious modern invention, were made necessary when elaborate funerals demanded time for their preparation. Wood in moist earth was virtually indestructible, with the result that the earth was condemned to become putrid, populated by 'festering tenants-in-perpetuity of the soil'. The condition of the new cemeteries had become that of the old graveyards, since coffins prevented the earth from exercising its function; they should be closed on sanitary grounds: 'We cannot thus outrage a Divine ordinance with impunity.'

The answer was a 'coffin of some lighter permeable material, such as wicker or lattice-work, open at the top, and filled in with any fragrant herbaceous matters that happened to be most readily obtainable. A layer of ferns or mosses for a bed, a bundle of sweet herbs for a pillow, and as much as it would still contain after the body had been gently laid in it of any aromatic or flowering plant for a coverlet . . . .' The pamphlet that reprinted Haden's letters was headed 'Lay her i' the earth'; it is possible that his original inspiration was literary and romantic.

The acceptance of this 'Earth to Earth' system, of allowing the body to decay naturally—it would not contaminate the adjacent earth—would mean that, after five or six years, it would be possible to bury again in the same ground; one thousand acres would bury a hundred thousand bodies for ever.

Haden also insisted that bodies should not be left long above ground; they should be buried while 'still grateful to every sense'. He reassured those afraid of premature burial: death cannot be mistaken, but it should be certified. To his second letter was attached a declaration, signed by six eminent doctors including the President of the Royal College of Surgeons and William Jenner, that the signs of death were as certain a few hours after it had occurred as days afterwards.

He attacked cremation as 'a wild project—to drive into vapour the bodies of the 3000 people who die weekly in Greater London alone, at a needless cost, an infinite waste, and . . . with an effect on the respirable air of the city that has yet to be estimated?' Moreover, the problem remained after cremation; it would be likely that room would have to be found each week in London for 3000 urns!

Haden's scheme did not lack supporters. Successive leaders backed his letters to *The Times*; the newspaper saw so many objections to cremation that it was heartily glad 'to learn on such excellent authority that the offending process is not really necessary', and that one had only to yield wisely to the dictates of natural laws. There was nothing needlessly revolting in Haden's suggested system.[6] A later leader commented that during the last ten or twenty years hostility to funeral display had grown, and that now an ordinary funeral cost far less than twenty years ago, allowing for the decline in the value of money. Haden had said especially the vested interests of the undertaker were dangerous; he should be licensed: *The Times* suggested that since the pecuniary interests of large numbers of people were involved, a Co-operative Society should be formed to carry out Haden's scheme.[7]

The Necropolis Company invented and patented the Earth to Earth coffin; a version was sold by such firms as Dottridges (see page 31). In 1885 a leader in *The Queen* commented frivolously on a prime image of Romanticism: 'Isabella, immortalised by Bocaccio and Keats, and rendered familiar even to the unpoetical public by the engraving of Millais' charming picture, might have conveyed her lover's head from place to place in her pot of basil without suspicion or offence, for the earth would have converted it into food for the plant that she was so fondly cherishing.' It added that a 'sanitarian' had kept a dead dog, covered with earth, in an open box in the centre of his sitting room, and that within a few weeks the dog had resolved itself into carbolic acid and watery vapour without offence. *The Queen* supported Seymour Haden; it declared its preference for the framed coffins covered in pulp, that gave way to the earth, recently adopted by the Earth to Earth Society. It declared that cremation meant that 'the foulest murder might be committed with impunity'.[8]

This last point was taken up by Haden in a paper, read at the Society of Arts in 1892, entitled 'Cremation an Incentive to Crime'. He asserted that Sir Henry Thompson's argument that only 102 exhumations had been made during the last twenty years, and that only one murder a year had been discovered through them, was completely false, and that, on the contrary, the text books positively bristled with such cases. A certain asperity had entered the discussion since the 1870s. Haden asked of cremation 'Is it a mere scientific fad, or does some ulterior aim, or aspiration more or less occult, lurk at the bottom of it?' He said, of Sir Henry's contention that burial was a cause of infection, that he constantly found himself obliged to 'contrast what I have always believed to be the ways of Nature with the ways, opinions, and statements of Sir Henry Thompson'. He called the crematoria chimneys 'vomitaria' and said that as a measure of public safety cremation should be declared a misdemeanour. He also said that coffins made of pulp were in daily use at Woking, and that since the patent had expired, anybody might make the coffin and sell it for much less than the Woking Company were now doing.

The first task of the newly founded Cremation Society was to find out whether cremation was legal. The answer of counsel was affirmative; money was subscribed; a piece of land in the Great Northern Cemetery was acquired. The building of a crematorium there was forbidden by the Bishop of Rochester, since the cemetery was consecrated ground. Another attempt was made. Freehold land was bought by Sir Henry Thompson in Woking, from the London Necropolis Company; Professor Gorini of Lodi supervised the construction of an apparatus, and on 17 March 1879 the body of a large horse was successfully cremated. The people of Woking marshalled themselves; led by their vicar, they appealed to the Home Secretary, who, on the pretext that cremation would cancel evidence of violence or poison, refused to permit it until sanctioned by Parliament. From 1879 to 1882, the Cremation Society had to restrict itself to words, not deeds. Then, on 8 October 1882, the first cremation in England in modern times took place.

In July 1876, Mrs Hanham, wife of Captain Hanham of Manston House, Dorset, had died; in June 1877 his mother, Lady Hanham, followed her. Both had expressed

97

a wish to be cremated. Captain Hanham determined to fulfil these wishes; he placed the bodies in elm within lead, and conveyed them to a temporary resting place, a mausoleum erected for that purpose; it was eventually to receive the urns.

For six years Captain Hanham sought to give effect to their wishes. He heard of the Crematorium at Woking, but the Home Secretary forestalled him. Formalities made him abandon the attempt to send the bodies to Italy for cremation; at one time he was confident that the United States would give him the facilities he needed, but that resource failed. He began to dread, being in poor health, that he himself would die before he could effect the business: he therefore took the matter into his own hands. He had a furnace built in his orchard, and burnt the bodies, coffins and all, with no nuisance to the neighbourhood, and 'without the slightest unpleasantness to those who stood within two feet of the white flame which promptly resolved the bodies to their harmless elements'.[9]

This well organized cremation provoked no riposte from authority. Oddly enough, it took a far less seemly attempt to legalize the process; this was the attempted cremation of his son by the inexpressibly shocking Dr William Price.

William Price had studied medicine in London; he practised from 1840 to 1893 in Glamorgan. He was a vegetarian, opposed vivisection and vaccination, regarded himself as a member of the ancient order of Druids, and practised free love. He had been tried several times for manslaughter but was always acquitted. At the age of eighty-three he fathered a child on his housekeeper, to whom he was not married. The child was named Jesus Christ (the housekeeper later had two others by him, Jesus Christ the second and Penelopan).

Jesus Christ died at the age of five months. On Sunday, 13 January 1884, the people of Llantrisant, returning home after their evening chapel, saw smoke ascending from the five-hundred-foot Caerlan Hill; on its summit they found Dr Price, clad in a druidical white garment, burning the body of his son with petrol. A tremendous furore ensued, at the end of which Dr Price carried home the partially consumed body and kept it under his bed for a week. He was brought to trial at Cardiff before Mr Justice Stephen, who advised the jury that no English law forbade cremation; the indignant and vengeful jury disregarded the judge, and persisted in attempting to find Dr Price guilty; finally the judge had to tell it outright to go away and find him not guilty.[10] Price claimed £3120 damages, and was awarded a farthing. On his death, he himself was cremated (plate 120).

This case proved that cremation was not illegal, and the Cremation Society issued a circular saying that it would cremate on request. But it was not yet legal; a bill brought forward in 1884 by Sir Charles Cameron to legalize it was voted out, being opposed by both the Prime Minister and the Leader of the Opposition. It was not legalized until 1902, years after crematoria had been established.

In 1885 the crematorium at Woking was completed; it accommodated its urns in niches in a columbarium. In 1888 an appeal was made for a chapel and waiting rooms; the subscription list began with the names of the dukes of Bedford and Westminster; only £1500 was raised, but the Duke of Bedford gave money to complete the scheme. Popular interest was at a high pitch (plate 119). The buildings at Woking exist still, in thirteenth-century Gothic style, with an alabaster catafalque, itself a memorial.

The second crematorium to open was at Manchester, where a local Cremation Society was formed in 1888. The Corporation refused to entertain any idea of supporting the Society's proposals, and the Society therefore formed a limited company; its buildings, in Romanesque brick, were opened in 1892. By 1895 a crematorium had been opened in Scotland, sponsored by a 'Scottish Burial Reform and Cremation Society' formed in 1891. Other crematoria gradually appeared; the age of swift, hygienic disposal had dawned before the death of Victoria.

William Robinson, the famous gardener, produced one of the most interesting and influential works connected with the cremation movement, *God's Acre Beautiful, or The Cemeteries of the Future*. It was first published in 1880.

The book is partly a manifesto for garden cemeteries and partly, one feels as a result, a tract for cremation. An idealistic spirit pervades it; despite the matter of fact central argument, it is suffused with golden nostalgia. The frontispiece (plate 118) strengthens this impression; one feels that the only thing lacking is the supremely appropriate—but supremely inappropriate, because pagan and hopeless —'Et in Arcadia ego'. Robinson put his individual case early in the book, with a sentiment in full harmony with the fashionable proclivities of the period: 'I propose to consider the subject from another point of view altogether—the aesthetic one— or that of the beauty of nature and art.' 'Art for art's sake' seems about to enter the graveyard.

Robinson began by flailing the cemeteries, quoting *The Lancet* of September 1874, which drew attention to certain metropolitan cemeteries that were 'rapidly becoming sources of peril not only to the neighbourhoods in which they were situated, but to the whole metropolis'; it instanced illness among mourners after burials, and called for action by the Home Secretary. He also quoted an issue of *The Times* of 1874 concerning the churchyard and church at Talland in Cornwall; the ratepayers had just voted against the formation of a Burial Board, despite pressure from the Inspector. Repeated burials had placed the church in a pit in which even primroses turned black.

Haden's 'Earth to Earth' system received short shrift; it had an ugly utilitarian aspect, and was simply the old system with the needless addition of basket coffins. Probably it would be even more injurious than the present system, since coffins had perhaps been invented to prevent the too rapid saturation of the soil. Robinson dismissed with scornful incredulity Haden's plan of raising and reclaiming the lowlands of Kent and Essex with decaying human bodies; 'anything more puerile and impracticable could surely not be thought of'—it would merely cause further pollution.

A new argument for cremation was brought forward by Robinson. It was that the poor were burnt anyhow. He quoted a correspondent of *Land and Water* who had encountered a grave-digger's son near a large metropolitan cemetery that, once in the depths of the country, was now surrounded by houses. The man was communicative, and imparted,

'the inner working life of the Necropolis, first drawing the broad distinction between the "privates" and the "commonses", alluding almost with pathos to the sacred soil devoted to the former, and detailing with professional *sangfroid* the management of the ground dedicated to the latter . . . he spoke like one who had seen something worth seeing when he exclaimed, "You should go in there of a night, sometimes, Sir, and see them burning the bones and the coffins. You see, they dig up the 'commonses' every twelve years (of course they dare not interfere with the 'privates'), and what they find left of them they burn."

The minute particulars of this exhumation and the subsequent cremation were described with a particularity of detail which I am sure I need not attempt; but the moral I draw from this little tale is, that if the poor are to be subjected to cremation at all, surely it would be at least as well to do it in the first instance, and to do it decently, as to postpone the operation for twelve years, and then allow it to be done anyhow! . . . a corpse buried in 1862 is dug up to-day (in 1874) and burned, very properly; and apart from the miasmatic exhalations of the grave there is an end of it; but . . . the earth . . . has now been thoroughly tainted, and its disinfecting powers having been largely exhausted, a new corpse, forsooth, is placed in the old grave . . . .'

Such details cleared the way to the encomium of the convenience, utility, and beauty of urn burial that was Robinson's main contribution to the cremation movement. Urn burial could, he said, be carried on for hundreds of years in graveyards the size of the present overcrowded London ones with no offence to the living. And since, 'by the common consent of mankind "God's Acre" is most fittingly arranged as a garden', and since the area set aside for urn burial need not occupy more than a fourth of the area of a large cemetery—this is insisted upon several times—the whole central area could be used as gardens and groves. It would be quite possible to have a private cemetery: near a large country house, for example, urn burial could lead to a family burial place being set aside within the park; 'a quiet enclosed glade in some sunny spot, chosen for its beauty, embowered in a grove of evergreen, the grass sprinkled with hardy native or naturalised flowers only'.

The tombs would enhance this scene of elegiac and antique calm, for the adoption of cremation would not mean the disappearance of tombs; in old Roman cemeteries, said Robinson, tombs still exist, with their undisturbed urns within. And 'the simplest urn ever made for the ashes of a Roman soldier is far more beautiful than the costly funeral trappings used in the most imposing burial pageant of modern times'. The book is illustrated with classical urns from the Vatican collections. Robinson drew a comparison:

'What a contrast there is between that picture of the noble Roman woman, surrounded by her maidens and friends, herself bearing her husband's ashes to the tomb, and the black array, the paid, half-besotted mutes, and the hideous box in which the remains of poor humanity are nailed up for a decay as needless as it is odious, to any one who has seen it or thought of it. What a gain it would be to get rid of much of this Monster Funereal, the most impudent of the ghouls that haunt the path of progress!'

The money spent on a funeral and burial could be concentrated on the urns or tombs; beautiful things could therefore be produced, enduring and legible stone records that would encourage art.

The garden should be natural and effective, with groves of oak and hardy native trees. Trees, or groups of trees, could be given as memorials; a beautiful 'tree-garden' could be created, and the interior groves could house all the beautiful green things that grow in our climate. The outer part of the cemetery should have the tombs and columbaria, an architectural covered way, and the churches (the word 'church' seems almost an intrusion in this context). The central portions should be 'quite free from the drill-master manner of marshalling plants, and sundry like effects of a too prevalent style of gardening'. A winter-garden should be built, in which 'religious or burial ceremonies could take place at inclement seasons—in an agreeable temperature, and in the midst of a variety of beautiful living things'.

This vision of a stately Claudian tomb landscape—'the views should be numerous and carefully considered'—is sympathetic to modern ears. There are significant differences between this and earlier ideals—those of the Ecclesiologists, for example. Although Robinson is never explicit (perhaps he was not so even to himself) one senses that stoicism, not hope, ruled this landscape; classical resignation, made possible by embowered trees, sylvan groves, and antique echoes, had taken the place of pious symbols and ecclesiastical abasements before the Saviour. A style is rarely adopted without reference to the extra-aesthetic conceptions of its originators; in Robinson's garden cemetery one feels that immortality is absent.

9 Angels and Spirits

'Yes! there is one more in angelic bliss,
One less to cherish, one less to kiss,
One more departed to Heaven's bright shore,
Ring the bell softly—there's crape on the door.'[1]

Crape on the door meant, for all who believed, that the door had opened for the defunct to a better land—or perhaps to a worse. The hopes of all, whether unsophisticated (plate 106), or sophisticated, were fixed on Heaven. Those of the former were perhaps more vivid. It is a pity that the Low Church and Nonconformist elements in English religious life had no visual tradition, for their more violent fancies might have made good art, different from the tired or blowsy (plate 122) elysiums of the orthodox. There are no convincing visions of the Established Church Heaven; its depiction as a physical place is rare, and its denizens either rarefied to attenuation (plate 128), arty (plate 124), or merely dull.

Nonconformist pieties sound as if, given pictorial form, they might have produced wonderful things; their intensity was heightened by the wretched conditions under which so many people lived. Bessy, the Darkshire mill girl close to death, with her 'dreams and Methodee fancies, and her visions of cities with goulden gates and precious stones', used the next world as a panacea for this, as did many others. And she, like them, could not bear that any doubt should be cast on the reality of her visions. To her, they were the only things that gave meaning to the waste and folly of this life. '. . . I think, if this should be th'end of all, if all I've been born for is just to work my heart and my life away, and to sicken i' this dree place, wi' them mill noises in my ears for ever, . . . I think if this life is th'end . . . I could go mad . . . .'[2]

The doubt—'Can these dry bones live?'—was an ominous threat to the spiritual peace of the thoughtful Victorian (plate 121). In the past, only those had not believed who had not wanted to believe, but now those who ardently wished to believe were at times unable to do so. Faith was fashionable, but new attacks were made upon it. Discoveries concerning the brain and the mind edged the soul away; Darwin's theories substituted for the handiwork of God, in all its marvellous and purposeful intricacy and detail of design, an impersonal, bloody and mindless selective process that worked by trial and error. He also disposed of the Fall, a doctrine central to orthodox Christianity. The geologists' hammers destroyed one picture of the world as they built another, a picture in which the City of God had no place; the reassembled Dinornis of Sir Richard Owen came to skeletal life only to tread heavily on the beliefs of the top-hatted and bewhiskered people who gazed at it in astonishment. And man without faith, man without hope, was to the mid-Victorian a monstrous aberration, a creature without a place in the Universe. He was a creature who 'built him fanes of fruitless prayer'; a

monster then, a dream,
A discord. Dragons of the prime,
That tare each other in their slime,
Were mellow music match'd with him.[3]

It is difficult for modern men, most of whom were born with doubt, to conceive of the horror doubt brought to men born with faith. Doubt became invasive; the agony was not to *know*—'O damned vacillating state'[4]—a certainty of atheism sometimes brought relief. The most august and the most conventional were not altogether free from doubt; Queen Victoria herself, reported the Dean of Windsor, 'asked me if there ever came over me (as over her) waves or *flashes* of doubtfulness whether, after all, it might all be untrue'.[5]

Science, which did so much to awaken infidelity or doubt, had also the opposite effect. Its stupendous discoveries, which realized the dreams of the magician in his tower, consolidated belief in the miraculous, the extraordinary, the unexplainable. The 'overwrought materialism' of the age was 'fevered by its own excess into spiritual dreams'; it gloried in 'the gas-jet flame of faith' that irradiated its 'coal-mine darkness . . . .'[6] And in a period when religion was, in a sense, as materialist as science, why should both not have their transcendental side?

'Fifty years ago any one would have said it was sheer impossibility to get a reply to a message sent to America in an hour. And, if the necessary conditions for the evolution of electricity were still unknown, the public would say a man was a knave or a fool who asserted that any force travelling with the velocity of light could produce mechanical action at the remote end of an indefinitely long wire.'[7]

In other words, why should God be more impossible than the gramophone, or the Resurrection than electric light?

The idea of progress, like the achievements of science, did not necessarily militate against belief. Perhaps only the Victorian age, with self-confident faith in its unique civilization, could have produced a new religion, boasting innumerable converts, that claimed that God had favoured *it* as the age to which he would send his personal messengers from the other side to proclaim and buttress the truth of Immortality. Moreover, Romanticism itself had helped to reassert the old order; the cult of the heart, the superiority of 'imagination' over reason, the assertion that there were irrational means of knowing, all helped to prevent a too easy conquest by materialism. This had its ridiculous side; when Carlyle's 'logic-cobwebs' were brushed too fervently aside, such spectacles as the midnight visit of the Countess of Caithness to Holyrood, led by her 'angelic guide' (Mary Queen of Scots) became possible. The Countess asserted, with the aid of the Apocalypse and the Pyramid of Cheops, that a new era had begun in 1881; its date, together with various occult emblems, decorated her writing paper.[8] But the great Romantics at times looked further along the path that men were treading than did many rationalists; if the common man, said Chateaubriand,

'shakes off the influence of religion, he will supply its place with monstrous opinions. He will be seized with a terror the more strange as he will be ignorant of its object: he will shudder in a churchyard, where he has set up the inscription

"Death is an eternal sleep"; and, while affecting to despise the Divine power, he will go to consult the gipsy, and, trembling, seek his destinies in the motley figures of a card.'[9]

The monstrous opinions have turned out to be political rather than religious, but this has hardly robbed the prophecy of its force.

The corporeal nature of Victorian religion encompassed a bearded, male, aged God and His hierarchy of ministers—Seraphim, Cherubim, Thrones, Dominions, Powers, Authorities, Princedoms, Angels and Archangels. The belief in angels was firmly founded; they were the companions of conformist and nonconformist. 'They never leave us. In sorrow they sympathize, in joy they rejoice, in prayer they unite with us; and in sin, alas! they behold us. In every varied scene of life, from the cradle [plate 126] to the grave [plate 117], they are ever with us, to soothe us in affliction, to warn us from evil [plate 127], to stimulate us to good [plate 2], if we disregard not their admonitions.' And, most of all, 'at the bed of death, angels do most especially minister'.[10] Angels and spirits were justified by classical tradition and by theology. As Professor W. F. Barrett, of the Royal College of Science, Dublin, said: 'Do not the Scriptures bear ample testimony to the nearness of the spirit world, and in past times the revelations of that world to this?' This tradition explains why so many eminent scientists could readily believe that Spiritualism might be true; it explains why they could contend in public without losing face; why Sir William Crookes, for example, could walk arm in arm with Katie King, and could grasp the corporeal hands of incorporeal spirits. And not only angels were corporeally true; so was their antithesis, the devil.

The Vicar of Islington, a man with an ecclesiastical future of some importance, said in 1853 (while castigating a clergyman who had dabbled in table-turning): 'He begins by asserting the personality of Satan, a truth in which all sober-minded Christians will agree with him.'[11] The devil was not demolished by science; science was called upon to explain the devil: 'I am under the impression that the devil can exercise his power upon men in no other way than by electro-biology', it was said in 1872.[12] It is not surprising that an enormous literature was produced by the orthodox connecting Spiritualism with Satanic agency, that the Pope was said to have expelled D. D. Home from Rome for his relations with the devil (fig 8), nor that J. A. Symonds, in common with many children—and adults—was 'persuaded that the devil lived near the doormat, in a dark corner of the passage by my father's bedroom. I thought that he appeared to me there under the shape of a black shadow, scurrying about upon the ground, with the faintest indication of a swiftly whirling tail.'[13]

The new faith of Spiritualism was the most astonishing religious movement of the nineteenth century. Orthodox religious belief, the doctrine of Progress, and Romanticism and Science, all assisted in its genesis. It claimed a scientific origin; in this it can be called the first modern heresy, doubly heretical in that its father-scientists were suspect to orthodox science. Oddly enough, these same scientists have some importance in the origination of modern psychological theory, which at times has curious affinities with aspects of Spiritualism.

The theory was that 'animal magnetism' was the medium of a mutual influence

FIG 8 'The Pope's Solution of "Table-Lifting" ' from *A Discovery Concerning Ghosts* by George Cruikshank, 1864. The sketch refers to the famous medium D. D. Home's being brought before the Inquisition at Rome. The table at which the Chief Inquisitor sat rose several times: 'The Pope is *infallible*, and as he can do *No wrong*, of course, whatever he does do, *must be right*, and as he suspected that the table was lifted with the assistance of the Spirit of "Old Nick" I merely made a sketch of the Pope's notion of the "Table Lifting" . . . .'

between the heavenly bodies, the earth and terrestrial organisms; Mesmer, the pioneer of hypnotism, was the discoverer of this magnetic influence—'. . . Mesmer, a pioneer in the realms of the imponderable, through whose stupendous revelations, miracle became converted into law, the supernatural into the spiritual and ancient alchemy into modern magnetism.'[14] From the hypnotist's couch, the 'mesmeric sleep', was evolved clairvoyance; hypnotized subjects or 'lucids' told of scenes and persons in the other world, and described apparitions to mourners. It needed only that the 'lucids' should be able to exercise these powers without the presence of an hypnotist for the medium to be created. In 1851, a 'Mesmeric Infirmary' was established in Wimpole Street; in the same year the 'Ghost Club', heavily backed by Trinity, was formed at Cambridge in order to examine Spiritualism. In 1852 American mediums, instructed by the 'Rochester knockings', in a 'systematic mode of telegraphy' (as described in scientific jargon by Emma Hardinge Britten), began to visit Britain.

British ground was fertile; as Kingsley said, 'few of us deeply believe anything'.[15] The new faith was seized upon, and not, at first, by the vulgar. As *The Nonconformist* said in 1875: 'Familiarity with spiritual manifestations and a firm conviction of their genuineness exist around us far more largely than is suspected, and especially is this the case in the upper classes . . . .' The upper classes, especially the women, were less employed than ever before in history; they entered into the fascinating spirit hunt with zest, and '. . . rapidly became converts. And all this in the present day, amidst its scepticism, its civilization and its glare of natural science.' The list of the distinguished claimed to be converts included representatives of Fashion, the Arts, Literature, Politics and the Sciences—Robert Owen, Lord Brougham, Lord Lytton, Lord Dunraven, Sir Edwin Landseer, Mrs Browning, Lord Crawford, Professors Wallace, Barrett and Crookes—and many others. Even Majesty did not escape rumours: it was whispered that John Brown, far from being Queen Victoria's secret husband or lover, was a medium between her and Prince Albert.

Spiritualism was a conscious antidote to modern unbelief, and a conscious replacement of established religion. In 1857 one of its devotees said that over half of the clergy doubted immortality and that the better half;[16] the one Church that really believed was the Romish Church; this was the 'one Church on earth where Spiritualism is in reality practised, and is the heart and core of the belief'.[17] The writer might, with justification, have gone on to claim the earlier Tractarian movement as an ally of Spiritualism; the difference between the two appears sometimes as much aesthetic as religious. Both held common ground—who, Tractarian or Spiritualist, wrote: 'we denounce as infidels all who cast doubt on miracles or inspiration. Spirit-raising pervades the whole of the Old Testament; every writer of the New devoutly believes in it . . , it is the undoubting belief of every nation in the world, savage and civilised'?[18] Spiritualism came just when it was most needed, when doubt and infidelity were turning the hearts of men cold; it 'was a refutation of atheism which it is utterly impossible to gainsay',[19] and would strike a death blow at the cold materialistic philosophy of the age. It is quite clear that to many Spiritualists their new beliefs were all that stood between them and a complete loss of faith: 'If spirits are not the authors of the communications received in their names, the whole theory of a hereafter . . . crumbles into the dust and ashes which underlie the unsustained assertions of theology.'[20]

One answer to all this was that Spiritualism was the real anti-Christian and hellish Church that was to come, for, as Robert Angus pointed out in *Spiritism—The Great anti-Christian Delusion of Scripture* (1872), the devil also possessed angels or spirits to serve his purposes: 'Beloved, believe not every spirit, but try the spirits whether they are of God . . . .'[21] Another objection was that to meddle with the spirits was to go far beyond sober sense and 'Christian propriety'; it was to meddle with sacred things, and thus to bring religion itself into contempt.[22]

When the Spiritualists used traditional religious imagery, as they often did, the result is conventionally acceptable. Thus 'Sachiel' was described in 1857 as of 'a majestic appearance, adorned with a long, loose robe of a purple and crimson hue, wearing upon his head a kind of coronet, beautifully decorated with purple and gold'[23]—not so far removed from a Burne-Jones angel (plate 128). Nor are many physical descriptions of the spirit world so original as to seem odd—a world 'covered with cities and mansions of dazzling gold, whose inhabitants were adorned in the most brilliant robes'.[24] John Bunyan and Thomas Traherne would have felt perfectly at home here, although they would have detected astrology and magic when the planets and spheres were invoked. But even such a literal Christian as Bunyan might have been perplexed to receive the kind of letter that Sir Charles Isham, for example, received from a nineteenth-century spirit:

'I am now residing in Jupiter, and am very happy, though thoroughly under the dominion of "King Saul" . . . . He is teaching me to fly gracefully, and says I am not a very troublesome pupil, except that I drop my feathers about . . . . I have a flower undergoing the process of materialization for you, and will enclose it in this letter if it is solid enough to stand the journey through the post.'[25]

106

It is not recorded whether this particular flower, after standing the journey through the spheres, *did* stand the journey through the post; many did, or were given directly by the spirit hands that were a feature of so many séances (plate 132). Thus Sir William Crookes related how a 'beautifully-formed hand rose up from an opening in a dining-table and gave me a flower; this occurred three times, in the light, in my own room . . . . I have retained one of these hands in my own, firmly resolved not to let it escape. There was no struggle or effort to get loose, but it gradually seemed to resolve itself into vapour, and faded in that manner from my grasp.'[26] The same well known scientist related elsewhere how other objects than flowers appeared; doves, or pigeons—which curiously combine in themselves echoes both of the Bible and of conjurors' hats—were often used by the spirits. Crookes was, in a locked and thoroughly searched room, presented with a 'live pigeon . . . an immense pyramid of flowers was found tastefully built up around a pot of tulips; later, the flowers were so completely removed that a strict search failed to find a single leaf. All that was left was the pot of tulips, on which was found a paper with very small writing, presenting the tulips as a gift to the author "from the Spirits".'[27]

The spirits' own verses may be apposite:

> Let all who doubt in revelation,
> Made by spirits from on high,
> Rest assured that explanation
> Will appear and satisfy.

'Spiritual'[28]

Flowers and doves—or pigeons—have a certain other-worldly consistency. The spirit 'Joey', called up by William Eglinton, produced more material evidence of his genuineness:

'For some time he moved his hands as if gathering something from the atmosphere, just as when he makes muslin. After some minutes he dropped on the table a massive diamond ring. He said, "Now you may all take the ring, and you may put it on, and hold it while you can count twelve." Miss M—— took it, and held it under the gaslight. It was a heavy gold ring, with a diamond that appeared much like one worn by a friend of mine worth £1000. "Joey" said the value of this was 900 guineas. Mr W—— examined it as we had done. He now made, as it seemed, and as he said, from the atmosphere, two diamonds, very clear and beautiful, about the size of half a large pea. He gave them into our hands on a piece of paper. We examined them, as we had the others. He laid the ring and diamonds on the table before him, and there next appeared a wonderful cluster of rubies, set with a large ruby about half-an-inch in diameter in the centre. These we all handled as we had the others. Last there came a cross, about four inches in length, having twenty magnificent diamonds set in it; this we held in our hands, and examined as closely as we liked. "Joey" took them all, and put them in paper and jingled them. He said, "I might leave the ring as a keepsake for Willie, but it might make him selfish."

He told us that the market value of the gems was £25,000. He remarked, "I could make Willie the richest man in the world; but it would not be the best thing, and might be the worst." He now took the jewels in front of him, and seemed to dissipate them, as one might melt hailstones in heat, until they entirely disappeared.'[29]

This interest in jewels *may* have faint memories of Biblical metaphor, but the interest in their value has a fleshly air.

Spirit photography (plate 125) was an extraordinary example of the harnessing of science in the service of religion; the results look to us now in every way spurious. Frederick Hudson himself, as related by Samuel Guppy in *Medium at Daybreak* (1874), was circumspect. He refused to guarantee any spirit photographs, and 'he made every person sign a book that they would ask no questions, or something to that effect'. Guppy rightly says that nobody after that had any right to comment; Hudson, he said, 'sold his spirit photographs as Tattersall sells his horses, "with all faults".' The same corporeality of manifestation occurred; the naïve and gullible Georgina Houghton related how, at Hudson's, 'while the third negative was in progress, I felt something on my head for a moment, and then a young rabbit (from Mr Hudson's rabbit-hutch in the garden wherein the studio is built) was placed in my lap .... There is a male figure behind ... but having had to move in consequence of the vagaries of the rabbit it is of course hazy.'[30]

Communication with the dead on this physical plane was, it was advised, made easier by various techniques; a cabbalistic complexity was occasionally involved, as in the following hocus-pocus with an egg laid by a dove:

'It is suggested that to the bath already prepared for use shall be added—as an experiment only—the half of the shell of the last egg laid by the Dove; this may be added seven minutes before the time when the bath is likely to be needed. It may be divided into three portions, and after the bath has been used, they should be removed, and kept from the light until they are again needed; they must be divided at this point, so that a portion of the egg may be retained in each piece. It will be well for the mediums connected with this photographic work to partake rather freely of eggs as an article of food, and previous to the photographic séances, the chief operator should bind a fold of linen about this part of the head (placing her hands across the forehead) to the back, which has been dipped in water in which eggs have been previously boiled.'[31]

Such a sect as that of the Spiritualists was bound to provoke opposition, and not only from opposing sects, but from those 'who considered themselves obliged to counter obvious trickery'. Ghosts and spirits have always attracted hilarity (fig 9), and when Cruikshank turned his attention to Spiritualists it was obvious that hilarity would be the order of the day. Cruikshank proved to his own satisfaction that since the spirits always wore clothes, and since theology did not permit the existence of ghosts of clothes (page 205), the spirits themselves were spurious.[32] He would, at his most charitable, probably have agreed with Scrooge, who at first saw in the ghost of old Marley merely a piece of ill-digested cheese—Dickens, by the way, appears to have been influenced in much of his ghost imagery by Spiritualist literature—or with Dr Zerffi, who said in 1875 that 'spectral visions, religious excitements, emotional extravagances, mysticism, and symbolic charlatanism are

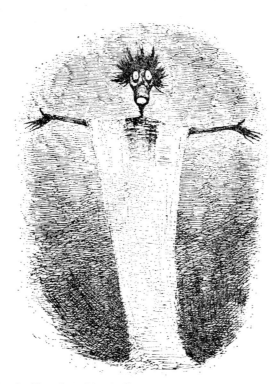

FIG 9 'O Meet me by the Moonlight Alone', from *Whims and Oddities in Prose and Verse* 1836.

merely products of a deranged balance between our vegetable or ganglionic and our cerebral or intellectual life'.[33]

Some spectral visions, at least, were of more systematic manufacture. A small book, *Gambols with the Ghosts*, advertised the wares of Sylvestre and Company, first established in 1872. In it (plate 133) is advertised a whole sequence of adventitious aids for professional mediums, including Instantaneous Spirit Writing, a Telescopic Reaching Rod, a Planchette, Bells, Tambourines and Self-Playing Guitars ('something very clever for clever people'). The more ambitious effects sound impressive. For example, 'Vest Turning or Matter through Matter' ('Any gentleman has his arms tied behind his back and is seated with the medium. In a moment, the vest of the sitter is found turned inside out without his coat being removed. Easily done in light or dark . . . no special garments . . . .') Or the 'Spirit Skull of Althoras' ('Placed on sheet of glass or any table, it will answer any question by working lower jaw . . . . Excellent when used in connection with the Rapping Hand . . . .' (plate 133) Or, most marvellous of all, one could buy 'Luminous Materializing Hands and Faces' ('For all materializing mediums, the production of luminous hands or faces is a *sine qua non* . . . .'); or, for fifty dollars, 'Luminous Materialistic Ghosts and Forms' ('We furnish these of all kinds and sizes. Full luminous female form and dress (with face that convinces) which can be produced in ordinary room or circle, appears gradually, floats about room and disappears. Nothing superior.')

Obviously, not every spirit that crossed the confines of the other world can have come from Sylvestre's catalogue. And in one category—that of the 'spirit' or 'automatic' drawings and paintings—the practitioners' sincerity immediately convinces.

109

In their day they aroused derision. John Nevil Maskelyne, the proprietor of the famous Egyptian Hall in Piccadilly, a self-dubbed 'Illusionist and Anti-Spiritualist', called 'automatic' painting 'a confused jumble of colours, rivalling Joseph's coat, or a bottle of mixed pickles'[34] (plate 115). Cruikshank declared that spirit drawings were reminiscent of paintings done in lunatic asylums (as they are); he said they were badly drawn, their design and composition was alien to all the rules, and they caricatured sacred subjects. These defects are now of course all virtues, but, quite apart from technical matters, the naïve fervour of the artists is compelling. Cruik-shank quotes the apocalyptic process through which one of these 'drawing mediums' attained her craft:

'Waking in the night, the *strange* drawing process instantly commenced, and I felt and saw within me the figure of an angel whose countenance resembled that of Christ, descending from a morning sky towards me, and bearing upon his shoulders a large cross, whilst from his lips proceeded these words—"Love, mercy, peace, but not till after death!" Again my soul *trembled with anguish*, for that strange portentous word "death" was ever written within me or without.'[35]

The word 'peace' was an obsession with mediums; a strange drawing of it by Mrs Alaric Watts (plate 131) has become richly suggestive to a post-Freudian age; indeed, it pictorially epitomizes the connexion between sex and death (which has a long literary tradition) in an extraordinarily explicit manner.

Mrs Watts was an artist of some talent (plate 116). In 1889 an account was given in *Light* of how the drawings were produced. She had at first practised automatic writing; she tried, for some reason, to check this power, and it changed into the delineation of forms. She also saw these forms in 'visions', which appeared some-times as she sat with closed eyes, sometimes as she awoke. She tried to escape them by drawing flowers; one day, as she sat sketching irises and talking to a friend, her pencil drew by itself the initials ARB—Angelico, Raphael and Blake—attached to a female head. These names (which do make up a mixed trio appropriate to her mixed style!) had frequently appeared in her automatic writing. Her usual practice was to draw on tracing paper, because she found when she first began to produce automatic drawings that the design changed and developed as she drew, making a confused effect; the tracing paper enabled her to trace the completed outlines and then to begin afresh at the point where the design became clear. In later years her power waned.

More remote and powerful are the drawings of Mrs Frederika Bodmer (1826–c. 1890, plates 129, 130). Her technique is quite extraordinary. At first sight many of the drawings look like lithographs, but the effect was produced with Indian ink, mapping pen, steel ruler and soft pencil. It is recorded that Mr Bodmer, an engineer who worked in the 1850s on the Welsh railways, worked over some drawings executed in outline 'when the trance was over'.

The weird imagery and surrealistic power of Mrs Bodmer's drawings almost divest them of any 'period' feeling; the even more fantastic automatic drawings of Georgina Houghton (plate 116) are completely un-Victorian. This detachment, in two fairly ordinary Victorian women, is sufficient proof, if proof were needed, of their sincerity. An explanation of the origin of the power that produced 'automatic' drawings, given by the husband of another lady medium, curiously anticipates both Surrealism and the modern interpretation of dreams. According to Mr Wilkinson, one third of our lives is passed in this 'wonderful state of detachment from the judging power'—sleep. In sleep 'the spirit walks about, and has a new power of vision, other and superior . . . . Angels guard it, now that it has lost for the time the judgment of the intellect; and its dreams, as we call them, have often more of inner truth than we can find in waking hours.'[36] This idea of sleep is as different from the Victorian notion of repose as the strange vitality of the automatic paintings is from the namby-pamby nature of much orthodox Victorian religious art.

Mr Wilkinson has other interesting things to say. He himself acquired the power of automatic writing. When he first tried it, he held the pencil without hope; it at last began to move, and finally sped across the paper with preternatural velocity; 'it literally ran away in spiral forms'. Afterwards, he could not lift his arm for several days. He attempted to explain these phenomena in terms that carry a weight of old-fashioned idealism—'all which is really beautiful must of necessity be true'. At the end of a long chapter proving the existence, physically and historically, of angels, he declared that the idea that the resurrection will be a revivification of the natural body at the last day was wrong: 'such a notion involves physical impossibilities'!

This fantastic paradox went unnoticed by its author. For (despite the significant fact that, even when faith seemed to be confirmed by the voices of the dead, the new Faith of Spiritualism strove continually to buttress itself with scientific proof), a scientific consistency was not looked for—Faith could always step in. There remained many to whom revelation by Faith was still perfectly adequate; the paradisical gardens with Seraphic children and the flower-like motifs of the lady mediums carry no hint of disquiet. But the worm nibbled at the bud; the equilibrium on which the whole edifice rested was fragile. Man toiled through life to find at the end perhaps not an angel shape (plate 117) but merely the precipice.

That most famous symbol of the withdrawal of belief, the ebbing tide on Dover Beach,[37] has a poignant accuracy. Death, the Bride (plate 134) was no longer crowned with lilies or roses, but with poppies—the emblem, as the Ecclesiologists recognized, of eternal sleep; she had become completely secularized.

The possibility that Faith had no foundation was looked at face to face; that agony over, the gaze was averted. Heaven became more remote; Death is still with us. And Death, to ordinary people as to Dido, is not a welcome guest. It is no longer celebrated. Our social customs have taken cognizance of the change, to such an extent that it is extraordinary to reflect that many Victorians are still alive. In place of the romantic and menacing pomp of the hearse and its sable attendants, the motor hearse glides swiftly to an anonymous destination. The external signs of grief are minimal. We do not frame and treasure memorial cards, nor scatter embroidered tears on our handkerchiefs; our little girls of eight do not laboriously stitch epitaphs, nor do we place ceramic figures of famous murderers and murderesses, together with the scenes of their crimes, on our chimney pieces. Nobody now talks of the moral influences of a cemetery. The whole apparatus, together with Seraphs, Angels and the Gates of Paradise, has passed into the realms of the fabulous.

Appendices

From 'Death in the Household'. *Cassell's Household Guide to every Department of Practical Life* 1874.

Funeral costing £3 5s.—Patent carriage, with one horse; smooth elm coffin, neatly finished, lined inside, with pillow, &c.; use of pall, mourners' fittings, coachman with hat-band; bearers; attendant with hat-band, &c.

Funeral costing £5 5s.—Hearse, with one horse; mourning coach, with one horse; stout elm coffin, covered with fine black, plate of inscription, lid ornaments, and three pairs of handles, mattress, pillow, and a pair of side sheets; use of velvet pall; mourners' fittings, coachmen with hat-bands and gloves; bearers; attendant with silk hat-band, &c.

Funeral costing £6 6s.—Hearse, with pair of horses; mourning coach and pair; strong elm coffin, covered with black, plate of inscription, lid ornaments, and three pairs of handles, mattress, pillows, &c.; use of velvet pall, mourners' fittings; coachmen with hat-bands and gloves; bearers; attendant with silk hat-band, &c.

Funeral costing £8 15s.—Hearse and pair of horses; mourning coach and pair; velvet covering for carriages and horses; strong elm coffin, covered with fine black, plate of inscription, lid ornaments, three pairs of cherub handles and grips, and finished with best black nails, mattress, pillow, and side sheets; use of silk velvet pall; two mutes with gowns, silk hat-bands, and gloves; four men as bearers, and two coachmen with cloaks, hatbands, and gloves; use of mourners' fittings; and attendant with silk hat-band.

Funeral costing £14 14s.—Hearse and pair of horses; mourning coach and pair, fifteen plumes of black ostrich-feathers, and complete velvet covering for carriages and horses; stout inch elm coffin, with inner lid, covered with black cloth, set with two rows all round of best black nails; lead plate of inscription, lid ornaments, four pairs of handles and grips, all of the best improved jet and bright black; tufted mattress, lined and ruffled, and fine cambric winding-sheet; use of silk velvet pall; two mutes with gowns, silk hat-bands, and gloves, eight men as pages and coachmen, with truncheons and wands, crape hat-bands, &c.; use of mourners' fittings; and attendant with silk hat-band, &c.

Funeral costing £23 10s.—Hearse and four horses, two mourning coaches, with pairs, nineteen plumes of rich ostrich-feathers, and complete velvet covering for carriages and horses; strong inch elm shell, covered with black; tufted mattress, lined and ruffled with cambric; and pillow; fine cambric winding-sheet, inch elm case to receive the above, covered with fine black cloth; lead plate of inscription, lid ornaments, four pairs of shield handles and grips, and furnished with two rows all round of best nails; use of silk velvet pall; two mutes with gowns, silk hat-bands, and gloves; eleven men as pages; and coachmen with truncheons and wands, crape hat-bands, &c.; use of mourners' fittings; and attendant with silk hat-band, &c.

Funeral costing £30.—Hearse and four horses, two mourning coaches, with pairs, nineteen plumes of rich ostrich-feathers, complete velvet covering for carriages and horses, and an esquire's plume of best feathers; strong elm shell, with tufted mattress, lined and ruffled with superfine cambric, and pillow; full worked fine cambric winding-sheet outside lead coffin, with inscription plate and solder complete; stout inch elm case, covered with superfine black cloth, set with three rows round, and lid panelled with best black nails; registered lead plate of inscription, lid ornaments to correspond, and four pairs of handles, and grips all of the best imperial black; use of the best silk velvet pall; two mutes with gowns, silk hat-bands, and gloves, &c.; twelve men as pages, feathermen, and coachmen, with truncheons and wands, silk hat-bands, &c.; use of the mourners' fittings; and attendant with silk hat-band, &c.

Funeral costing £53.—Hearse and four horses, two mourning coaches with fours, twenty-three plumes of rich ostrich-feathers, complete velvet covering for carriages and horses, and an esquire's plume of best feathers; strong elm shell, with tufted mattress, lined and ruffled with superfine cambric, and pillow; full worked glazed cambric winding-sheet, stout outside lead coffin, with inscription plate and solder complete; one-and-a-half-inch oak case, covered with black or crimson velvet, set with three rows round, and lid panelled with best brass nails; stout brass plate of inscription, richly engraved; four pairs of best brass handles and grips, lid ornaments to correspond; use of silk velvet pall; two mutes with gowns, silk hat-bands and gloves; fourteen men as pages, feathermen, and coachmen, with truncheons and wands, silk hat-bands, &c.; use of mourners' fittings; and attendant with silk hat-band, &c.

APPENDIX B
Expenses of funerals
What is the cost of porters, the men who bear staves covered with black?—The cost of the mutes varies from 18s. to 30s. In some cases of respectable persons, where silk scarfs or fittings, including hat-bands and gloves, are used, 5l. 5s. is charged to families for those fittings. To parties in moderate circumstances, two guineas would be charged for the fittings and the pay.

What is the charge for the person who walks with a scarf?—The usual charge to a respectable family would be a guinea, besides fittings, scarfs, gloves, and hat-bands, which would altogether amount to about two guineas and half for this man.

What is the charge for the plume of feathers borne on the head before the hearse? —The charge for the feathers would be about two guineas; then there is the man's gloves, scarf, and fittings, which make it about three guineas and a-half.

What is the charge per man bearing batons ?—The charge, including silk fittings, will be about 22s. each man.

What is the charge for each man bearing a wand?—About the same price.

How many men of this description would be required for what is deemed a respectable funeral ?—About twenty men; for if the coffin be a leaden one it would require about eight men to bear it.

What other charges are there of the same kind ?—There are velvets attached to the hearse, including feathers, and feathers to the horses, which makes from ten to fifteen guineas more.

What is charged for the pall ?—From one to four guineas would be charged for the use of the pall.

What is it usual to give to the clergyman ?—A silk scarf of three yards and a half, a silk hat-band, and black kid gloves.

What may be the expense of this ?—About two guineas to the parties.

Is anything usually given to the clerk ?—Yes, the same as to the minister.

Is anything given to the sexton ?—Yes, they do in respectable families, or rather the undertaker does so, for his own gain. The cost of the whole,—minister, sexton and undertaker, will be about seven guineas to a respectable family, but it is usual to compound the matter by giving them money; I generally give the minister 18s., and the clerk 15s., and the sexton, perhaps, 15s.

APPENDIX C

From the Hardman Registers (deposited with the Victoria and Albert Museum, London)

Funeral a/ct of the late Earl of Shrewsbury

Articles lent and returned

6 Plated Candlesticks (Exhibition C. Sticks)	,, ,, ,,
8 Brass Herse Lights No. 903	,, ,, ,,
8 ,, Branches for 4 Lights No. 3427	,, ,, ,,
4 ,, Standing Lights with 7 Branches ea. 2316	,, ,, ,,
2 ,, Elevation C. Sticks No. 2150	,, ,, ,,
1 ,, Holy Water Vat No. 1172	,, ,, ,,
1 Plated Sprinkler	,, ,, ,,
8 Brass Torches No. 1947	,, ,, ,,
2 Plated Processional C. Sticks	,, ,, ,,
13 Cases, Packing and Carriage of do	50 ,, ,,

A Spanish Mahogany Coffin   long   wide   at top,   deep,
    covered with rich crimson Genoa silk velvet   21 ,, ,,

Gilt Coffin Furniture as under

6 Handles, with eyes and back plates, with Lions on Cap of Main-
    tenance & twisted wires @ 67/6   20 5 ,,

8 side clips	„	„	„
A Plate for Lid, of Cross, supported at bottom by Talbots	„	„	„
A Plate with Inscription for Head	„	„	„
A Plate with Shield & Coronet for Foot	„	„	„
Edging all round	„	„	„
1150 Large Pins	„	„	„
800 gold headed screws	78	15	„
Men's Time fixing above furniture on Coffin	2	16	„
(The whole Engraved, Beaten and Saw pierced)			

Brass Furniture for Herse

48 Standards 11 in. high, twisted pillars, frilled pans & dowel sockets No. 3426 @ 13/6	32	8	„
3 Countersunk screws each	„	„	„
4—4 Light Branches for intersections of Roof, with twisted pillars, 2 ft. 8 in. high, with dowel sockets No. 3428 @ 50/-	10	„	„
An 8 Light Corona, with frilled pans, crestings, & Inscription painted on Band, with Cross with Beaten Leaves, rising from centre, & dowel socket, height from socket to top of Cross, 6 feet, dia. of Corona 2 feet No. 3431	12	10	„
4—7 Light Branches for Gables, with twisted pillars 1ft. 6 in. high, with dowel sockets No. 3429 @ 53/-	10	12	„
8 Four Light Branches for Herse lights 3427 charged after return @ 11/-	4	8	„
8—7 Light Branches held by Talbots, with plain pillars, 2 feet 8½ inches high with dowel sockets No. 3430 @ 50/-	20	„	„
2 Wrot. Iron Curtain Rods No. 3432 see entry below	4	18	„
8 Saw Pierced Beaten Gilt Crowns with 8 roses and 8 screws each 63/-	25	4	„

For Funeral Car

4 Brass Poles 8 ft. 7 in. long, with Cross at top (3 ft. twisted) with 4 Iron Plates & Rings No. 3425 @ £3	12	„	„
To Black Cloth & Hangings for do from Miss Brown &c.	13	18	6
16 countersunk screws	„	„	„

Large Hatchments in Frame painted with Arms Supporters &c.	17	10	„
Small Hatchments in Frame painted with Arms Supporters &c.	7	10	„

Hangings for Chapel at Alton

To 173¾ yards Black cloth	3/-	26	1	3
„ 395¾ „ „ „	3/6	69	5	1½
„ 399¾ yards Serge	2/4	46	12	9
„ 12 Wrappers		„	13	9
„ 243¾ yards Blk. Bullion Fringe	6d.	6	1	10½
„ 126½ „ 1 in. White Orris Lace	2½d.	1	6	4½

				£	s	d
,, 251¾ ,, 1½ in. White Orris Lace		3d.		3	2	11
,, 72 ,, 2 in. ,, ,, ,,		4½d.		1	6	,,
,, 80 ,, Black Lustre		7½d.		2	10	,,

Alterations in Herse to carry Body of Earl (Charged elsewhere)   ,,   ,,   ,,

Mr. Denny's Work at Alton
To Joiners & Carpenters Work as pr. Mr. Denny's Bill

	£	s	d
For Herse	16	10	,,
,, Funeral Car	1	6	3½

Upholsterers' Work

	£	s	d
To Upholsterers Time, sewing and hanging cloth in Chapel, Alton & St. John's Chapel, includg. Travelling Expenses of men from Birmingham	20	11	,,
5000 Brass Chair Nails @ 2/6	–	12	6

	£	s	d
To Painting & Gilding Herse & Shields	43	18	2

To Hangings for St. John's Chapel & School

		£	s	d
,, 250 yards black cloth	3/6d	43	15	,,
,, 138 yards Serge	1/-	6	18	,,
,, Sundries as per Bill		11	5	9

Herse to Stand in Centre of Chapel

	£	s	d
To Mr. Myers Bill for Making do	58	,,	,,

Work from Miss Brown's

	£	s	d
To A Pall of Black Velvet with Inscriptions	192	10	,,
,, 4 Black Velvet Copes, with Silver Lace &c.	64	,,	,,
,, 1 Richer do do with Embroidery	39	,,	,,
,, A Black Cloth Antependium for High Altar	21	10	,,
,, A Do Do Do ,, St. John's ,,	19	10	,,
,, A Do Do Super Altar ,, High ,,	2	15	,,
,, A Do Do Dossell ,, ,, ,,	31	,,	,,
,, A Set of Curtains ,, ,, ,,	21	10	,,
,, A Black Cloth Dossell ,, St. John's ,,	18	15	,,
,, A Set of Curtains ,, ,, ,,	9	10	,,
,, Servings for Herse of Inscriptions &c.	110	,,	,,
,, Hangings for Funeral Car	10	,,	,,

Wax Candles as per Mr. Parkers Bill

	£	s	d
To 375 lbs. of Wax @ 2/2	40	13	7
,, 3 Cases for do	,,	15	,,

	£	s	d
To Drawings & Designs made by Edwd. W. Pugin and I. H. Powell Esqrs	40	„	„
Expenses of Choir			
To Cash paid to Organist & Choir of St. Chads for Services, including Travelling Expenses	49	2	6
Allowances for Surplices, Books &c.			
To Loan of Surplices from St. Chads	5	„	„
„ Washing do after use	1	4	6
„ 40 Black cloth caps for Choir @ 1/-	2	„	„
„ Cab & Sundries	„	3	„
To Travelling Expenses for Mr. Hardman & E. W. Pugin including Expenses at Hotel	25	9	4
To Mr. Joyce, for superintendance of Funeral	10	„	„
To Sundries, various incidental Expenses	31	10	10
To Extra Expenses not included in Estimate for Shrewsbury Funeral Hangings for Talbot Gallery			
To 140 yards black cloth @ 3/-	21	„	„
„ 30 „ Serge @ 2/4	3	10	„
To Mourning Coaches & Hearses pr. F. Dees' Bill			
To 11 Pairs of Horses, with 8 mourning Coaches 63/- pair	34	13	„
„ Full State Ostrich Plumes & Velvets to 22 Horses @ 5/- ea.	5	10	„
„ 11 Men @ 7/6 ea.	4	2	6
To Funeral Car, see folio 474	„	„	„
To Conveyance of Mourning Coaches & Horses, by Railway, Special Train			
To Special Train	25	„	„
„ 12 Drivers @ 12/6	7	10	„
To Hire of Knives, Forks & Plates & charge for attendant			
To T. E. Lisseters' Bill	6	19	„
To Printing Funeral Cards see Entry Revd. Dr. Winters a/ct, folio 477			
To 200 Admission Cards, procured by Revd. Dr. Winter	„	12	„
„ Stationery Expens, Postages &c. paid by Revd. Dr. Winter	„	14	2
„ Medical attendance on Sick Boy, injured by an accident from Herse	2	11	6

In the case of funerals of persons of moderate respectability costing, say about 60*l.*, how many of such men as those described would there be attending it?—About fourteen.

For a curate, or person of that condition, would there be that number and array? —Yes.

What would be the expense of the funeral of a person of the condition of an attorney?—From 60*l.* to 100*l.*; but this would not include the expense of tomb or monument, or burial-fees.

If a person of such a condition were buried, would it be of about twenty attendants, with such an array as that described?—Yes; for such a person the cost would be about 100 guineas, exclusive of the burial-fees.

There would then be the same number of attendants as those mentioned, about twenty men?—Yes, about twenty men.

The funeral being ordered of an upholsterer, is it not usually provided by an undertaker?—Yes.

In how many cases of funerals will there be 'the second profit?'—In nearly two-thirds of the cases of burial in the upper classes.

Is the same observation applicable to the funerals amongst the middle classes?— Yes; I think in nearly the same proportion.

How much of the profit will be the profit of the upholsterer?—Nearly half: if the funeral costs 50*l.* to the upholsterer from the undertaker, it will cost about 100*l.* from the undertaker to the family.

Is there much credit given in the business to respectable families?—Not much; for as soon as letters of administration are taken out the funeral expenses are discharged.

The average expense of the funeral of an adult of the labouring class being about 4*l.*, exclusive of the burial fees, and that of a child about 30*s.*, what may be stated to be the ordinary expense of the funeral of a tradesman of the lowest class, as ordinarily conducted?—Of the very lowest class—of a class in condition not much beyond that of a mechanic, the funeral expenses might be from 10*l.* to 12*l.*

What would be the ordinary expense for the funeral of a child of a person of this class?—The ordinary expense would be about 5*l.*

What would be the ordinary expense of the funeral of a tradesman of a better class?—From 70*l.* to 100*l.*

What do you consider would be a low average for the ordinary expense of the whole class of tradesmen's funeral?—About 50*l.* would, I consider be a low average for the whole class.

What may be considered the average of ordinary expenses of the funerals of children of the class dying below 10 years of age?—About 14*l.*

Might 100*l.* be taken as the average expense of the funeral of a person of the condition of a gentleman?—No; they range from 200*l.* to 1,000*l.* I think that 150*l.* would be a low average.

What may be considered the ordinary expense of the funeral of a child of this class?—About 30*l.* would be the average.

What may be the ordinary expense of the funerals of persons of rank or title?— The expense varies from 500*l.* to 1500*l.*

Notes to the Text

CHAPTER I

1 Elizabeth Barrett Browning 'The Cry of the Children' 1844
2 *Report from the Select Committee on the Health of Towns* June 1840
3 Edwin Chadwick *Supplementary Report on the Results of a Special Enquiry into the Practice of Interment in Towns* 1843
4 Ibid.
5 *Report . . . on the Health of Towns* June 1840
6 Report by James Smith *Parliamentary Proceedings* 1845, vol. 18. Quoted by E. R. Pike *Human Documents of the Industrial Revolution in Britain* 1966
7 Rev. Whitwell Elwin *Parliamentary Proceedings*, Lords, 1842. Quoted by Pike, op. cit.
8 Cecil Frances Alexander (1818–95) from *All Things Bright and Beautiful* 1848
9 Edwin Chadwick *Parliamentary Proceedings*, Lords, 1842, vol. 26
10 Chadwick, op. cit. 1843
11 Rev. James Vaughan, MA, *Sermons to Children preached in Christ Church, Brighton* 1868
12 Charles Dickens *Martin Chuzzlewit* 1843–4
13 Chadwick, op. cit. 1843
14 Ibid.
15 Lady Eddisbury to Lord Eddisbury September 26 1848. v. *The Ladies of Alderley* edited by Nancy Mitford, 1967
16 Chadwick, op. cit. 1843
17 Return to an Address of the House of Commons June 1857. Complaining of the system of burials within the Metropolitan Police District etc.
18 Charles Dickens 'The Raven in the Happy Family', from *Household Words* 1850–9
19 Ibid.
20 Ibid.
21 Mrs Stone *God's Acre or, Historical Notices Relating to Churchyards* 1858
22 Thomas Lovell Beddoes (1803–49) 'The Phantom Wooer'
23 Chateaubriand *The Genius of Christianity*. Quoted in J. Halstead *Romanticism: selected documents*, London, 1969
24 Ibid. De Musset *The Confession of a Child of the Century* 1836
25 Hans Andersen 'The Nightingale'
26 *Inheritance* quoted in the *Quarterly Review* no. 146 1844
27 Chadwick, op. cit. 1843
28 Quoted in W. E. Houghton *The Victorian Frame of Mind* 1957
29 Charles Dickens 'The Uncommercial Traveller' after 1860
30 Houghton, op. cit.
31 Charles Dickens *Martin Chuzzlewit* 1843–4

CHAPTER 2

1 Charles Dickens *Martin Chuzzlewit* 1843–4
2 Ibid.
3 Ibid.
4 Ibid.
5 Washington Irving 'Rural Funerals', *The Sketch Book of Geoffrey Crayon, Gent.*
6 Charles Dickens 'The Raven in the Happy Family', from *Household Words* 1850–9
7 Washington Irving, op. cit.
8 'Review of Ecclesiastical Art Exhibition at Croydon' quoted in *Ecclesiastical Art Review* February 1878
9 Edwin Chadwick *Supplementary Report on the Results of a Special Inquiry into the Practice of Interment in Towns* 1843
10 *Quarterly Review* no. 146 1844
11 Ibid.
12 Information kindly supplied by Mr Tom Last
13 *Quarterly Review* loc. cit.
14 *Report from the Select Committee of the House of Lords on the Burial Acts* 1856
15 Dickens 'The Raven in the Happy Family', op. cit.
16 Dickens *Martin Chuzzlewit* 1843–4
17 *Ecclesiastical Art Review* loc. cit.
18 Chadwick, op. cit.
19 Ibid.
20 Ibid. Also quoted in *Quarterly Review* no. 146 1844
21 *Report from the Select Committee on the Health of Towns* June 1840
22 Ibid.
23 Chadwick, op. cit.
24 *Report . . . on Improvement of the Health of Towns* June 1842
25 Chadwick, op. cit.
26 Dickens *Martin Chuzzlewit*
27 Chadwick, op. cit.
28 *Quarterly Review* loc. cit.
29 *Ecclesiastical Art Review* loc. cit.
30 *The Ecclesiologist* September 1845
31 Ibid April 1846
32 J. C. Loudon *On the Laying Out, Planting and Managing of Cemeteries and on the Improvement of Churchyards* 1843
33 *Quarterly Review* loc. cit.
34 *The Ecclesiologist* April 1846
35 *Ecclesiastical Art Review* loc. cit.
36 D. R. Gwynn *Lord Shrewsbury, Pugin and the Catholic Revival* 1946. Introduction by Rev. S. Gosling
37 Washington Irving, op. cit.
38 Mrs Stone *God's Acre or, Historical Notices Relating to Churchyards* 1858
39 *Ecclesiastical Art Review* loc. cit.

CHAPTER 3

1 G. A. Walker *Gatherings from Graveyards* 1839
2 The mss of Jeremy Bentham (British Museum) 'Auto-Icon, or Further Uses of the Dead to the Living'
3 Rev. Canon Clayton MA 'Happy Dying', *Home Words* 1873
4 *Quarterly Review* no. 146 March 1844
5 Mrs Stone *God's Acre or, Historical Notices Relating to Churchyards* 1858
6 Walker, op. cit.
7 Ibid.
8 *The Queen* April 1880
9 Edwin Chadwick *Supplementary Report on the Results of the Special Inquiry into the Practice of Interment in Towns* 1843
10 *The Weekly Despatch* 23 December 1838
11 *Illustrated London News* March 16 1850
12 Walker, op. cit.
13 *Quarterly Review* 1840
14 Walker, op. cit.
15 *Quarterly Review* no. 146 1844
16 *Report from the Select Committee on the Improvement of the Health of Towns— Effects of Interment of Bodies in Towns* June 1842
17 Ibid.
18 Walker, op. cit.
19 *Report . . . on the Improvement of the Health of Towns . . .* June 1842
20 Ibid.
21 William Eassie *Cremation of the Dead* 1875
22 J. C. Loudon *On the Laying Out, Planting and Managing of Cemeteries and on the Improvement of Churchyards* 1843
23 *Report from the Select Committee on the Health of Towns* June 1840
24 Ibid.
25 Walker, op. cit.
26 *Report . . . on the Improvement of the Health of Towns . . .* June 1842
27 Ibid.
28 *Sanatory Progress, being the Fifth Report of the National Philanthropic Association for the Promotion of Social and Salutiferous Improvements etc.* 1850
29 *Report . . . on the Improvement of the Health of Towns . . .* June 1842
30 *Report . . . on the Health of Towns* June 1840
31 *Report . . . on the Improvement of the Health of Towns . . .* June 1842
32 Chadwick, op. cit.
33 *Report . . . on the Improvement of the Health of Towns . . .* June 1842
34 Ibid.
35 *Report . . . on the Health of Towns* June 1840
36 Ibid.
37 *Report . . . on the Improvement of the Health of Towns . . .* June 1842
38 Ibid.

39 *Report . . . on the Improvement of the Health of Towns . . .* June 1842
40 Ibid.
41 *Sanatory Progress . . . 1850*
42 Ibid.
43 Ibid.
44 *Dr John Simon City Medical Reports, No 1* 1844. Quoted by E. R. Pike *Human Documents of the Industrial Revolution in Britain*
45 Loudon, op. cit.
46 *Report on the Improvement of the Health of Towns . . .* June 1842
47 Ibid.
48 Ibid.

CHAPTER 4

1   *Ecclesiastical Art Review* February 1878
2   *Quarterly Review* no. 146 1844
3   Edwin Chadwick *Supplementary Report on the Results of the Special Inquiry into the Practice of Interment in Towns* 1843
4   *Quarterly Review* loc. cit.
5   Ibid.
6   *Cassell's Household Guide to Every Department of Practical Life* vol. 3
7   *Quarterly Review* loc. cit.
8   A. Welby Pugin *An Apology for the Revival of Christian Architecture in England* 1843
9   Chateaubriand *Genius of Christianity*, v. Halsted *Romanticism: selected documents,* 1969
10 *The Ecclesiologist* January 1845
11 Ibid.
12 George Blair *Biographic and Descriptive Sketches of Glasgow Necropolis* 1857
13 J. C. Loudon *On the Laying Out, Planting and Managing of Cemeteries and on the Improvement of Churchyards* 1843
14 *Quarterly Review* loc. cit.
15 J. H. Markland FRS *Remarks on English Churches, and on the Expediency of Rendering Sepulchral Memorials Subservient to Pious and Christian uses* 1843
16 *Quarterly Review* loc. cit.
17 Ibid.
18 Chadwick, op. cit.
19 Charles Dickens 'A Popular Delusion', from *Household Words* 1850–9

CHAPTER 5

1   *Report on a General Scheme for Extramural Sepulture* 1850
2   *The Ecclesiologist* August 1844
3   Ibid. September 1844
4   Ibid. August 1844
5   Ibid. January 1845
6   George Blair *Biographic and Descriptive Sketches of Glasgow Necropolis* 1857

7   A. Welby Pugin *An Apology for the Revival of Christian Architecture in England* 1843

8   *The Ecclesiologist* January 1845

9   Rev. Edward Trollope FSA *Manual of Sepulchral Memorials* 1858

10 J. H. Markland FRS *Remarks on English Churches, and on the Expediency of Rendering Sepulchral Memorials Subservient to Pious and Christian Uses* 1843

11 *Quarterly Review* 140 1842

12 Trollope, op. cit.

13 Ibid.

14 *The Ecclesiologist* January 1845

15 Ibid.

16 Ibid.

17 *A Tract upon Tomb Stones by a Member of the Lichfield Society for the Encouragement of Ecclesiastical Architecture* 1843

18 *The Ecclesiologist* January 1845

19 *Ainsworth's Magazine* vol. 11 1842

20 *The Ecclesiologist* January 1845

21 Ibid.

22 Ibid.

23 Ibid.

24 Pugin, op. cit.

25 *Ecclesiastical Art Review* February 1878

26 *The Ecclesiologist* January 1845

27 Ibid.

28 Ibid. November 1845

29 J. C. Loudon *On the Laying Out, Planting and Managing of Cemeteries and on the Improvement of Churchyards* 1843

30 Markland, op. cit.

CHAPTER 6

1   Charles Dickens *David Copperfield* 1849–50

2   *The Shops and Companies of London and the Trades and Manufactories of Great Britain* edited by Henry Mayhew 1865

3   *Woman's World* 1889

4   Ibid.

5   *The English Woman's Domestic Magazine* vol. 20 1876

6   Charles Dickens *Dombey and Son* 1846–8

7   Quoted by C. Willett Cunnington *English Women's Clothing in the Nineteenth Century*, London, 1948

8   Anthony Trollope *The Prime Minister* 1875–6

9   *The Queen* 1880

10 Anne Buck 'The Trap Re-baited', *Proceedings of the . . . Costume Society* 1968

11 George Eliot 'Mr Gilfil's Love-Story', *Scenes from Clerical Life*

12 D. C. Coleman *Courtaulds: an economic and social history* 1969

13 *The Queen* July 1872. Quoted by Anne Buck, op. cit.

14 *Enquire Within upon Everything* 1856. Information supplied by Dr Phillis Cunnington

15 Ibid.

16 *The Practical Housewife.* Information supplied by Dr Phillis Cunnington

17 *The Queen* 1880

18 Quoted by C. Willett Cunnington, op. cit.

19 *Illustrated London News* 1852

20 Quoted by Margaret Flower *Victorian Jewellery* 1951

21 Charlotte M. Yonge *The Daisy Chain* 1856

22 *The Queen* 1880

23 Ibid.

24 *Woman's World* 1889

25 *The Queen* 1880

26 *The Ladies of Alderley* edited by Nancy Mitford, 1967

27 Mrs Gaskell *Cranford* 1853

28 Charles Dickens *Nicholas Nickleby* 1838–9

29 C. Willett Cunnington, op. cit.

30 *The Queen* 1880

31 Ibid.

32 *Dearest Child, Letters between Queen Victoria and the Princess Royal* 1858–61 edited by R. Fulford. Quoted by Anne Buck 'The Trap Re-baited', *Proceedings of the . . . Costume Society* 1968

33 *Letters of Mrs Gaskell* 1832–65 edited by J. A. V. Chapple and A. Pollard 1966. Quoted by Anne Buck, op. cit.

34 *The Lady's Pictorial* 1901

35 Quoted by Anne Buck, op. cit.

36 *How to Dress Well on a Shilling a Day by Sylvia* c. 1875. Quoted by Anne Buck, op. cit.

37 Yonge, op. cit.

38 Quoted by Anne Buck, op. cit.

39 Ibid.

40 Alison Adburgham *Shops and Shopping* 1964

41 Ibid.

42 *Myra's Journal of Dress and Fashion* 1881

43 Ibid.

44 *Illustrated London News* December 1861

45 Henry Mayhew, op. cit. Quoted also in Adburgham, op. cit.

46 Ibid.

47 Richard Davey *A History of Mourning*, Jay's, Regent Street

48 Ibid.

49 Mrs Stone *God's Acre or, Historical Notices Relating to Churchyards* 1858

50 Anthony Trollope *The Prime Minister* 1875–6

51 *Ecclesiastical Art Review* February 1878

52 *Woman's World* 1889

53 *The Lady's Pictorial* February 1901

54 Ibid.

55 *The Lady's Pictorial* February 1901
56 Ibid.
57 Ibid.
58 Ibid.
59 Ibid.
60 Telegram, collection of Miss Diana Holman Hunt
61 Ibid.
62 Princess Marie Louise *My Memories of Six Reigns* 1956

CHAPTER 7

Quotations from *The Times* and other journals, numerous in this chapter, are not
individually acknowledged.
1 Alfred Lord Tennyson 'Ode on the Death of the Duke of Wellington' 1852
2 Queen Victoria to King of the Belgians 23 November 1852. V. Benson and
   Esher *Letters of Queen Victoria* 1907
3 Ibid. Memorandum by Prince Albert 17 September 1852. 'Victoria wishes the
   Army to mourn for the Duke as long as for a member of the Royal Family.'
4 Ibid. Queen Victoria to King of the Belgians 17 September 1852
5 Ibid. 22 September 1852
6 From an eye witness account recorded in 1940 by Mr Frederick Mead: BBC
   Sound Archives
7 Ibid.
8 *Illustrated London News* 27 November 1852
9 Joan Stevens *Victorian Voices* La Société Jersiaise 1969
10 From the diary of William Windle (1818–99), in the possession of Dr Windle,
   Brighton
11 Stevens, op. cit.
12 William Windle, op. cit.

CHAPTER 8

1 Lord Stowell '*Gilbert* v. *Buzzard*'. Quoted in *The Times* 16 June 1875
2 *A Tract upon Tomb Stones by a member of the Lichfield Society for the Encouragement of Ecclesiastical Architecture* 1843
3 Thomas Hardy (1840–1928) *The Impercipient (at a Cathedral Service)*
4 Bishop Fraser of Manchester quoted in William Robinson *God's Acre Beautiful* 1880
5 William Eassie *Cremation of the Dead* 1875
6 *The Times* 12 January 1875
7 Ibid. 17 June 1875
8 *The Queen* 16 May 1885
9 Related in William Robinson, op. cit., Appendix 11
10 *Pharos* May 1969

CHAPTER 9

1 Mrs Braddon *Lady Audley's Secret* 1862

2 Mrs Gaskell *North and South* 1855

3 Alfred Tennyson 'In Memoriam' 1849

4 Tennyson, quoted by W. E. Houghton *The Victorian Frame of Mind* 1957

5 Quoted by Elizabeth Longford *Victoria R. I.*, London, 1964

6 'Poems of Alfred Tennyson' *Quarterly Review* no. 140 1842

7 Article by Professor W. F. Barrett *The Nonconformist* 6 October 1875

8 Countess of Caithness *A Midnight Visit to Holyrood*, v. Emma Hardinge Britten *Nineteenth Century Miracles . . . etc.* 1883

9 Chateaubriand *Genius of Christianity*. Quoted in J. Halstead *Romanticism: selected documents*, 1969

10 Mrs Stone *God's Acre or, Historical Notices Relating to Churchyards* 1858

11 Daniel Wilson *Satanic Agency not connected with Table-Turning* 1853. A reply to Rev. N. S. Godfrey *Table-Moving tested, and proved to be the Result of Satanic Agency*

12 Robert Angus *The Great Anti-Christian Delusion of Scripture* 1872

13 John Addington Symonds, quoted in Houghton, op. cit.

14 Emma Hardinge Britten *Nineteenth Century Miracles . . . etc.* 1883

15 Charles Kingsley, quoted in Houghton, op. cit.

16 J. G. H. Brown *A Message from the World of Spirits, showing the state of men after death* 1857

17 *The Spiritualist* 6 April 1877

18 *Weekly Despatch* May 1868

19 George Sexton *God and Immortality viewed in the Light of Modern Spiritualism* 1873

20 Britten, op. cit.

21 I John 2: 1–6

22 David Wilson, op. cit.

23 J. G. H. Brown, op. cit.

24 Ibid.

25 Quoted by John Nevil Maskelyne *Modern Spiritualism. A short account of its rise and progress* 1876

26 William Crookes *The Phenonema of Spiritualism* 1875

27 William Crookes, quoted by Emma Hardinge Britten, op. cit.

28 J. G. H. Brown, op. cit.

29 John S. Farmer *'Twixt Two Worlds: A Narrative of The Life and Work of William Eglinton* 1886

30 Georgina Houghton, *Chronicles of the Photographs of Spiritual Beings and Phenomena Invisible to the Material Eye* 1882

31 Georgina Houghton, op. cit.

32 George Cruikshank *A Discovery Concerning Ghosts* 1864

33 Dr G. G. Zerffi *Lecture on Historic Ornament . . . at South Kensington, etc.* 1875

34 John Nevil Maskelyne, op. cit.

35 George Cruikshank, op. cit.

36 William Martin Wilkinson *Spirit Drawings: A Personal Narrative* 1869

37 Matthew Arnold 'Dover Beach'

A Short Bibliography

Books mentioned elsewhere are not included

Anonymous *The Spirit at Home: the Confessions of a Medium* 3rd ed., 1861

Barbauld, A. L. *Hymns in Prose for Children* London

Bennett, A. R. *London and Londoners in the 1850s and 1860s* London, 1927

Brangwyn, W. C. *Gothic Memorials: being sundry sketches for mural monuments, headstones, etc.* Wolverhampton and Ipswich, 1861–72

Briggs, A. *They Saw It Happen, 1879–1940* Oxford, 1960

Briggs, A. *Victorian People: A Reassessment of Persons and Themes 1851–67* London, 1954; Chicago, 1970

Brown, J. G. H. *Important Revelations from the Spirits of Swedenborg the Swedish Spiritualist and Joseph Smith the Mormon Prophet* London and Nottingham, 1857

Burgess, F. *English Churchyard Memorials* Lutterworth, 1963

Burgess, L. M. *The Child's Guide to Spiritualism* Boston, 1874

Burn, W. L. *The Age of Equipoise* London, 1968

Bush, D. *Mythology and the Romantic Tradition in English Poetry* Oxford, 1969

Bywater, J. C. *The Mystery Solved: or, a Bible exposé of the spirit rappings* Rochester, 1852

Cole, G. D. H. and R. Postgate *The Common People 1746–1946* London, 1962

Cooper, Thomas *The Purgatory of Suicides* London, 1845

Cope, G. (ed.) *Dying, Death and Disposal* London, 1970

Crookes, Sir W. *Psychic Force and Modern Spiritualism: a reply to the 'Quarterly Review' and other critics* London, 1871

Cunnington, C. W. and P. *The History of Underclothes* London, 1951

Cunnington, P. and C. Lucas *Occupational Costume in England* Oxford, 1967

Dingwall, E. J. *Very Peculiar People* London, 1950

Dobler, Herr (G. W. S. Buck) *Exposé of the Davenport Bros.* Belfast, 1869

Doyle, R. *Bird's Eye View of Society* London, 1864

Fischel and Boehn *Modes and Manners of the XIX Century* London, 1927

Gauld, A. *The Founders of Psychical Research* London and New York, 1968

Gernsheim, H. and A. *Queen Victoria: a Biography in Word and Picture* London, 1959

Holland and Sons *Funeral Books* (Victoria and Albert Museum)

Jones, B. *Design for Death* London, 1967

Jones, P. H. (ed.) *Cremation in Great Britian* London, 1945

Henderson, P. *William Morris* London, 1967

Kelke, W. H. *The Churchyard Manual* London, 1851

Lewis, R. and A. Maude *The English Middle Classes* London, 1949

Lindley, K. A. *Of Graves and Epitaphs* London, 1965

Macdonald, A. J. *Monuments, grave-stones, burying grounds, cemeteries, temples, etc.* London, 1848

Macdonald, W. *Spiritualism identical with ancient Sorcery, New Testament Demonology and modern Witchcraft, etc.* New York, 1866

Mayhew, H. *London Labour and the London Poor* London, 1862

Mackail, J. W. *The Life of William Morris* London, 1899

Myers, F. W. H. *Human Personality and its Survival of Bodily Death* London, 1903

Porter, G. R. *The Progress of the Nation . . . from the Beginning of the Nineteenth Century* London, 1851

Praz, M. *The Romantic Agony* Oxford, 1951

Quarterly Review 'Spiritualism and its Recent Converts', 1871

Sitwell, O. and M. Barton *Victoriana* London, 1931

Journal of the Society for Psychical Research London, June 1903

Speight, Alexanna *The Lock of Hair* London, 1871

T.F.G. *Heaven opened: or, Messages for the bereaved from our little ones in glory, etc.* London and Glasgow, 1870

Temple, N. *Seen and Not Heard* London, 1970

Walker, G. A. *Burial—grand incendiarism. The last fire at the Bone-House in the Spa-Fields Golgotha, or the minute anatomy of Grave-digging in London* London, 1846
Interment and disinterment etc. . . . letters to . . . the Morning Herald London, 1843
On . . . intramural burying places, with practical suggestions for the establishment of national extramural cemeteries London, 1851
Practical Suggestions for the establishment of National Cemeteries London, 1849

Ward-Jackson, C. H. *A History of Courtauld's* London, 1941

Wood, R. *Victorian Delights* London and New York, 1967

Young, G. M. *Victorian England* London, 1936

Zerffi, G. G. *Spiritualism and Animal Magnetism* London, 1871
Dreams and Ghosts, 1875

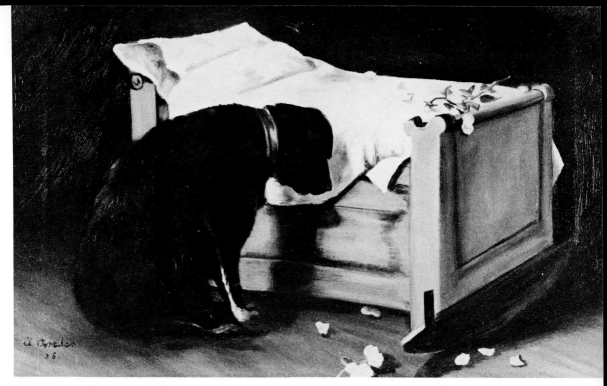

1 *The Empty Cradle* by W. Archer (1839--1935). Oil on canvas 16 × 22 in. (40.6 × 56 cm). [1]
Museum of Childhood, Edinburgh

2 *A Token for Children* by the Rev. J. Janeway. A Victorian reprint (1844) of a seventeenth-century classic. *Museum of Childhood, Edinburgh*

Silver locket and chain, late Victorian: engraved with the Good Shepherd and, on the reverse, 'Nell, in memory'. 'The Right Way': shell cameo with a child and guardian angel, gold frame. *Cameo Corner Ltd*

'Immortality': embossed tin painted black white, and in colours. *Castle Museum, York*

3 Grave decoration of a child mourning over a broken rose, late Victorian, bisque porcelain. *Museum of Childhood, Edinburgh*

4 Child asleep lying on a cross, holding a palm, *c.* 1860. Plaster with stearine finish. Figures of this kind, kept under a glass dome, were used in order to head off tactless questions about the disappearance of a child. 'There's your little brother dear. He's resting.' *Museum of Childhood, Edinburgh*

'The Little Mourner' by Frederick Sandys, from *English Sacred Poetry*, 1862. Woodcut.

The Funeral of Cock Robin attributed to Richard Doyle (1824–83). This subject was extremely popular in Victorian days, treated often in children's books (fig 1) and paintings. An interesting lithograph shows children re-enacting the funeral, having constructed a hearse very like William Morris's (plate 55). *Collection Alexander Martin*

7 Memorial cards of a family 1843–56;
laid on black velvet and framed.
Such cards were frequently hung on
the wall. *Stoke on-Trent City Museum
and Art Gallery*

8 Sampler, 1859. Cross stitch in
coloured wools and black silk. 'Jesus
Wept in Rememberance etc'.
Manchester City Art Galleries

9   Selection of memorial cards, 1870–
c.1900. Many are embossed, some
silvered, on a background of black.
The emblems used include ivy (clinging and evergreen, a reference to
undying affection), angels, weeping
willows and a broken column – the
last often symbolized a violent or
premature death, such as that of a
soldier. *Castle Museum, York;
Leicester Museums and Art Gallery;
the Trustees of the London Museum*

In Loving Memory

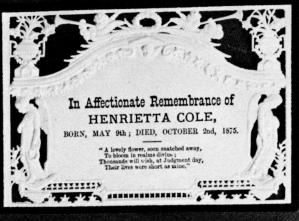

In Affectionate Remembrance of
HENRIETTA COLE,
BORN, MAY 9th; DIED, OCTOBER 2nd, 1875.

"A lovely flower, soon snatched away,
To bloom in realms divine;
Thousands will wish, at Judgment day,
Their lives were short as mine."

In Affectionate Remembrance of
ROBERT ASKEW STEVENS,
Who Died June 5th, 1871.

Aged 55 Years.

"The Lord thy God is a merciful God, he will not
forsake thee."—Deut., iv., 31.

Interred at Nunhead Cemetery.

Rest in the Lord.

In
Affectionate and Loving Remembrance of
SARAH ANN BURDITT,
Who Died May 19th, 1874.

AGED 9 YEARS

O, fare ye well my darling girl
Your mother's pleasure and her joy
The treasure of your father's heart,
'Tis hard, my darling girl, 'tis hard to part.

AND FORBID THEM NOT O,
FOR OF SUCH IS THE KINGDOM OF HEAVEN

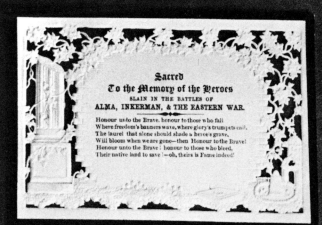

Sacred
To the Memory of the Heroes
SLAIN IN THE BATTLES OF
ALMA, INKERMAN, & THE EASTERN WAR.

Honour unto the Brave, honour to those who fall
Where freedom's banners wave, where glory's trumpets call,
The laurel that alone should shade a hero's grave,
Will bloom when we are gone—then Honour to the Brave!
Honour unto the Brave! honour to those who bleed,
Their native land to save!—oh, theirs is Fame indeed!

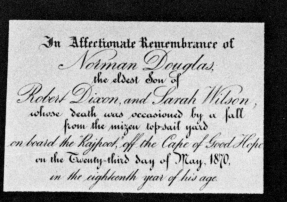

In Affectionate Remembrance of
Norman Douglas,
the eldest Son of
Robert Dixon, and Sarah Wilson,
whose death was occasioned by a fall
from the mizen top-sail yard
on board the Rajpoot, off the Cape of Good Hope
on the Twenty-third day of May, 1870,
in the eighteenth year of his age.

In affectionate remembrance of
Nathaniel Briggs, J.P.
who died at
Cliffe Cottage, Rawden,
September 23rd 1880.
in the 73rd year of his age.

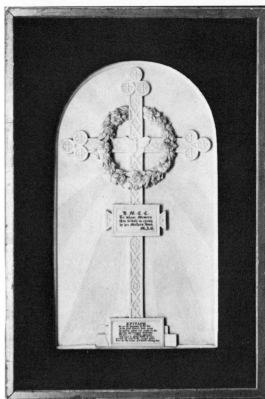

10 Pottery plaque depicting a marble obelisk on a black background in memory of the seventy-seven miners entombed at 'The Diglake Colliery Audley Jan 14th 1895. The Lord's Will be done.' *Stoke-on-Trent City Museum and Art Gallery*

11 Memorial plaque carved by the mother of the deceased: a butterfly in the centre of a cross and a wreath of emblematic flowers; marble, framed in ebony, gilt and dark purple velvet, and glazed. The inscription runs:
HMCC
To whose Memory this tribute is carved by her Mother's Hand. MAC
Epitaph
So we the blossoms of the day
As the field flowers fade away
To mortal gaze we seem to die
But like the winged Butterfly
We quit our earthly chrysalis
And clad in plumy robes of bliss
Ascend for ever to the realms above
Freed by the cross of Christ's atoning love.
Collection Miss Barbara Jones

12 Tea plate, *c.* 1840, Staffordshire earthenware: printed with a grave-digging machine at work; the grave-diggers, seated on a tombstone, play cards. One of a set of plates prophesying the effects of the Industrial Revolution – in this case on death. *Brighton Museums*

13 Plate (one of two) issued in memory of the victims of the Swaithe Main Colliery Explosion, 6 December 1875: printed in black; in the centre bearing the name of the 'coal owner', a tomb with a cross, angels and a weeping willow. *Stoke-on-Trent City Museum and Art Gallery*

14 A 'funeral teapot', late nineteenth century. Staffordshire, decorated in black and gold, with blue forget-me-nots. *Brighton Museums*

12

13

14

...O. F......S. MANN...

Who underwent the Penalty of the Law, on Tuesday, November, 13, 1849, at Horsemonger Lane ... for the Barbarous Murder of PATRICK O'CONNER, Esq., at No. 3, Minver-Place, Bermondsey.

A COPY OF VERSES.

I PRAY attend to my Lamentation,
A dreadful deed I will now unfold,
And you will find that the bare relation
Will make your very blood run cold.
It's of a horrid and cruel murder,
As ever stained the page of crime,
Committed on the 9th of august,
Eighteen hundred and forty nine;

Alas! upon that fatal evening
O'Conner came to our house to dine,
But little thought that his grave was waiting,
His body to consume in lime:
Soon he arrived, and all things being ready,
He asked for water to wash his hands,
When on the stairs he was basely murdered,
And fell beneath the assassin's hand.

The murderers then to conceal the body
They mangled, cut, and bruised him sore,
And in a sack they quickly bound him,
And buried him him beneath the kitchen floor,
Then to his dwelling they quick repaired,
To Greenwood Street, in Mile End Road,
They robbed and plundered, and stole his jewels,
all for the sake of accursed gold.

Now being possessed of these victim's riches,
In concert they contrived the plan,
For to escape—but we find that Justice
Pursued them to a foreign land.
Where they are taken in put in prison.
In irons strong were brought back with speed
Was then examined and soon committed,
To answer for the dreadful deed.

Now three days after this horrid murder,
The God of Justice brought things to light,
Beneath the kitchen floor they found him,
Which proved to be a most dreadful sight;
They raised the stones and soon discovered
The mangled form of O'Connor lie,
tied neck and heels with a rope together;
But soon the body was identified.

George Frederick Manning, and his wife Mari
Charged with the highest crime in law,
Are guilty found, and condemn'd together,
May God in mercy receive their souls:
Then pity all who see us suffer,
Man and wife on the fatal tree;
For years to come will be remembered
The Manning's deeds in Bermondsey.

THE extraordinary and deep interest excited by the almost unparalleled tragedy which has so strongly agitated the public mind, has induced us to give a more than usually connected detail from the first entrance of the characters in the fearful drama, to its awful *denouement* on the scaffold, as the reward which human laws—we dare not say humanity—afflicts on the perpetrators of such deeds of blood!

GEORGE FREDERICK MANNING, was the son of a Sergeant in the Somerset Militia was lessee of the market tolls, and some turnpike trusts, and for some yea's kept the Bear Public house at Taunton, much respected in every relation of life. He died in 1844, leaving his widow, and his favourite son, George, his representatives. His mother soon after died, and he thus became possessed of the ground ... to his late father's property. He subsequently was in the service of the Great Western Railway Company as Guard, ... no doubt implicated in the extensive robberies committed on that line, a no less a sum than £4000 was ... from the train of which Manning was guard; however, it is certain that he was connected with the mail robberies ... when both he and his ... fe were taken into custody, but dismissed in conse-

... amined the body, and discovered extensive fractures, and extracted a large pistol bullet. Suspicion immediately pointed to the Manning as the assassins, and steps were immediately taken their apprehension. Manning was apprehended at Jersey, and his wife in Edinburgh. T... were forthwith conveyed to England, and finally committed for trial to Horsemonger Lane G...

The TRIAL commenced on Thursday, Oct. 25, at the Old Bailey, before the Lord C... Baron Pollock, Mr Justice Maul, and Mr. Justice Cresswell. The Attorney General (Sir J... Jervis), Mr. Clarkson, Mr. Bodkin, and Mr. Clark appeared for the prosecution; Mr. Serge... Wilkins, and Mr. Charnock were for the male prisoner, and, Mr. Ballantine and Mr. Parry Mrs. Manning. The Clerk of Arraigns having read over the indictment, on being called upon plead, the male prisoner exclaimed in a loud firm tone, "Not Guilty."—Mr. Ballantine then p... on behalf of the female prisoner ... by a jury de medietat's ling... but the application was then overruled, and she pleaded, in a voice almost inaudible, "Not G... ..., ... manner, stated the case for the prosecution, proceeded to call witnesses, who clearly established the facts already stated; after which Serje... Wilkins, in a somewhat coarse but ingenious address, endeavoured to throw all the blame on the

---

GEORGE FREDERICK MANNING, was the son of a Sergeant in the Somerset Militia was lessee of the market tolls, and some turnpike trusts, and for some yea's kept the Bear Public house at Taunton, much respected in every relation of life. He died in 1844, leaving his widow, and his favourite son, George, his representatives. His mother soon after died, and he thus became possessed of the ground ... to his late father's property. He subsequently was in the service of the Great Western Railway Company as Guard ... no doubt implicated in the extensive robberies committed on that line, a no less a sum than £4000 was ... from the train of which Manning was guard; however, it is certain that he was connected with the mail robberies in January last, when both he and his wife were taken into custody, but dismissed in consequence of no property being found in their possession. Poole and Nightingale, his confederates, were sentenced to 15 years transportation. This event caused him to leave the White Hart Inn at Taunton, and he opened a beer-shop in the vicinity of the Hackney Road, London, but he closed this, in consequence of the absconding of his wife, at the wish of their victim O'Connor, with whom he was no doubt cohabiting. Manning traced his wife, made up matters, and took possession of the house, No. 3, Minver Place, Bermondsey, where the murder was committed.

MARIA MANNING's maiden name was MARIA De ROUX, born at Lausanne, in Switzerland, in 1822, and inherited a small patrimony from her parents, who are both dead. About six years since she served in the family of Sir Lawrence Palk, at Hald n House, Devonshire; while travelling to and fro with Lady Palk on the Great Western Railway, she became acquainted with Manning. At the decease of Lady Palk, in 1846, she obtained a situation with Lady Blantyre, daughter of the Duchess of Sutherland, at Stafford House. While attending her Ladyship on a brief continental tour, she met with O'Connor, on board of a London and Boulogne boat, who was so struck with her appearance and manners, as to offer her marriage. On her return in 1847, she was frequently visited by both O'Connor and Manning, the latter, however, seems to have the most favoured suitor, and on the 27th of May, 1847, she was married to him at St James's Church, Piccadilly.

PATRICK O'CONNOR arrived in London from Ireland, in February, 1842. He had letters of recommendation from his brother, the Rev. Dr. O'Connor, of Templemore, County Tipperary, and through the ... of several noblemen high in office, he at length obtained a situation as the Customs, as Gauger at the London Docks. His acquaintance with Mrs Manning has already been noticed, and that an improper connection existed between them is quite certain- and that Manning was aware of the fact is equally apparent.

The murder was no doubt committed on the evening of Thursday, August 9. On the previous day she posted an invitation for O'Connor to dine with them at half-past 5 o'clock, and he was last seen on his way to Bermondsey to comply with the invitation.

On the 13th of August the Mannings precipitately left their house, and on the following day their landlord found the house unoccupied, and on the 17th. the Police havingobtained access to the premises, made a diligent search, and in the back kitchen, under the flagged pavement, about four feet deep, was found the body of Patrick O'Connor, thrust into hole, the legs being bound back to haunches covered with lime, and naked. The body being disinterred, was ... identified, and a set of ... from deceased's mouth, by Mr. Lockw... a surgeon, who afterwards ex-

MARIE MANNING.

16 Contemporary broadsheet on the execution for murder on 13 November 1849 of George and Maria Manning. Mrs Manning (bottom right) wore a black satin dress to the scaffold; Dickens wrote indignantly to *The Times* on the levity of the mob. *Madame Tussaud's Ltd, London*

17 Paper model of a mausoleum made by Charles Peace: its main component is a memorial card of the same model as Plate 66. Charles Peace was hanged for murder in 1879. [2] *Madame Tussaud's Ltd, London*

18 Chimney-piece ornaments, 1848. Staffordshire earthenware. James B. Rush, the murderer; Emily Sandford, his housekeeper, Potash Farm, where they lived; and Stanfield Hall, where the murders were committed. [3] *Brighton Museums*

1

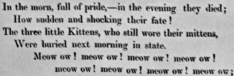

In the morn, full of pride,—in the evening they died;
How sudden and shocking their fate!
The three little Kittens, who still wore their mittens,
Were buried next morning in state.
Meow ow! meow ow! meow ow! meow ow!
meow ow! meow ow! meow ow! meow ow;

20

21

19 *A Funeral Bearer* by Rev. Septimus Buss, *c.* 1830–40. Tin plate 14^1/$_2$ × 11 ft (4.6 × 3.4 m). White was used at the funeral of a child or perhaps a young girl. The pendant to this painting shows a mute dressed entirely in black. *The Trustees of the London Museum*

20 *Death and Burial of the Three Little Kittens*, from Dean's New Series of Large Toy Books 1860. *Collection Ronald Horton Esq.*

21 *The Lying in State of the Duke of Wellington at Chelsea Hospital* Lithograph coloured by hand; lettered 'Chas. Burton, Litho. Published for the Proprietor by J. and R. Jennings, 62, Cheapside, London. Printed by Standidge and Co.' *Victoria and Albert Museum*

THE LOVELY MUST DEPART!

How may the mother's heart
Dwell on her son, and dare to hope again?
The spring's rich promise hath been given in vain.
The lovely must depart!
Is he not gone, our brightest and our best?

'Yet mourn yet not as they
Whose spirits' light is quench'd' for him the past
Is seald. He may not fall, he may not cast
His birth-rights hope away!
All is not here of our beloved and bless'd,
Leave ye the sleeper with his God to rest!

22 *The Common Lot* by J. Bouvier. From a series of coloured lithographs illustrating poems by Mrs Heman, published by William Spooner c. 1860. *Museum of Childhood, Edinburgh*

23 *The Last Moments of Raphael* by H. N. O'Neill. The Royal Academy catalogue of 1866 described the painting:

> The great painter is about to die on his thirty-seventh birthday; the fatal Roman fever has run its course. The evening light which catches the summit of Monte Mario, shows that the hour of death is near. Raphael died between half-past four and five in the afternoon of a spring day, which is seen shining cheerfully in at the open window. The unfinished picture of *The Transfiguration* has been uncovered, and the painter's friends, Giulio Romano, Peruzzi, Giovanni da Udine, Marcantonio, and Cardinal Bibiena are gathered around the couch.

Bristol City Art Gallery

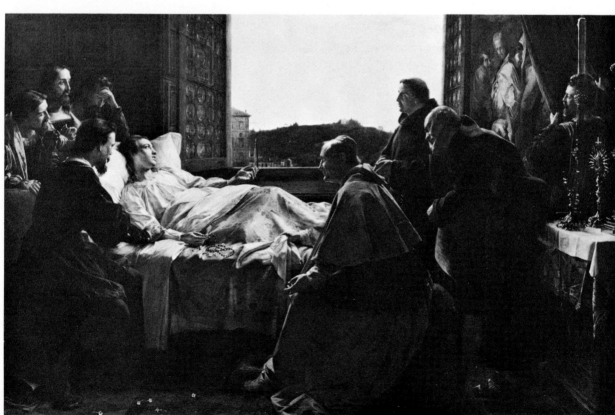

24 *The Lovely must Depart* by J. Bouvier. From a series of coloured lithographs illustrating poems by Mrs Heman, published by William Spooner *c.* 1860. *Museum of Childhood, Edinburgh*

25 *The Last Moments of HRH The Prince Consort* by W. I. Walton. Coloured lithograph printed by C. J. Culliford. Closely related to and probably done after an anonymous painting of the scene at the Wellcome Institute of the History of Medicine. Queen Victoria is on the right of the bed; Prince Edward on the left. At the far left are four doctors, Watson, Clark, Ferguson and Jenner, who signed the last medical bulletin. The number of people present and the elaborate nature of the décor contrast strongly with the simplicity of popular representations of the scene. *Museum of Childhood, Edinburgh*

26 'An Altar hung for a Funeral Mass', plate 73
of *Glossary of Ecclesiastical Ornament and Costume*
by Augustus Welby Pugin. *Brighton Public Libraries*

27 Firescreen, 1884, enclosing a painting of
a view of the mausoleum of the Hesse
family at the Rosenhohe. Queen Victoria's
second daughter, Princess Alice Grand
Duchess of Hesse (1843–78) was buried
there. *From Osborne House, by gracious
permission of Her Majesty The Queen*

28 'Automatic' drawing, *c.* 1870 by Mrs Alaric
Watts (died 1903). Coloured inks applied
by reed pen, and watercolour, on tracing
paper. *The Society for Psychical Research*

29 *Study for the Neild Memorial Window* by Sir Matthew Digby Wyatt. Watercolour
24⁷/₈ × 21 in. (63 × 53 cm) J. C. Neild (*c.* 1780–1852) was a famous miser who left
£ 500,000, the whole of his property, to Queen Victoria. He was buried in the chancel of
North Marston Church, Bucks; in 1855 the Queen restored the chancel and inserted a
window in his memory. *Royal Institute of British Architects*

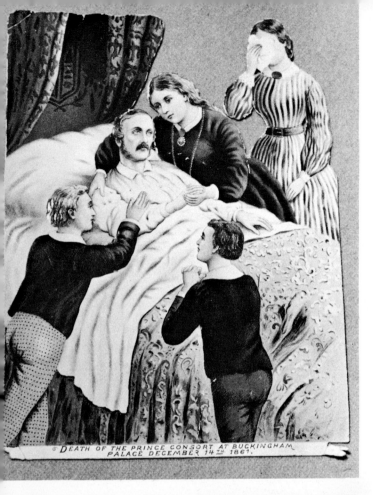

DEATH OF THE PRINCE CONSORT AT BUCKINGHAM
PALACE DECEMBER 14TH 1861.

30 'The Death of the Prince Consort at Buckingham Palace', from a volume of cut-outs produced towards the end of the Queen's reign. *Collection Mrs Betty O'Looney*

31 White marble cross on wood. The inscription 'Auf Wiedersehen Frogmore March 16 1861', and the cypher 'VM', refer to the death of Queen Victoria's mother, Victoria Mary Louisa, Duchess of Kent (1786–1861). An inscribed wall panel commemorates her death in a first floor room at Frogmore. *From Osborne House, by gracious permission of Her Majesty The Queen*

White lawn mourning handkerchiefs belonging to Queen Victoria and to her daughter Princess Helena, embroidered in white and black. The Queen's is bordered by a Greek key pattern interspersed with forget-me-nots. The initials are formed of willow leaves. *The Trustees of the London Museum*

32 Queen Victoria and Princess Alice with the bust by Theed of the Prince Consort. Photograph by Prince Alfred, Windsor Castle, 1862, the first year of the Queen's widowhood. This, like many similar photographs, contains the Prince's bust; in others, the Queen is reading beside it; in some, almost the whole Royal Family is present. The astonishingly histrionic pose of the Queen in this photograph is alien to modern sensibility; this, however, was a Romantic age. *By gracious permission of Her Majesty The Queen*

33 Mourning ear trumpet, late nineteenth century, made of 'Vulcanite', covered with ribbed silk, and decorated with lace and ribbon, on a silk cord. *Collection Miss Barbara Jones*

Mourning handkerchief of Queen Victoria, of fine linen lawn, embroidered with the royal monogram in white and black, and white formalized tears (white was considered deeper mourning than grey or mauve). *The Trustees of the London Museum*

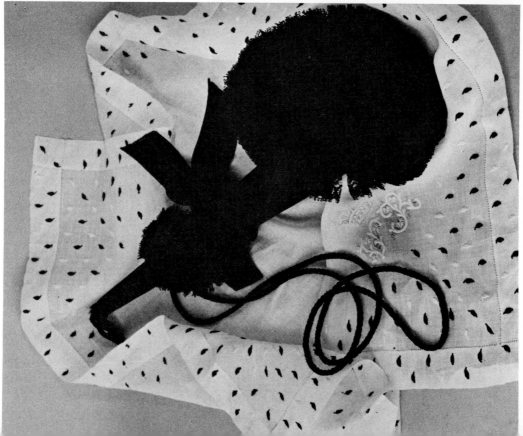

HIS LATE ROYAL HIGHNESS
PRINCE ALBERT.
Born Aug.t 26.th 1819. *Died Dec.r 14.th 1861.*

34 Commemorative ribbon for Prince
Albert, signed R. Schweizer, 1861.
Woven silk. *Worthing Library, Museum
and Art Gallery*

Granite cross, Celtic design with the
cypher 'VR 1862' within a wreath of bay
(symbol of immortality), in metal. This
probably commemorates the ceremony
of 21 August 1862 when Queen Victoria,
accompanied by six of her children, laid
the first stones of the Cairn built at the
top of the Craig Lairigan 'To the beloved memory of Albert the Great and good
Prince Consort'. *From Osborne House,
by gracious permission of Her Majesty The
Queen*

35 *Hope* by Carl Schmidt. Painted porcelain: an anchor, the symbol of faith, and
a branch of yew, symbol of immortality,
within a border 'Victoria: May 24 1863'
and the text 'Seid frohlich in Hoffnung:
Geduldig in Trubsal' (be joyful in hope,
patient in trouble). The gilt frame is
ornamented with forget-me-nots. After a
watercolour drawing by Victoria, the
Queen's eldest daughter, given to her
mother for her birthday on 24 May 1863.
The Queen had then been a widow for
eighteen months. *From Osborne House,
by gracious permission of Her Majesty
The Queen*

VICTORIA
Seid fröhlich in Hoffnung.
Geduldig in Trübsal.
MAY. 24. 1863.

36 *Design for a Christening Cup* by Edward Henry Corbould (1815–1905). Signed and dated 'Feb. 1864 Osborne'. Watercolour $20^{1}/_{2} \times 36^{1}/_{2}$ in. (52×92.7 cm). Designed for Prince Albert Victor (1864–92), the cup was a gift from the Queen for her grandson's baptism. The completed design, much like that in the sketch, was executed by Messrs Elkington and Company and finished in December 1865. Queen Victoria composed the inscriptions, and the verses were by Mrs Prothero, wife of the Rector of Whippingham. *By gracious permission of Her Majesty The Queen*

37 'Design for the Albert Memorial' by Sir George Gilbert Scott, RA (1811–78). This was possibly the design submitted to Queen Victoria in January 1863, showing the monument in Kensington Gardens, with groups of spectators. The face of the statue of the Prince Consort is a photograph, cut out and attached to the main sheet. This drawing, made before the addition of another storey to the spire, shows details in the design of the canopy and of the statue of the Prince which differ from those of the completed monument. *Victoria and Albert Museum, London*

38 Jug commemorating Prince Albert made by the Old Hall Pottery, Hanley. Stoneware, moulded with the Prince's portrait, orders, dates of birth and death, and the royal arms, registered design mark for 9 April 1862. The same design occurs in other materials (e.g. Parian ware) and by other firms. *Brighton Museums*

40 Satin rosettes, late nineteenth century. [5]
Mourning cockade for a coachman's hat, late nineteenth century, Pressed fibre with fabric bow. *Collection Miss Barbara Jones*
False horse's tail, late nineteenth century. [6] *Messrs W. J. Crane and Sons Ltd*
Mourning toque of Princess Marie Louise, 1901. The long veil completely covered the face and hair, and in front reached down to the waist.
Record of events connected with the death and funeral of Queen Victoria. *The Trustees of the London Museum*

39 'The Temporary Sarcophagus, Royal Mausoleum Frogmore 1864', photograph, coloured by E. H. Corbould (1815–1905). The sarcophagus, seen from outside the opened doors of its protective enclosure, is enclosed in a Gothic ormolu frame, which incorporates lilies in the design, of a type often used for memorial purposes. [4] *From Osborne House, by gracious permission of Her Majesty The Queen*

41 Hatchment, first half of the nineteenth century. The rules of heraldry make it possible to deduce the sex and status of the deceased; this is that of a man whose wife survived. Hatchments were suspended against the wall of a deceased person's house for six to twelve months; they were then removed to the Parish Church. A hatchment was seen in a London street in 1928. *Bristol City Art Gallery*

42 Undertaker's hatchment; an undertaker's shop-sign in the form of a mock hatchment, formerly in use at Northiam, Sussex. *Collection Mrs N. Perigoe*

43 *Barnard's Furnishing Undertaker*. Anonymous, *c.* 1850. Watercolour. A typical lower class undertaker's shop. *Brighton Museums*

44 Top hat *c.* 1890. The hat of an undertaker, with black silk 'weeper' ends. *Worthing Library, Museum and Art Gallery*

Half-mourning parasol. White satin heavily edged with black. Summer parasols were often almost covered in crape, with no lace or fringe for the first year, if carried by a widow. Afterwards, mourning fringe could be put on. *Whitby Literary and Philosophical Society*

45 'The Funeral of the Late Archbishop of York', *Illustrated London News* 1847 'The Hearse, it will be seen, was of Gothic design – in appropriately solemn taste.' The outer coffin was covered with silk velvet ornamented with gilt lace.

46 *The Funeral Procession of the Late Mr James Braidwood* [7] by C. J. Culliford after A. L. Butler. Coloured lithograph. *Guildhall Library and Art Gallery*

47 'The Funeral of Lord Palmerston', *Illustrated London News* 1865. The print clearly shows the feather tray and the draped staves. Lord Palmerston had provided a vault for himself at Romsey Cemetery, after the sanitary inspector, following the ban on intramural burials, had closed the family vault at Romsey Abbey. However, the Queen desired his burial at Westminster. The funeral was arranged by Bantings of St James Street: it was remarked that the hearse, with its armorial bearings, was 'somewhat too glaring for the vehicle of death'. The pall was of black velvet and white satin; the coffin was crimson; the mourners cast their rings into the vault. The London clubs draped in black.

48 Card of admission to St Paul's Cathedral for the Duke of Wellington's funeral service. *Hampshire County Museum Service*

Ticket to the St James's Club, to view the Duke's funeral; black bordered. Part of the ticket has obviously been retained. *The Trustees of the London Museum*

Coffin furniture, mid-nineteenth century large embossed tin plaque, ornamented with angels, palms, clouds, a crown, and the Holy Ghost; painted in black and gilt. [8] *Castle Museum, York*

49 A hearse-plume and a horse-plume: each 'feather' consists of many feathers bound together, with the edges clipped. Side cloths for horses: black velvet and white appliqué. *Collection W. A. Marr of James Recknell & Co., London E8*

Two mutes' staves, brass mounted with wreaths and inverted torches on ebonized wood. *Collection W. H. Scott*

50 Undertaker's bill (1897) and trade card.

Gold locket, with a photograph of a child, on the reverse inset with a cross in blue enamel. *Castle Museum, York*

Gold locket and chain, engraved with a leaf design and enamelled with a cross in blue, containing two locks of hair. *Worthing Library, Museum and Art Gallery*

Gold mourning brooch, *c*. 1850, with a design of willow tree and tombstone worked in hair. *Collection Miss Barbara Jones*

Mourning cross, in gilt metal inset with jet. *Castle Museum, York*

51 Grave clothes, late nineteenth century. Dress in white brushed cotton, the sleeves slit open, backless; decorated with panels of matching brushed cotton, stamped with floral designs, and white satin scalloped ribbon; satin bar at the neck. The resemblance between grave clothes and baby clothes is interesting. *Castle Museum, York*

52 Hearse, coach built, with glass panels decorated in silver and gilt with emblematic flowers, iron scroll work on the roof, the body painted black and gold. The coach lamps are missing. Built in the latter half of the nineteenth century by Kay's of Margate; owned by Partis, Undertaker's at Faversham. $12^1/_2 \times 7^1/_2 \times 5^3/_4$ ft $(3.8 \times 2.3 \times 17.5$ m$)$. *Maidstone Museums and Art Gallery*

53 Hearse in wood and cast iron, the glass windows etched with emblematic flowers. It could be used as a hand hearse, without horses. Bought by Northiam Parish Council to commemorate the Diamond Jubilee of Queen Victoria. *Northiam Parish Council*

54 Child's coffin box, late nineteenth century. The wooden box is ebonized and gilded; each side is engraved and silver gilded; the rounded ends are decorated with cast iron. This type of box, attached to an ordinary carriage, saved the expense of a full-sized hearse. *North of England Open-Air Museum, Beamish Hall, Co. Durham*

55 Photograph of the hearse used for the corpse of William Morris. The funeral took place on 6 October 1896. [9] The gravestone, with a coped top, was designed by Philip Webb. *William Morris Gallery, Walthamstow*

56 ENGLISH MOURNING JEWELRY
(from left to right) Bracelet, *c.*
1860–70, enamelled gold, with pearls
and diamonds. Brooch, *c.* 1860-70,
gold with onyx and pearls. Four
bosses, *c.* 1840, enamelled gold, with
pearls and diamonds. Necklace,
c. 1860, enamelled gold with pearls.
Victoria and Albert Museum, col-
lection bequeathed by Lady Cory

57 *Queen Victoria after Death* by Sir
Hubert von Herkomer (1849–1914).
Watercolour $22^3/_4 \times 16^3/_4$ in. (58 × 43
cm). [10] Inscribed 'Painted direct
from Her Majesty Queen Victoria
Jan. 24 1901'. The painting is enclosed in a heavy ebonized frame.
From Osborne House, by gracious
permission of Her Majesty the Queen.

58 *Dreams*, by William Millner. Oil, 24 × 20 in. (61 × 50.8 cm). This extraordinary painting epitomizes the morbid romanticism peculiar to the nineteenth century. *The Picadilly Gallery*

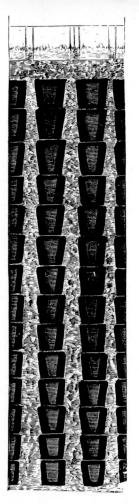

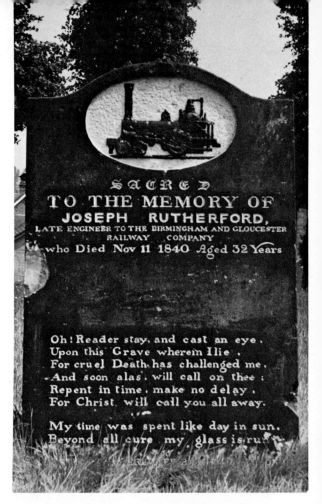

SACRED
TO THE MEMORY OF
JOSEPH RUTHERFORD,
LATE ENGINEER TO THE BIRMINGHAM AND GLOUCESTER
RAILWAY COMPANY
who Died Nov 11 1840 Aged 32 Years

Oh! Reader stay, and cast an eye,
Upon this Grave wherein I lie,
For cruel Death has challenged me,
And soon alas, will call on thee:
Repent in time, make no delay,
For Christ will call you all away.

My time was spent like day in sun,
Beyond all cure my glass is run.

59

62

59 'Section showing number of Coffins in each Grave in London Cemetery' from *On the Laying Out, Planting and Managing of Cemeteries and on the Improvement of Churchyards* by J. C. Loudon, 1843. [11]

60 Tombstone 'to the Memory of Joseph Rutherford', 1840.

61 'Enon-Chapel Cemetery, and Dancing Saloon', from *Sanatory Progress, being the fifth report of the National Philanthropic Association for the promotion of Social and Salutiferous Improvements etc.* 1850

62 'The Lying in State of the Sixteenth Earl of Shrewsbury in St Peter's Chapel, Alton Towers', *Illustrated London News* 1852. [12]

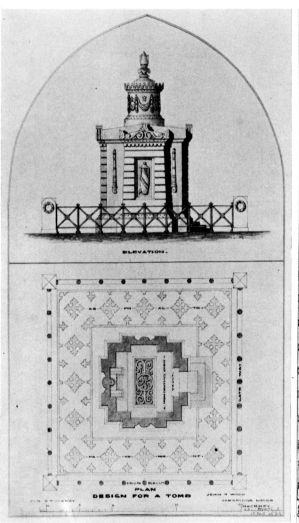

63 *Design for a Tomb*, plan and elevation by J. T. Wood *c.* 1835. Pen and wash; in the 'pagan' style, with urns, wreaths and inverted torches. *Royal Institute of British Architects*

64 Headstones, from *Monumenta, Designs for Tombs, Monuments, Headstones, Gravecrosses etc. with Working Details*. Published by J. Hagger, mid-nineteenth century. *Messrs Ernest Smith (Nottingham) Ltd*

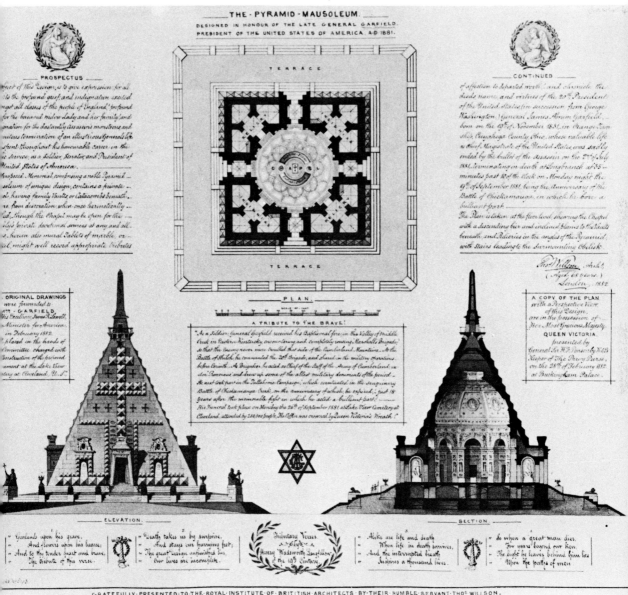

65 Plan, elevation and section for *The Pyramid Mausoleum designed in honour of the late General Garfield, President of the United States of America, AD 1881*, at Cleveland Lakeview Cemetery by Thomas Willson (born 1814). Pen and wash, signed and dated 1882. The original drawings were forwarded to Mrs Garfield in 1882 and a copy of the plan with a perspective view was presented to Queen Victoria. It is difficult to imagine a more eclectic design. *Royal Institute of British Architects*

66 Memorial card to Charles Davey, 1881. Embossed, with black flock and silvered decorations, $13^1/_4 \times 11^3/_4$ in. (33.7×29.8 cm). The patent was registered by Wood, July 1871. Cards of this elaborate nature were intended to be framed and hung on the wall by relatives and friends of the deceased. *Collection Mrs Barbara Morris*

67 *Sketch-design for the Monument of His Eminence Cardinal Wiseman* (died 1865) by C. A. Buckler (1824–1905). Pencil and sepia wash. Cardinal Wiseman's monument, transferred from Kensal Green to Westminster Cathedral, is by E. Welby Pugin. *Royal Institute of British Architects*

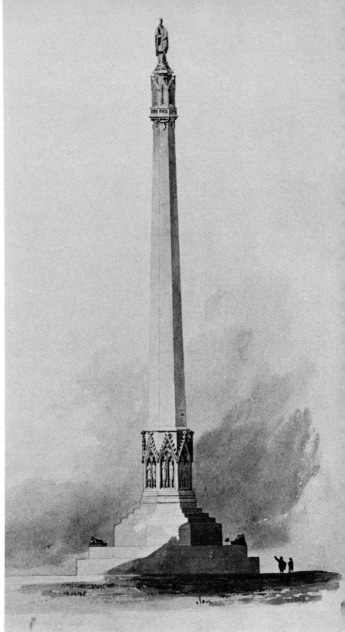

68 *Design for an Octagonal Monument in Gothic Style* by J. Trubshaw (1777–1853). Pen and watercolour. *Royal Institute of British Architects*

69 *Design for a Monumental Column in Gothic Style* by S. C. Fripp. Pen, sepia and wash. The size of the adjacent figures indicates the scale. *Royal Institute of British Architects*

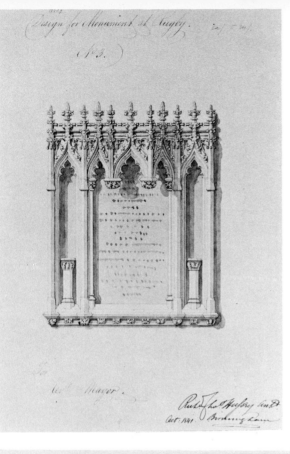

70 Design for a Gothic wall monument 'For Revd Mayor' for the Church of St Andrew, Rugby, by Richard Charles Hussey, signed and dated 1841. Pencil and sepia wash. *Royal Institute of British Architects*

71 'Examples of modern costume adapted to sepulchral brasses', *An Apology for the Revival of Christian Architecture in England* by A. Welby Pugin 1843. *Brighton Public Libraries*

Mourning brooch, Gothic design in gold, an agate within a serpent swallowing its tail (a symbol of eternity). Engraved on reverse: 'N. M. Rothschild Esq. ob 28 July. At. 58 HLC' *The Trustees of the London Museum*

Jet pendant in the form of a cross encircled by a mourning wreath, *c.* 1890. *Worthing Library, Museum and Art Gallery*

✠ EXAMPLES OF MODERN COSTVME ADAPTED TO SEPVLCHRAL BRASSES

72 Motif showing the globe surrounded by various other commemorative monuments, set in a circle, for the title-page of *The Competition for the Erection of the Nelson Monument* London 1841. Pencil. Signed and dated 1839. *Royal Institute of British Architects*

Projected design by John Coldicutt for the Lord Nelson monument, Trafalgar Square, London; a hemispherical globe surrounded by water; perspective design seen from behind the portico columns of the National Gallery. Pencil and coloured washes. *Royal Institute of British Architects*

74 Graveyard obelisk painted with forget-me-nots and lilies of the valley and inscribed in memory of Eliza and William Carter of John Street, Hanley, 1888. Staffordshire earthenware. The obelisk is pierced on the base (*bottom left*) to take flowers, and when so used, was turned upside down, the obelisk being stuck into the earth. It was probably made at Hanley and may be a unique object made by a local potter for his family or a friend; the naïve nature of its double use suggests this. *Brighton Museums*

75 Chalice, London 1868. Silver-gilt, decorated with enamels, semi-precious stones and stained glass; maker's mark of Jes Barkentin. Designed by William Burges (1827–87) a leading designer and propogandist of the Gothic style. His close connexion with the Ecclesiological Society began in 1845; he shared its reforming fervour. The chalice was given as a memorial, in line with reformist theory. It is inscribed 'MEMENTO: DOMINE: JOHANNIS: BAKER: GABB ET: MARIAE: UXORIS: EIUS: QUI: HUNC: CALICEM: IN: VSUM: ECCLESIAE: S. ANDREAE: DE: WELLS: STREET: DEDERUNT: ANNO: SALUTIS: MDCCCLXVII.' *St Andrew, Kingsbury*

76 Highgate Cemetery, London: from *The Pictorial Times*, 27 April 1844. *Collection Dr Phillis Cunnington*

77 Highgate Cemetery, London 1971

78 Highgate Cemetery, London 1971:
the catacombs.

79 *Design for the Entrance to a Cemetery.* Anonymous. Watercolour on card. The cemetery has the two chapels, one consecrated,
the other not, as established by legislation.
In this case there are two entrances also,
one for each chapel. *Royal Institute of
British Architects*

80 'Entrance gateway for a new cemetery' (NB 'Shillibeers Funeral Omnibus') from *An Apology for The Revivial of Christian Architecture in England* by A. Welby Pugin, 1843.

81 *Design for an Entrance to a Cemetery*, plan and elevation by Alfred Batson. Pen and wash, signed and dated 'AB 20 April 1839'. This dignified design could, with no alteration whatsoever, be used with perfect propriety for the entrance to a gentleman's park. *Royal Institute of British Architects*

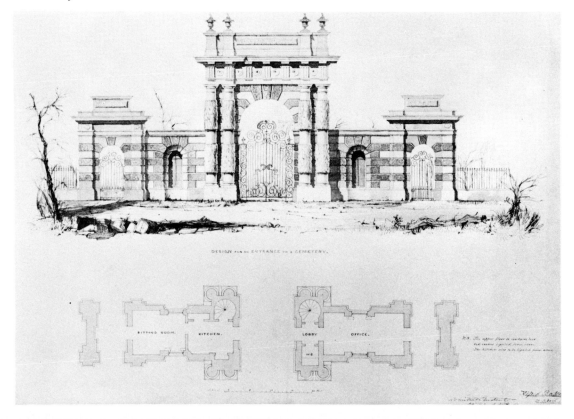

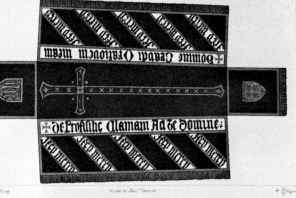

82 Funeral palls, from *A Glossary of Ecclesiastical Ornament and Costume* 1844 by A. Welby Pugin (1812–52). *Brighton Public Libraries*

83 LEFT: Parian wreath of roses and lilies-of-the-valley, for use on a grave, *c.* 1880. *Stoke-on-Trent City Museum and Art Gallery*

RIGHT: A group of *immortelles* under a glass dome [13]: the flowers include roses and lilies.

84 'Design for Laying Out and Planting a Cemetery on Hilly Ground' from *On the Laying Out, Planting and Managing of Cemeteries: and On the Improvement of Churchyards* by J. C. Loudon, 1843

85 'The Starved-Out Undertakers', *Punch* January–June 1850.

82
83

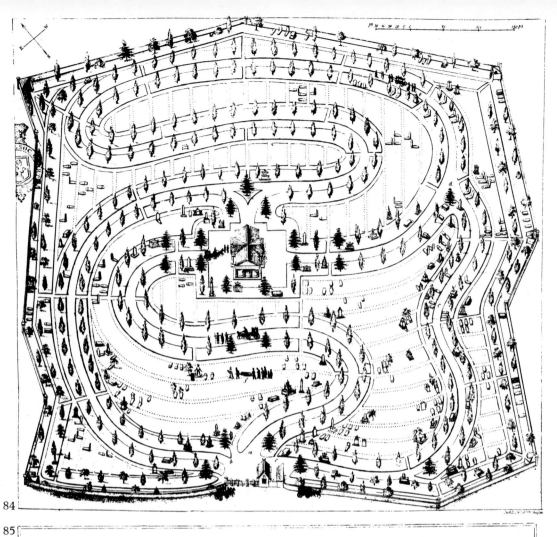

84

85

THE STARVED-OUT UNDERTAKERS.

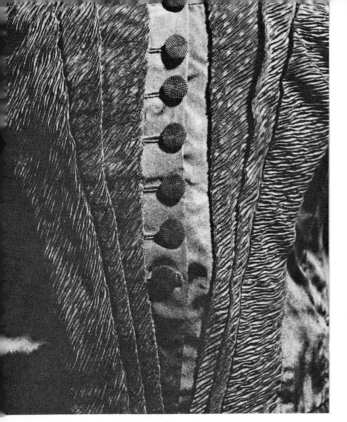

86 Detail from the bodice of a dress worn by Queen Victoria in 1894 (aged seventy-five), when in mourning for the Duke of Clarence, elder brother of the future King George V. The dress belongs to the first stages of mourning and is heavily trimmed with crape. The buttons are covered with a crape-like material. The waist measurement is 48 inches. *The Trustees of the London Museum*

87 Detail of the bodice of a half-mourning day dress, late 1880s: black cord silk with black bead and jet trimming. The effect, although black, is glittery. *Museum of Costume, Bath*

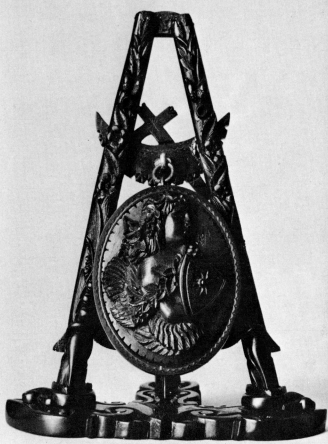

89   90

◄88 Three hair ornaments: aigrette, comb and hair pin, in French jet. *The Trustees of the London Museum*

MOURNING RINGS

Black enamel and gold, set with pearls, inscribed 'In Memory Of', *c.* 1840.

Gold, with a plait of blond hair inset, inscribed on the back 'J. Etheridge Died Dec. 16th 1855 Aged 78.' *Both Worthing Library, Museum and Art Gallery*

Gold with a glass cameo of a white urn on a black background. Engraved 'T. Grey died May 1839.' *Manchester City Art Galleries*

Serpent ring in gold and black enamel, set with a topaz. Inscribed inside the ring 'Hannah Rothschild died Sep. 5th 1850.' *The Trustees of the London Museum*

Gold, and blue enamel; inscribed 'LANDSEER'. Worn by William Powell Frith *RA* in memory of Sir Edwin Landseer. *Royal Academy*

89 Whitby jet mourning necklace and pendant, *c.* 1870. Tied with black ribbon, carved with ferns, forget-me-nots and a lily. The jet is partly matt and partly polished.

Carved Whitby jet mourning brooch *c.* 1880. Leaf pattern set with a gold-framed window containing plaited hair. *Whitby Literary and Philosophical Society*

Whitby jet cameo mourning necklace and pendant, *c.* 1870. *Collection Lady Chapman*

Gentleman's mourning watch chain in jet.

90 Carved and engraved easel in Whitby jet, supporting an oval pendant carved with a female figure in high relief holding a shield and a spear; on the reverse a monogram; a cross, forget-me-nots, acorns and lilies of the valley are included in the motifs. *Whitby Literary and Philosophical Society*

91 Necklace with pendant cross, and earrings in woven hair with gilt fittings, *c.* 1845 Hair jewelry became increasingly of a generalized sentimental nature, but the cross probably indicates the specifically memorial nature of the necklace.

Cross and beads in carved ivory, the cross with lilies, on the obverse the commemorative date 28 November 1887, and an entwined cypher. Ivory was frequently used for mourning jewelry. *Museum of Childhood, Edinburgh*

Memorial badge, celluloid. Inscribed 'In Memoriam: George Dawson MA: Died Nov 30 1876.' Dawson was a much loved Birmingham politician and social reformer. *City Museum and Art Gallery, Birmingham*

92 Courtauld's crape sample card dated January 1899; photograph of women 'finishing operators' dated 1859; background of late-nineteenth-century crape. *Messrs Courtauld Ltd*

Jet pendant shaped as a book, engraved 'Sophia'. *Whitby Literary and Philosophical Society*

93 Silk bookmark 'Forget Me Not', with a vase containing forget-me-nots. *Maidstone Museums and Art Gallery*

MOURNING BROOCHES
Gold (*top left*), reversible, with hair in the shape of plumes of feathers and pearls on both sides. *Collection Miss Barbara Jones*

Gold acanthus frame (*middle left*), a gold oval surrounded in black enamel containing hair. *Collection Mrs W. H. Scott*

Gold (*bottom left*), the frame with forget-me-nots and columbine, a bunch of flowers (forget-me-nots) in hair work with turquoise and gold decoration; the brooch swivels: on the reverse a photograph of an elderly lady (about 1865) in widow's cap. *Cameo Corner Ltd*

Gold (*top right*), 'In Memory'.

Pinchbeck with ivy design (*middle right*), reversible: dark and light brown hair on a mauve ground on one side, painted photograph on the other (*c.* 1870)

Gold with plume in hair (*bottom right*). *Collection Miss Barbara Jones*

FORGET
ME NOT

FORGET THEE?-BID THE SUN FORGET
TO RISE WITH GOLDEN RAY,
FORGET THEE?
BID THE SILVER MOON
SHINE NOT AT CLOSE OF DAY,
WHEN IN THE CLEAR BLUE
VAULT OF HEAV'N
THESE GLORIOUS ORBS ARE NOT
THEN, BUT I PROMISE
NOT TILL THEN,
BY ME THOU'LT ... BE FORGOT.

93

94 Mantelshelf ornament by Obadiah Sherratt of Burslem. Pre-Victorian. Earthenware. Watch-stand (the watch pointing to a quarter to twelve) with sun, moon, and stars: angels, one with a tomb-stone inscribed 'Time Flyes' and the raised legend in black 'Prepare to meet thy God'. [14] *Worcestershire County Museum, Hartlebury Castle*

Jet jewelry
Tiara (*top*), with graduated balls and disc design. *Museum of Costume, Bath*

Necklace with pendants (*centre*). *Collection Lady Chapman*

Bracelet (*centre right*) with inset porcelain medallion, with the arms of the nineteenth Hussars in mauve.

Bracelet (*bottom right*) with silver monogram EHI. *Whitby Literary and Philosophical Society*

Locket with photograph (*bottom left*). *Collection Miss Barbara Jones*

96 Memorial postcard of Queen Victoria, the postage-stamp box edged with black, underneath '22nd January 1901' (the date of the Queen's death). Obverse a photograph of the old Queen. *Museum of Childhood, Edinburgh*

Autograph letter from Queen Victoria, from Hyères to Edith, Lady Lytton, a lady-in-waiting, dated April 3 1892. The Queen was in mourning for the Duke of Clarence, who had died in January. The black-edged letter was in the envelope adjacent to it bearing the Queen's large black seal, unbroken. *Collection Miss Mary Lutyens*

Black-edged mourning envelope with a cross.

Jet jewelry: aigrette and brooch, in French jet. *The Trustees of the London Museum*

◄95 Mug with a spray of flowers on one side, and on the reverse in gold, 'A Present from the Staffordshire Potteries to Thomas Cooper Author of the Purgatory of Suicides.' *Stoke-on-Trent City Museum and Art Gallery*

Half-mourning pinafore (in the background), black taffeta trimmed with purple satin and coarse black and white lace. *Collection Mrs Victor Sheppard*

BLACK KID GLOVES,
4-BUTTONS, 2s. 6d. PER PAIR.
Per Post, 2s. 7d.

BLACK KID GLOVES,
2-BUTTONS, 1s. 11d. PER PAIR.
Per Post, 2s.

THE "ÆSTHETIC."   THE "HOURI."

EVENING DRESSES.
BLACK NET, TULLE, AND SPANISH LACE.

Messrs JAY prepare for the Season a variety of BLACK EVENING DRESSES, which they can confidently Recommend both for correctness of Fashion and Economy in Price. Designs and Prices Post Free.

JAY'S, THE LONDON GENERAL MOURNING WAREHOUSE, REGENT STREET, W.

97 Advertisement for Jay's General Mourning Warehouse, 7 May 1881

98 Two dresses from *Jay's Manual of Fashion*, Spring 1862. [15] *Collection Mrs A. F. V. Scott*

The Ghiva.   The Benitza.

JAY'S — 247, 249, 251, REGENT STREET.
By Appointment to the Queen & Her Royal Highness the Duchess of Cambridge.

99 'Buying a Mourning Hat-Band',
Punch 1864

100 *Little Sister's Gone to Sleep*. Popular
ballad, later nineteenth century.
Collection Dr Phillis Cunnington

A boy's mourning dress, *c.* 1860, of
white duck with black braid trimming, black tassels, and buttons of
French jet. *Museum of Costume, Bath*

Customer. "A SLIGHT MOURNING HAT-BAND, IF YOU PLEASE."
Hatter. "WHAT RELATION, SIR?"
Customer. "WIFE'S UNCLE."
Hatter. "FAVOURITE UNCLE, SIR?"
Customer. "UM—WELL, YES."
Hatter. "MAY I ASK, SIR, ARE YOU MENTIONED IN THE WILL?"
Customer. "NO SUCH LUCK."
Hatter (to his Assistant, briskly). "COUPLE O' INCHES, JOHN!"

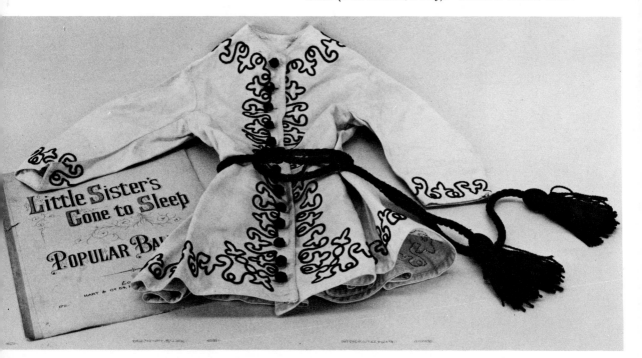

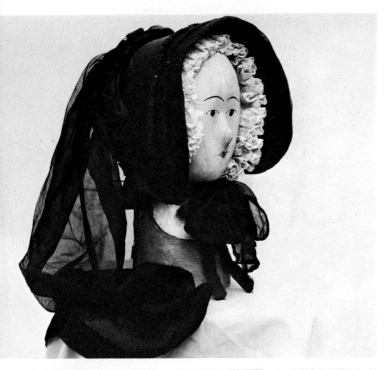

101 Full mourning bonnet, *c.* 1890.
Bands of crape over a stiffened
foundation, crape knot and semi-
circular black tulle veil; on a
mid-nineteenth-century hat-
stand. *Worthing Library, Museum
and Art Gallery*

102 Wedding dress: black satin, with
'cuirass' bodice, ruching around
the hips, tied-back skirt, bustle
and train; trimmed at collar,
cuffs and bustle with applique
motifs of black braid, beads and
lace. Made by 'Miss Canham,
27 Belgrave Place, Bradford'.[16]
*Whitby Literary and Philosophical
Society*

103 'Mourning Toilettes', *The English
Woman's Domestic Magazine* vol.
20 1876.

104 Widow's cap (1870s) in spotted stiff black net, wired and covered with frills of white silk tulle; an elastic strap at the back to go beneath a chignon. Trimmed with black emblematic flowers and leaves made out of feathers, sequins, jet beads and wax; long 'falls' of white tulle. This type of cap was worn by old ladies. *Museum of Costume, Bath*

Hat stand, mid-nineteenth century. Leather with painted face. *Brighton Museums*

Widow's cap (1880). White pleated muslin, with reconstructed 'falls'; on its own box. *Museum of Costume, Bath*

Mourning braid in black and white, marked $6^1/_4$d.

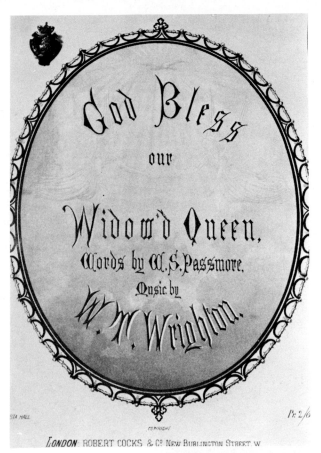

105 *God Bless our Widow'd Queen* by W. S. Passmore and W. T. Wrighton. Sheet music. The verse runs:

Father of Mercies, at whose will
Both Queens and Princes reign:
Who dost the proudest realms o'er-rule,
And life and death ordain;
Since it hath pleased Thee hence to call,
Good Albert from earth's scene;
Be Thou the lone one's comfort now,
God bless our widow'd Queen!

Collection Dr Phillis Cunnington

106 Queen Victoria, with Princess Alexandra of Denmark and the Countess of Caledon. Photograph, November 1862, taken eleven months after the Prince Consort's death. The Queen, in full widow's mourning, wears a Marie Stuart's widow's cap; her dress is virtually covered with crape. *By gracious permission of Her Majesty The Queen*

107 Death mask of Arthur Wellesley, First Duke of Wellington (1769–1852). Bronze. Taken three days after death. *From Walmer Castle, Deal, by courtesy of the Department of the Environment*

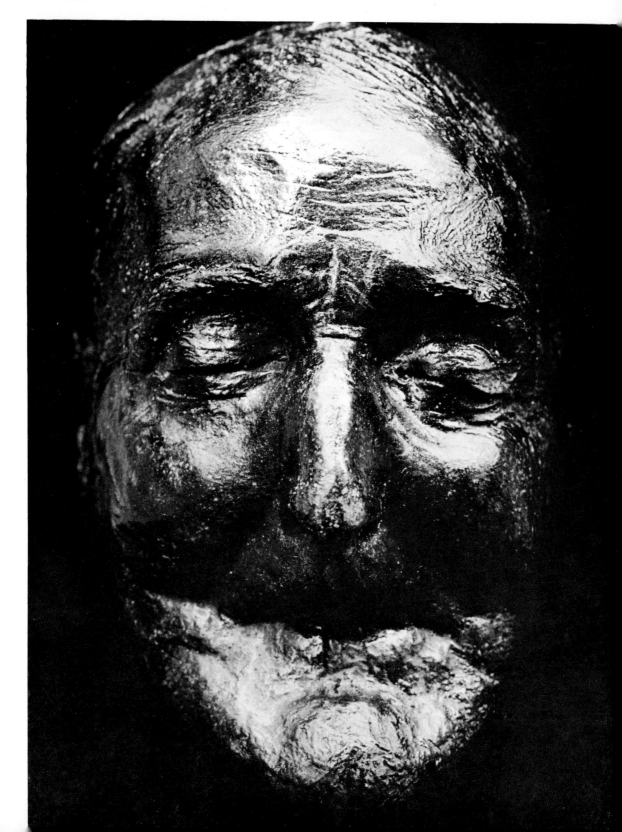

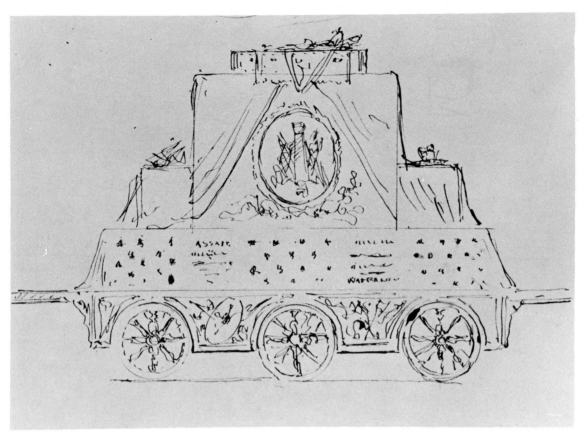

108 *Sketch for the Wellington Car* by Richard Redgrave RA, 1852. *Victoria and Albert Museum, London*

109 *Funeral-Car of the Duke of Wellington.* Lithograph in black and beige. 'Designed from the general idea suggested by the Superintendent of the Department of Practical Art by the Art Superintendent, Mr Redgrave, RA. The Constructive and Ornamental Details by Professor Semper. The Details Relating to Woven Fabrics and Heraldry by Octavius Hudson, Professor. Published by Ackerman and Day.' It was not at first intended to use the canopy in the procession: the coffin was to be the pre-eminent object. *Victoria and Albert Museum, London*

110 'The Funeral of the Duke of Wellington: the Decorations of Temple-Bar.' *Illustrated London News* 1852.

111 *Wellington's Funeral Car passing Apsley House, 18 November 1852* by Louis Haghe. The original watercolour painting for the chromolithograph. *Guildhall Library and Art Gallery*

112 *Arthur Wellesley, 1st Duke of Wellington K.G* (1769–1852), by G. Abbot, after Alfred Crowquill. Published by Samuel Alcock & Company, 18 June 1852. The model, made just before the Duke's death, was 'shown at the soirée given by the President of the Institution of Civil Engineers, at the close of last session. The likeness of the great original, and the unstudied life like position of the figure, were the subject of general admiration throughout the evening.' The Duke is seen seated in the House of Lords. *Collection Victor Percival Esq*

Ticket to the funeral. *Collection Mrs A. F. V. Scott*

113 'Sketch for the monument to the Duke of Wellington, St Paul's Cathedral' by Alfred Stevens (1818–75). Pen and ink on tracing paper; inscribed 'retraced from another tracing of Mr Stevens' original sketch'. *Royal Institute of British Architects*

114 White antimacassar, in cotton thread crochet work. English, *c.* 1852. A humble tribute to the memory of the Duke of Wellington: the tomb, urn and weeping willow follow a standard sampler pattern. *Brighton Museums*

115 'The Funeral of His Late Royal Highness The Prince Consort: the Hearse', *Illustrated London News* 1861.

THE FUNERAL OF HIS LATE ROYAL HIGHNESS THE PRINCE CONSORT: THE HEARSE.

116 'Automatic' painting by Georgina Houghton (died 1887). Watercolour and gouache on paper. Opposite is inscribed 'The Flower of William Stringer who entered the Spirit-Life 10 July 1817'. [17] *The Society for Psychical Research*

117 *The Bourne from which no Traveller Returns* attributed to John Martin (1789–1854). Oil
30¹/₂ × 19³/₄ in. (77.5 × 50 cm). *The Elton Collection*

118 'A Cemetery of the Future' by William Robinson, FLS. Frontispiece to *God's Acre Beautiful, or the Cemeteries of the Future*, First edition London: 1880.

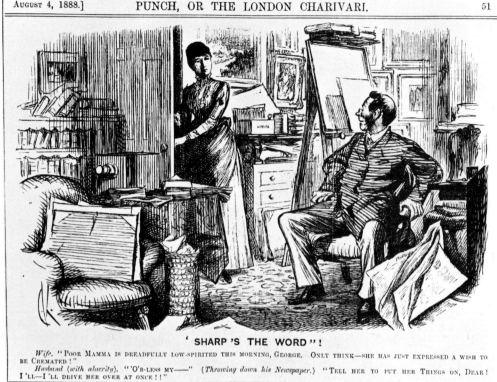

' SHARP 'S THE WORD ' ' !

Wife. "Poor Mamma is dreadfully low-spirited this morning, George. Only think—she has just expressed a wish to be Cremated !"

Husband (with alacrity). "'O'b-less my——" *(Throwing down his Newspaper.)* "Tell her to put her Things on, Dear ! I 'll—I 'll drive her over at once ! !"

119 'Sharp's the Word!' *Punch* August 1888.

120 Photograph of the cremation of Dr William Price. *The Welsh Folk Museum, St Fagan's, Cardiff*

121 *The Doubt: 'Can these Dry Bones Live?'* by H. A. Bowler c. 1856. Oil on canvas. 24 × 20 in. (61 × 51 cm). *Tate Gallery*

122 *The Fields of Bliss* by John Martin (1789–1854) Mezzotint, engraved by the artist after his painting (1852) of the same title. *Collection Mr Derek Rogers*

123 A 'two roads' chart: the roads to Heaven and Hell: hand drawn, from a scrap album. *Museum of Childhood, Edinburgh*

124 *The Blessed Damozel* by Byam Shaw. Oil on canvas 37 × 71 in. (94 × 180 cm). The aesthetic angels here might have come from the chorus of 'Patience'; since when have peacock feathers (*far left*) been an angelic attribute? *Guildhall Art Library and Gallery*

125 Spirit photograph from the Hudson Collection of Spirit Photographs. [18] *Collection Dr E. J. Dingwall*

126 'The Royal Children asleep, with a Guardian Angel' *c*. 1845. Staffordshire earthenware. *Brighton Museums*

127 *Child and Guardian Angel c*. 1890. Coloured lithograph, perhaps German for the English market. *Victoria and Albert Museum, London*

128 *An Angel of the Hierarchy Cherubim* by Sir Edward Coley Burne-Jones, Bt (1833–98). One of ten cartoons for stained glass designed in 1873 for the south transept window of Jesus College Chapel, Cambridge. Pencil, sepia and watercolour, $48 \times 23^1/_2$ in. $(122 \times 60$ cm). *City Museum and Art Gallery, Birmingham*

129, 130 'Automatic' or 'spirit' drawings by Mrs Frederika Bodmer (1826–85/90). Indian ink and pencil. Selected from seven volumes of drawings executed between 1855 and 1875. *Society for Psychical Research*

131 'Peace', automatic drawing by Mrs
Alaric Watts (died 1903). Watercolour
and gouache on paper. *The Society
for Psychical Research*

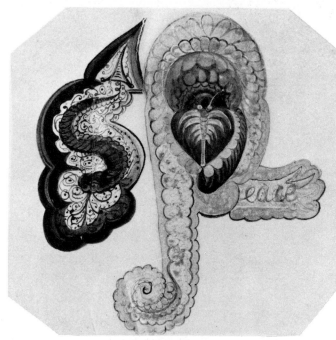

133 Book (*top*) *Mind Reading, Spiritualistic Effects, Mental
and Psychical Phenomena and Horoscopy:* Ralph E.
Sylvestre and Co, 16th edition.

Rapping hand (*bottom*): life size model with lace cuff.
Probably controlled pneumatically by concealed rubber
tubing. The code normally used was one rap for yes,
two for no, and three for doubtful or unknown. [19]
Harry Price Library, University of London

132 Illustration of spirit hands from
*Twixt Two Worlds: A Narrative of
The Life and Work of William
Eglinton* by John S. Farmer 1886

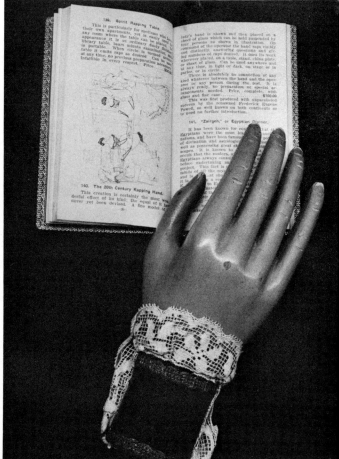

134 Study for *Death the Bride* by Thomas Cooper Gotch (1884–1931). Oil on canvas,
15¹/₂ × 12 in. (39.4 × 30.5 cm). Death is here secularized with pagan poppies and an
ambiguous smile; there is no hint of either Old or New Testament. *Kettering Museum
and Art Gallery*

Notes to the Illustrations

1   Dogs were given a firm place in the Victorian language of grief: Landseer's *Faithful Hound* and *Shepherd's Last Mourner* had a large litter. The *Quarterly Review* mentioned in 1861 'the dog who, not many years since, attended his mistress's funeral in a black cloak' at Winchester.

2   Charles Peace was said to have made this model while awaiting execution. 'The fellow had a passion for an ambitious mausoleum and spent his spare moments when not burgling in designing the most gorgeous one possible. It was to be finished in marble and gold and to have a troupe of cherubims playing around the summit.' (from *Answers*, 12 December 1888)

3   Such objects reveal an intense interest in crime and the violent death that rewarded it. The spectacle of a public execution was intensely popular; Dickens describes one thus:

'For this interesting event everybody made holiday. Not only the inhabitants of the adjacent villages and towns, but the sight-seers of the whole district, flocked to the exciting scene, all dressed 'in their best', having made up pleasure-parties of threes, and fives, and sevens, in gigs and taxed-carts, and market-carts—with large parties in light wagons and covered vans, as if to a gipseying or 'the races',—and all in the highest glee. But, the mass of the assemblage consisted principally of smocked frocked labourers, their highlows and gators spattered with mud, and their steps heavy with a number of miles they had travelled to 'the hanging'. There were hardly any respectable people observable in the crowd, but a most disgusting number of women. Some of these had gay flowers in their bonnets, and evidently set up for rustic belles; others were mothers with their infants in their arms; others were elderly matrons, presiding at the head of their families, and from the elevation of the domestic spring-cart pointing out to their young daughters how they could best see the execution.' (*Cain in the Fields* 1851)

The hangman shared this popularity; Dickens objected that 'it is not good for the hangman to flourish in the public papers like the toastmaster at a public dinner'. A more serious objection, to authority, was that public hangings took away the terror of the death penalty; they were abolished in 1868.

4   The coffin containing the remains of the Prince Consort was brought from the Royal Vault beneath St George's Chapel at Windsor, and placed in the temporary sarcophagus on 18 December 1862. It remained there until placed in the permanent tomb in 1868.

5   Carriage horses went into mourning with their owners; the bright headbands on the bridle beneath the ears were replaced by black ones with satin rosettes for the rich, wool for the poor.

6   False horses' tails were used to 'improve' the appearance of funeral horses. The best horses were specially imported from Belgium. Mares and geldings were not used:

their coats were inclined to turn brown. The bearing-rein was cruelly used to bow the horses' heads.

A record (in the BBC Sound Archives) of the Albin Brothers, an undertakers' firm in south-east London, describes how their fathers used to go to Flushing and buy three black stallions for 100 guineas; they would have cost £60 each in London. These stallions were hard to handle; their heads had to be kept apart, or they would fight. The 'feather tray' or 'lid of feathers' was often difficult to carry in the wind; the undertakers' assistants were armed with truncheons to guard against body-snatchers.

The Albin Brothers said also that their funeral processions walked up to ten miles, starting at 9 a.m. and ending at 10 p.m.; they stopped every twenty minutes at the nearest pub. The 'Thatched House' at Leightonstone had at times more than forty funeral coaches outside it.

7   Mr Braidwood, the Superintendent of the London Fire Brigade, was killed on 22 June 1861, in the greatest London fire since the seventeenth century, when £2 million of damage was done. He was in the street, giving brandy to his men, when a warehouse fell and buried him. His funeral was a great event: the London Rifle Brigade the Tower Hamlets Volunteers, all public and private fire brigades, the City and Metropolitan Police, etc. attended: the procession was over a mile long. Every avenue leading to Watling Street was blocked; the windows and roofs of houses were crowded; shops closed, and every church save St Paul's rang a funeral peal. The hearse and fifteen mourning coaches went to Abney Park; the service for the hero was held in the Presbyterian chapel of the cemetery.

8   Pugin wrote, 'nothing can be more hideous, than the raised metal work called *coffin furniture*, that is so generally used at the present time: heathen emblems, posturing angels, trumpets, death's heads and cross bones, are mingled together in a glorious confusion, and many of them partake of a ludicrous character'. (*Glossary of Ecclesiastical Ornament and Costume* 1844)

9   The coffin containing the corpse of William Morris was met at Lethlade Station by a farm wagon, with a yellow body and bright red wheels, drawn by a roan mare, and led by a Kelmscott carter. The wagon was wreathed in vine and strewn with willow, over a carpet of moss. 'No red-faced men in shabby black to stagger with the coffin to the hearse, but in their place four countrymen in moleskin bore the body to an open hay cart festooned with vines, with alder and with bullrushes and driven by a man who looked coeval with the Anglo-Saxon Chronicle.' A wreath of bay, and a piece of Broussa brocade, were laid on a coffin of unpolished oak with wrought iron handles. 'It was the only funeral I have ever seen that did not make me ashamed to have to be buried.' (W. R. Lethaby)

10 Queen Victoria's interest in death is well known, and especially her cherishing of Albert's memory—the laying out of his clothes and the bringing of his shaving water every day until her death, the immobilization of his rooms, the photograph of him on his deathbed that hung next to her head wherever she slept. Despite this interest she disliked black funerals. At Osborne, the mortuary chamber was hung in crimson; her pall was in white satin sumptuously embroidered in colours; the draperies that hung along the route taken by the funeral—'more of a triumphal march than a funeral cortège'—were violet not black. Her corpse was surrounded by flowers:

'The Royal ladies themselves at Osborne took from the first the sad and beautiful duty of placing fresh flowers each day in a room in which the late Monarch's mortal remains temporarily rested. Our dear Queen loved lilies of the valley and of these quantities were placed near her. Arum lilies and great white trumpet lilies and white orchids were also used for this beautiful purpose.' (*The Lady's Pictorial* February 1901)

11 In order to solve the problem of continuing over-population of graveyards Loudon proposed:

'That no graves should be made except on ground that never was opened before; when only one coffin was placed in a grave, it should not be less than 6 ft below the surface; that, when more than one coffin was to be contained in the same grave, each coffin should be separate from the other by a layer of earth not less than 6 ft in thickness; that all burying in vaults and catacombs be discontinued; and that no new burial grounds be formed in London within two miles of St Paul's, nor in country towns within half a mile of their suburbs. Such a law would at once prevent interments from being made in most of the London burial grounds, while it would admit all of the unoccupied ground, whether in London or out of it, being used; and thus no injustice would be committed towards those who have recently enlarged their burying-ground; it would, at the same time, check the disgusting and dangerous practice of burying ten or twelve bodies close upon one another in one grave, now practised both in the old churchyards and in the new cemeteries.'

12 The lying-in-state of the Earl (plate 12) differed poignantly from that of the Duke (plate 21). The former's Gothic chapel, by Pugin, had been draped with black cloth, to exclude all light, and the altar hung with black velvet, with a white cross in the centre. The catafalque was cruciform, a shape beloved by the Ecclesiologists; its gabled roof, supported on twelve gilded pillars, was finished by carved crestings, from which rose standards of light; coronas of light surmounted the points of the gables. The roof was covered in black cloth, embroidered with coronets and the letter S in gold; on two of the gables were foliated crosses, with the sentence '*In hoc signe spes mea.*' The edges of the coffin were engrailed with gilt metal work; at its foot the Shrewsbury arms were engraved in gilt metal. The pall, of black velvet, bore a cross in white velvet across its centre, and the arms of the Earl in gold; the family motto was worked in gold on crimson velvet, running bend-wise across the whole pall. At each angle were the initials of the Earl, and in gold at each end: '*Requiem aeternam dona eis Domini et lux perpetua luceat eas.*' This shares with Wellington's fantasy only the heraldic emphasis and the gorgeous solemnity; the baroque design and heathen symbolism of the Duke's catafalque outraged every Ecclesiological tenet.

13 In 1888 (*McGough* v. *Lancaster Burial Board*) a case arose because the Board had made a rule, prior to selling graves, that prohibited glass shades on graves.

'There is a great deal of irritation up and down the country against the restrictions that burial boards put upon the kind of memorials that the poor choose to place on their graves, particularly those glass shades with wreaths made of some indestructible material inside. They appear to be a form of memorial which I believe is not admired by cultivated people, but which certain classes use very largely and I suppose do admire. Up and down the country there are a great many burial boards which actually refuse to allow them to be put on a grave, even by people who have bought a

203

grave space. If that were subject to ecclesiastical authority, I am sure it would be allowed.' (*Report from the Select Committee on Burial Grounds* July 1898)

14 Although pre-Victorian, the watch stand is of a type commonly seen during Victoria's reign. The legend occurs often: death may strike at any time, and the evangelical emphasis was on the state of mind at death—the implication is that one's guard should never slip, and one should be good all the time.

15 These dresses belong to the second stage of mourning, and are described thus:

'THE GHIVA
Head-dress of white flowers, with band of black velvet two inches wide, placed in form of a triangle over the flowers. Bouquet to correspond. Dress of black tulle: the skirt fouillioné, fastened in the form of diamonds, with a ruching of tulle and satin-ribbon; tunic to the waist, trimmed round with two flounces of tulle, edged with satin ribbon, caught back with large rosettes; full berthe to correspond.

THE BENITZA
This truly magnificent Bodice is made in Genoa Velvet, and is trimmed elaborately up each seam with a superb trimming, most chaste in design. Round the bottom of the Bodice and up the front is a splendid netted fringe, with cut jet beads inserted, producing a remarkably dressy and stylish effect. Head-dress: Velvet and jet coronet, with small plume of black or white ostrich feathers, placed over the left ear. Dress of black Glacé, with flounce about a quarter of a yard deep at bottom, edged with velvet, and headed with rich velvet trimming, in squares, about five inches apart, caught across with two straps, finished at the ends with a rich silk or jet button; the velvet trimming headed with a narrow Glacé frill, bound with velvet to correspond, with flounces at bottom.'

16 This dress, which appears to be unique, was worn by Mrs M. Gardner, JP, of Kingston-upon-Hull, whose father had died only a month previously. The usual procedure would have been to postpone the wedding. It is said that there is a contemporary photograph in existence of the bride wearing the dress, but this has not been traced. In its absence, the reconstruction of the veil and gloves is theoretical. The fact that such an elaborate dress is high-necked, indicating that it could not have been an evening dress, is in favour of a firm tradition, although one eminent costume expert has pronounced firmly against it, and doubts must remain.

17 Inscribed opposite the painting is:

'We must begin by giving a slight insight as to the Spirit flowers of individuals for the comprehension of those persons who may see this drawing without having been prepared for it by acquaintance with the collection of Georgiana the Holy Symbolist. Such flowers may be termed spontaneous records of human life, for, from earliest infancy do they grow (in Spirit realms) in complete correspondence with the development of the being they represent, whose character is thus expressed by the colour, size, and shape of their own Spirit flower; from the heart of which yellow filaments recording each action of their lives; such as are good rising as a sweet incense towards Heaven, such as are faulty or evil going downwards, representing those actions which must be repented of, and as far as possible atoned for. May the knowledge of such records induce all to pray for Grace so to govern their own souls that their flowers may henceforth emit only upwards.

In this flower may be discerned a character of great decision, from the preponderence of the dark blue powerful fibres . . . the deep red shows a loving nature, but not exactly a tender one . . . . His faith in His God was the main spring of his life. This is shown in the flower by the yellow colouring, and also by the many representations of The Eye of The Lord . . . he passed unregrettingly from the earth life to the Spirit-world . . . .

Above the flower we have symbolised The Shaddowing Wing of the Most High, sheltering His Servant, and making him ever feel that whatever disappointments might meet him upon earth, there could be none when he looked upwards to The Fountain of Life, Love and Hope.'

18 Mr Frederick Hudson was probably the most popular and best known of all Victorian spirit photographers. His studio in Palmer Terrace, Holloway Road, London, was visited by nearly all the well-known Spiritualists of the period. He was assisted in producing the photographs by such prominent mediums as Miss Frances Cook, whose materialized spirit-form, Katie King, walked arm-in-arm with Sir William Crookes, and also her friend, Frank Herne, whose fraudulent practices were condemned by Spiritualists.

19 Sylvestre advertises, with an illustration very like this hand (plate 133), the 'Spirit Rapping and Writing Hand. This is an excellent model of a lady's hand and forearm, with lace cuff and sleeve. Bears minute examination. When placed on table or sheet of glass, it at once raps out any numbers or answers desired. Including full instructions how to cause hand to write answers to questions propounded by audience . . . $2.50.'

'Ghosts of Stockings', from *A Discovery Concerning Ghosts* by George Cruikshank 1864.

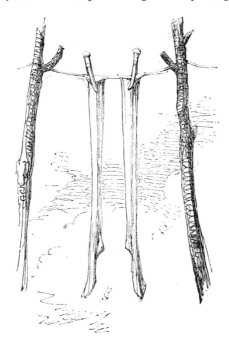

Index

Numbers in italics refer to plate numbers.